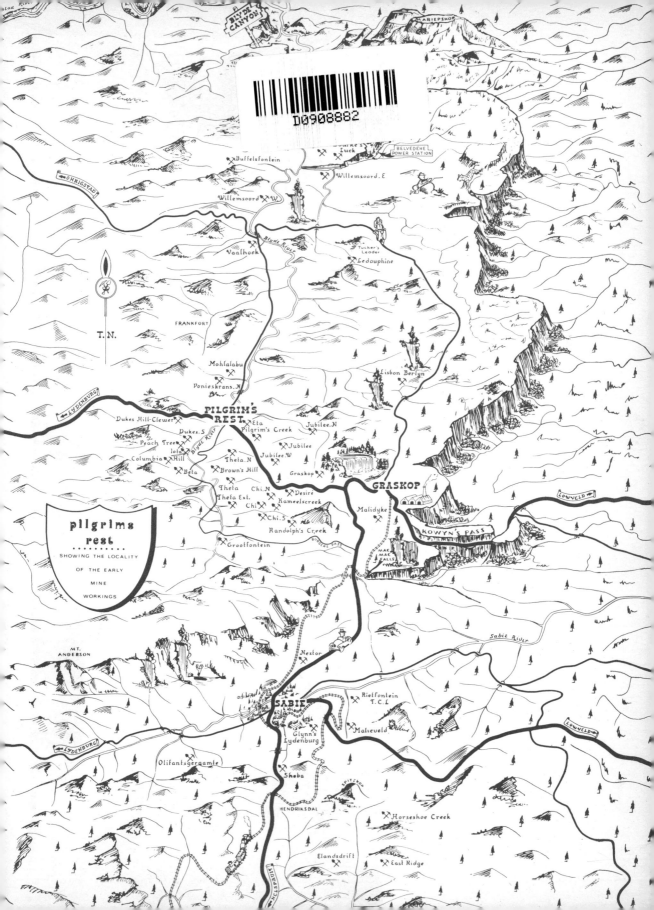

To Bob - Nancy,

Best Wishes,

Rod.

1979.

A. P. CARTWRIGHT

VALLEY OF GOLD

Illustrations by P.W. Wheeler and
Roy Taylor
End Papers by Cartography Department,
Rand Mines Limited.

HOWARD TIMMINS
CAPE TOWN

New and completely revised
version of the book
first published under this title
in 1961

Third Edition 1978

ISBN 0 86978 043 3

Citadel Press 🐚 *Lansdowne*

CONTENTS

ILLUSTRATIONS

FOREWORD

In a sense I am the "father" of this book for it is some fifteen years since I came to the conclusion that the gold mines of the Pilgrim's Rest district would provide an author with a remarkably good story and so help to keep alive a fascinating era in our history. But I had to find a suitable author. I called in my friend Paddy Cartwright and sent him off to look at a part of South Africa he had never seen before. He returned full of good stories and enthusiasm for his subject. Today he tells me that I am not only the father of the book he wrote then, and of this new version of it that is now being published, but also that I fathered his career as an author for this was the first book he published under his own name.

If this is true I am more than pleased that I had this inspiration for both the book and the author have proved themselves and gone from strength to strength since then. The original *Valley of Gold* was printed in 1961, reprinted almost immediately and, not long afterwards, a third time. Then, for reasons that I have never clearly understood, it went out of print altogether and became completely unobtainable — except as an expensive item of Africana. For the past ten years everybody in any way connected with Transvaal Gold Mining Estates, Limited, the company that managed the mines, has been pestered with the question: "Can't you get me a copy of *Valley of Gold*? The answer has always been "No".

Now I am very happy to welcome the book in new guise and to wish it and the author continued success. It comes out at the right time, for in 1973 we shall be celebrating the 100th birthday of our great gold mining industry which to all intents and purposes began at Mac Mac and Pilgrim's Rest. Anyone who doubts that claim should read the book.

I recommend it not only to those who visit the area, but also to every South African as a really rich slice of our history.

P.H. ANDERSON

The Gate House,
Valley Road,
Parktown,
Johannesburg.

14th September, 1972.

CHAPTER I

A MINING COMPANY IS BORN

No one is certain when gold was first unearthed by primitive man but there is evidence that it was known and used by the Egyptians as early as 4,000 B.C. Since then it has been discovered and mined, in one way or another, on every one of the five continents. Yet despite the high value that the human race has always set upon the metal one learns with astonishment that all the efforts of man and machines over nearly 6,000 years of recorded history have produced only a little more than 50,000 tons of it or, since we record our stocks in Troy ounces, let us say 112-million pounds. What is even more surprising is that four-fifths of all this gold has been won in the course of the last 100 years*.

It was in the 19th century that the systematic hunt for gold, set in motion by world demand, began in earnest. Hundreds of prospectors, tough characters, many of whom had worked in mines in Europe, began to roam the great open spaces of the undeveloped countries. Their discoveries were to lead to the wild gold rushes of the 19th century, the most famous of which was the great stampede to the Californian alluvial diggings in 1848. Spurred by rumours that said that here any man might make a fortune, more than 150,000 men, and some women, took part in this wild adventure. Not many of them made much more money than they would have made in any other job in America at that time, but they did discover a pleasant land in which to live and bring up their children and they gave the United States some of its hardiest, most enterprising citizens.

The Californian field was still producing gold when a second great rush took thousands of men to Australia where many of them prospered and some great mines were founded. There was one other great rush after this, perhaps the wildest of them all for it lured thousands of ill-equipped men to Alaska where the ground in which the gold was discovered was hard frozen for five months in the year and often had to be thawed by fires before digging could begin. The annual output of Alaska when production was at its peak was, I estimate, about the same as the annual output of today's West Driefontein mine. Nevertheless that was a great deal of gold in those days, enough to make some thousands of hardy men tramp in Indian file through snow storms carrying all their worldly belongings on their backs.

The Alaskan gold was discovered in 1896. Ten years earlier the great South African gold field had been discovered in the bleak and rocky area known as the Witwatersrand. Today the annual output of this field amounts to more than three-quarters of the entire gold production of the free world. For almost 90 years it has been the most profitable mining operation the

---

* For the statistics of gold recovery see "Gold: Its Beauty, Power and Allure" by C.H.V. Sutherland, published by Thames and Hudson, London.

world has ever known, its earnings almost equally divided between share-holders throughout the world and the State Treasury of South Africa. When people say: "Of what use is gold?", they should see what it has done for South Africa and its people, white and black. While the rest of Africa has advanced at the pace of the snail this country has raced ahead, financed by the profits of its gold mines. And gold has built other industries that now employ 6-million men and women and will fill the gap when the last gold mine crushes the last ton of ore at some distant date in the 21st century.

However, it would be wholly wrong to suppose that gold mining in South Africa began with the discovery of the outcrop of the Main Reef on the Witwatersrand and the founding of the city of Johannesburg. Nor is it true to say that the first planned mining operations began at De Kaap in 1882 and that Barberton was the first mining town. There had been discoveries and proclamations earlier than this and "splashes" of gold had been found in many parts of the country over a period of twenty years. But the fact is that profitable gold mining (as opposed to making money and losing it by trying to enlarge the mine) began long before Barberton and Johannesburg were names on anyone's map. It began 100 years ago as it had begun in other parts of the world with a rush to "pan" alluvial gold in mountain streams — that is what this story is about.

ii

The directors of the new company met for the first time in the offices of Hermann Eckstein & Co. at the corner of Simmonds and Commissioner Streets, Johannesburg, on May 20, 1895.

In the chair was a small, sprucely-dressed man with an incisive manner which suggested that he had attended many board meetings, that he knew exactly how long this one would last and what it would achieve. If, watching the proceedings, you had come to the conclusion that this dapper little man was in complete control you would have been right. For this was Lionel Phillips, first Chairman of Rand Mines Ltd., a director of 20 or 30 other mining companies, successor to Hermann Eckstein as Wernher, Beit's representative in Johannesburg, President of the Chamber of Mines and well on the way to his first million.

If Phillips spoke with authority it was not without reason. Behind him were the accumulated resources of Julius Wernher and Alfred Beit, Rhodes's partners, and behind them, if they needed capital for new ventures, the Rothschilds and Rudolph Kahn, the banker. The firm of Wernher, Beit and Co. issued no prospectuses and no invitations to the public to subscribe for shares. They got the capital they needed from the immense resources of their holdings in De Beers and from the banking houses of Europe. They had faith in Phillips. They said he had "a nose for gold". He had come to Johannesburg from Kimberley, where he had held every conceivable type of job in the diamond mines. He had found his feet very quickly on the Rand

2

and showed shrewdness and vision in pegging claims and buying ground. On the one occasion when he and one of the partners in the firm had disagreed Phillips had gone ahead and bought the ground "for his own account". The Lionel Phillips Block had become the Bonanza Mine. Phillips had been right and the partner wrong. When, quite unexpectedly, Eckstein died in 1893, Phillips was obviously the man they needed to take his place.

The new company was another example of Phillips's "nose for gold" and of his determination that, wherever gold was to be found, the firm of H. Eckstein & Co. should get in early. It was to be called the Lydenburg Mining Estates Ltd. It might with more geographical accuracy have been called the Sabie River Mining Estates Company, or the Lowveld Exploration Company. But the name is of significance, for it shows that Phillips was looking far beyond the somewhat meagre array of claims, mining rights and freehold properties with which the new company was to begin its career. What he was looking at, in fact, was a vast area of uninhabited country in the Eastern Transvaal where gold had been found in all sorts of unexpected places. There had been alluvial gold and nuggets, there had been rich "leaders" and pockets and now there were indications of reef. All the signs seemed to show that the whole area was "honeycombed" with gold, but no one could say with certainty precisely where it would be found. Some believed that it lay below the granite where the low country began at the foot of the Drakensberg. Others believed that it was locked up in the mountains and must be blasted out of the rock. But they all were certain that it was there.

If Lionel Phillips had thought it necessary to address his fellow directors at this inaugural meeting, he would have said words such as these: "Gentlemen, this company has been formed to acquire mines, claims and mineral rights over an area that is bigger than the Witwatersrand as we know it today. We shall buy any property that seems a reasonable prospect, provided we can get it at a reasonable price. You may say that this is a gamble but, if we look at the history of the district, we see that gold has been found there for the past 25 years. We know the gold is there. What we have still to discover is how much of it there is and how to mine it . . ."

But there was no need to explain the objects of the company to the directors. They knew the district better than he did.

Two of them were mere striplings — Abe Bailey, aged 30, and Percy FitzPatrick, aged 33. But both had packed a life-time of experience into their early years.

FitzPatrick, the son of a judge, had left his home at the Cape to seek his fortune on the very diggings which the company now hoped to acquire. He had starved as a digger, then worked as a storekeeper and a transport driver — adventures which in due course were to inspire him to write the immortal "Jock of the Bushveld". He had "gone broke" again in Barberton, had been befriended by Alfred Beit, had escorted Sir Winston Churchill's father, Lord

Randolph Churchill, on his expedition to Rhodesia and had returned to Johannesburg to join H. Eckstein & Co. He was, therefore, an employee of the firm that controlled the new company, but this did not mean that he was a figurehead. Indeed, he was the best informed man on the board. He had walked every yard of the rough road that ran from Lydenburg to Lourenco Marques, had visited mining properties throughout the district and knew who was to be trusted and who not.

Bailey, a somewhat brash young man, had quarrelled with his father and turned his back on what might have been a prosperous career at Queenstown in the Cape. At the age of 20 he had arrived at Barberton and proceeded to earn his living. Professional boxing, digging, storekeeping, selling insurance, playing poker — all things were alike to Abe Bailey. Never was a young man less in need of the assistance of a wealthy father than he. Someone said of him about this time: "Put Bailey down in the middle of the Kalahari Desert and he'd make a living out of the snakes". In one way and another he made more than a living at Barberton. When the crash came and the companies folded up he bounced out of the district, having made and lost a fortune, but far from penniless.

Somewhere along the way he had acquired, at a very reasonable figure, an interest in a number of small mines and undeveloped claims in the district in which Hermann Eckstein & Co. were now interested. Thus we find him on the board with his holdings in the New Clewer Estate (Clewer was Bailey's "trademark" all his life), the Jubilee Mine and the claims he had pegged or bought being exchanged for a very considerable holding in the company. Phillips must have decided that he would be a useful man to have on the board, and to Bailey this association with the house of Eckstein (Johannesburg had just begun to call it "The Corner House") the most powerful financial organisation of the day, was the chance of a life-time. He had much learn about company promotion and management. This was the beginning.

A fourth director was H.G. Glenny, who represented an organisation known as the Transvaal and General Association Ltd. Since Eckstein's owned this company he may be regarded as another Eckstein nominee.

The fifth, and perhaps the most important of them all, was a man named D.H. Benjamin, a London financier of some renown.

His importance lay in the fact that he held a controlling interest in a company called the Transvaal Gold Exploration and Land Company, of which Bailey was also a director, that had been producing gold in the Lydenburg area since 1883 and which, in 1894, had achieved a record and impressive output valued at £69,853.

Benjamin's name long ago faded from the history of the South African gold mining industry. Yet he deserves to be remembered as one of the very earliest of the pioneers. I cannot give you many biographical details for none of his contemporaries seems to have known much about him. He was an associate of that mysterious character, Baron Grant, who gave London its

"The deed of concession was signed by the members of the Triumvirate . . . ."

famed Leicester Square and who had fingers in many pies.

The legend has it that Benjamin was a London financier, a man of considerable means. One day in the seventies he picked up the *Illustrated London News* and read an article (with pictures) about the alluvial gold diggings of the Transvaal. There were the usual stories of the nuggets found in creeks and the rich "patches" of free gold found in river gravel. This set him wondering as to where this gold had originated and whether there might not be more gold in the hills.

He was so interested that he sailed for Cape Town where he found that people could talk of nothing but the diamond fields. They had heard of the Lydenburg gold rush, but knew less about it than he did. At some time or another he must then have visited the alluvial diggings in the Pilgrim's Rest area and decided that this was where he would take his plunge. What guided him I cannot say. We do not know what means he used to achieve his ends or who acted as his agent. All that is certain is that, in 1881, he suddenly appeared in the *Staats Courant* as the holder of a mining concession granted him by the South African Republic. The concession granted him all rights over six farms at the foot of Pilgrim's Hill, north-east of Lydenburg, and it included the village of Pilgrim's Rest, such as it was in those days, and the creek where hundreds of diggers had sifted every cubic foot of gravel and found thousands of ounces of gold.

The deed of concession was signed by S.J.P. Kruger, Vice President of the Republic, M.W. Pretorius and W. Hollard, members of the triumvirate*, and

---

* The Triumvirate governed the South African Republic temporarily, in 1881-82, until a Presidential election could be held.

5

Benjamin's signature was witnessed by W.E. Bok, the State Secretary and E.J. Jorissen, the State Attorney.

It read: "Granted and assured by the Government of the South African Republic to Mr. David Benjamin of Cape Town in the Colony of the Cape of Good Hope on this, the 10th day of November, 1881, in consequence and by virtue of a Resolution passed by the Honourable Volksraad in its sittings of the 7th November, 1881".

"The Government of the South African Republic hereby grants and assures to the said David Benjamin, his successors or assignees, the full, free and exclusive right to all Gold Reefs and other mines, minerals, ores and precious stones of whatsoever nature now in, on or under the farms and lands named 'Ponieskrantz', 'Ledovine', 'Waterhoutboom', 'Grootfontein', 'Belvedere' and 'Driekop' (otherwise known as 'Pilgrim's Rest') situate in the district of Lydenburg in the South African Republic, or such portion thereof as is now in his possession, further granting to him the exclusive right to prospect and to work the said Pilgrim's Rest or his portion thereof on the following conditions . . ."

The conditions were simplicity itself. Benjamin was to pay the Republic £1,000 a year for the concession, and the government reserved to itself the right to convert this into a payment of 2½ per cent on all precious stones and minerals found there. He had to acquire the freehold of all the farms (which was not so difficult once all digging and prospecting were stopped). He had also to erect within two years machinery to the value of £10,000 and to have at least 25 labourers at work.

He had also, and this was the most difficult of the clauses in the deed, to settle the fair claims of all licensed diggers on the property. How he succeeded in carrying out this part of the agreement remains wrapped in mystery. It is said that it cost him two years of argument and £70,000. There were still hundreds of diggers in the area, and they regarded the granting of this concession as an attempt to jump their claims. It can have been no easy task to meet their demands and tell them to pack up and go.

As far back as 1875 the South African Republic, hard pressed for revenue, had amended the gold law to provide for concessions such as this.

The revised section of the law said: "Where gold on a proclaimed gold field is not found in sufficient quantities to pay individual diggers, or where individuals do not wish to dig, it shall be lawful to give out such localities by concession to companies. For the application for such concessions the said companies must be properly constituted and must give evidence that at least one-third of the requisite capital has been paid up and that it is a bona fide company".

To this clause the diggers took violent exception. As far as they were concerned there was no such thing as a "worked out" field. The government, they said, was taking the bread out of their mouths and, as we shall see, this section of the law remained a bone of contention for many years to come.

However, whether they liked it or not, Benjamin got his concession and proceeded to float a company.

Thus was founded, in 1882, one of the very earliest of the Transvaal gold mining companies and one of the few outside the Witwatersrand whose shareholders lived to bless its name. It was called the Transvaal Gold Exploration Company. It installed a gas engine and a mill at Pilgrim's Rest and produced its first gold in 1883. And its output rose each year — from £1,576 in 1886 to £39,000 in 1893 and an impressive £69,000 in 1894.

There is no mention of the Transvaal Gold Exploration Company in the minutes of that first meeting of the directors of Lydenburg Mining Estates in May 1895. The meeting was concerned with such mundane matters as paying out one S. Brangham for 22 claims, buying 300 acres of ground at Graskop and arranging the transfer to the company of the farms Elandsdrift and Hendriksdal, owned by Eckstein's.

But, reading between the lines as one has to do today, there is not the least doubt that the real purpose of the new company was to acquire the assets of the Transvaal Gold Exploration Company, including that valuable concession over the six farms near Pilgrim's Rest. Benjamin's presence on the board, the name "Lydenburg", the increase in the company's gold output from £39,000 in 1893 to £69,000 in 1894, all point the same way. One visualizes a series of meetings between Alfred Beit, Lionel Phillips, Benjamin and Bailey, at which the terms of a merger were discussed. And to men who knew the difficulties of mining in that far-off wilderness of the Eastern Transvaal the prospect of having The Corner House to supply the capital, the mining engineers and the know-how, to say nothing of the prospect of participating in other flotations, must have been extremely attractive.

How they worked, those directors of early mining companies! Soon after the first meeting of the board of the new company Beit and Phillips set off to inspect the workings in the area. That meant a ten-day journey in a mule wagon, a hair-raising scramble down the slopes of mountains. It meant camping out in wild country where lions and buffalo were still to be seen, crawling into adits on the slopes of hills, inspecting pegs and panning samples of payable "dirt".

Their fellow directors had given them a free hand to buy properties and agreements with claim holders. On their return Phillips said that they had made a thorough inspection of the company's properties in the Lydenburg area, and had inspected Frankfort, Spitzkop and many other centres. They had come to the conclusion that it would be highly desirable in their own interest to purchase the properties of the Jubilee Company and the Clewer Estates Company. Both these companies were in such a forward state that ehey would at an early date be paying dividends. Lydenburg Estates ought to absorb them. He had therefore made an offer of 50,000 shares to each company.

Benjamin intervened at this point. He said that, though he acquiesced in this decision, he did not think these purchases were wholly advantageous to the shareholders as he considered the price was far too high. Time was to show how wrong he was.

The buying of small mines, syndicates, holdings, claims and mining rights continued. The company bought the B.I. Syndicate's property, half of the farm "London", the Ross Hill Syndicate, 14 shares in a romantic property called "Olifantsgeraamte" (literally "Elephant's Skeleton"), property owned by B.T. Bourke of Pretoria, the Pilgrim's Mining and Estate Company (this turned out to be an unregistered company owned by the Bourkes) and a dozen other properties.

Within three months of its formation it owned a mixed bag of properties extending from the Lowveld, south of where Sabie stands today and practically in what is now the Kruger National Park, to ground north of Pilgrim's Rest and 30 miles east of Lydenburg. It looked as though Phillips was buying "by guess and by God", but in fact he bought only where there were indications of gold-bearing reef. His intention clearly was to secure a firm foothold in a district that he and Beit both thought might prove to be a second Witwatersrand. There was no outcrop to guide them as they had been guided on the Rand. The whole area was a geological jigsaw puzzle. But, though it was a gamble, they meant to be first in the field.

On August 9, 1895 a special meeting of the directors was called to consider a cable received from Wernher, Beit Ltd., London. It came as no surprise to the board. It reported that, as the result of "certain negotiations" in London, it was now definite that the Transvaal Gold Exploration Company was prepared to consider an offer from Lydenburg Mining Estates.

It was then resolved to create new capital and offer Transvaal Gold Exploration 270,000 shares in the new company. But the London directors of the older company, with a production of £300,000* worth of gold behind them, asked for more. They finally settled for 300,000 shares of £1 each and retained the rights that their 5,000 shares in the Jubilee Mine and 43,000 shares in Grootfontein gave them. To the disinterested observer it must have looked as though T.G.E. was absorbing Lydenburg Mining Estates.

The new company, which had begun life with a capital of £200,000 in May 1895, increased this to £340,000 and finally to £640,000 in the first nine months of its existence, of which the former shareholders and directors of Transvaal Gold Exploration owned over 300,000. These London shareholders were to have a considerable say in the management of the company for years to come.

The first of their requests was that the new company should change its name to commemorate the merger and, since Johannesburg was anxious to placate London, Lydenburg Mining Estates Ltd. vanished after having existed

---

* For purposes of calculation the £ sterling may be regarded as the equivalent of R2, though at the time its purchasing value was probably R6.

for only nine months, and became Transvaal Gold Mining Estates Ltd., the name it has borne ever since.

It now owned properties that covered 200,000 acres and extended over 30 miles. It had acquired mineral rights over another 70,000 acres. It owned a number of small mines and stamp batteries, hundreds of undeveloped claims and old workings in river beds and on hillsides. But there were less than 20 buildings in the whole area. The only road in the whole district was the wagon track that ran from Lydenburg down precipitous hills to Pilgrim's Rest and then crawled down the edge of the Berg and across the Lowveld to Lourenco Marques. The railhead was at Machadodorp, 60 miles away. Far to the east lay the remains of the old Selati line, which had been built from Komatipoort on the Portuguese border to the Sabie River, where Skukuza camp now stands in the Kruger National Park. This had been designed to serve the gold fields. But the Selati Railway Company, which had its head-quarters in Brussels, went bankrupt about this time and the 50 miles of track it had built ended abruptly on the south bank of the Sabie, of no use to anyone though it had cost a fortune in money and many lives to build.

The Transvaal Gold Mining Estates, therefore, started its career with one of the most difficult mining propositions in history. Its properties were scattered over a vast area which was inaccessible by any means except ox wagon. Every ton of supplies it needed had either to climb the Drakens-berg from Lourenco Marques or else be transported first by rail to Machado-dorp then by ox wagon to Lydenburg and down the fantastic hillside track that led to Pilgrim's Rest. There was virtually no labour, very little timber and no coal. Before mining could begin every conceivable requirement of the mine and the men who were to work it had to be hauled over the hills. The exception was the mine at Pilgrim's Rest which, thanks to Benjamin's enterprise, was a going concern.

Those far-off shareholders in London may just possibly have been able to imagine what the country in which their mines were situated looked like (they were shown pictures of the mountains surrounding Pilgrim's Rest). What they cannot possibly have imagined were the other difficulties their directors faced. They did not know that within a matter of months three of them would be in the Pretoria jail.

Floating companies by this time was child's play to Lionel Phillips, with the House of Eckstein and Alfred Beit behind him. But all through 1895, while presiding at meetings such as I have described, he was deeply interested in another proposition, the biggest gamble of his life. He was chairman of the Reform Committee, which was secretly planning a revolution against the government of the South African Republic. His code name for the plan which he, Cecil Rhodes, Frank Rhodes, John Hays Hammond and Jameson had prepared was, appropriately enough, "The Flotation". Deeply involved with him were Percy FitzPatrick and Abe Bailey.

Meetings of the directors of the Transvaal Gold Mining Estates Company continued at intervals throughout the year. So did the secret meetings of the "Reformers". Then, on December 29, 1895, Jameson startled the world when, at the head of 500 men, he crossed the Bechuanaland border and made for the Rand. Ten days later Phillips, FitzPatrick and Bailey surrendered themselves to the police and were marched from Pretoria station to the jail.

In the uproar that followed the affairs of mining companies were neglected, and Transvaal Gold Mining Estates was no exception. The first annual meeting was postponed and postponed. Eventually it was set down for July, 1896. But on that day the news spread that the Reformers were to be released, and when the time arrived for the meeting to begin there was no quorum, though some of the new directors (Phillips, FitzPatrick and Bailey having resigned) were in their places. Three days later, on July 11, 1896, Phillips, his sentence of death commuted to a £25,000 fine, was released and carried shoulder high by a cheering throng from Park Station to the Stock Exchange.

Then, on July 16, and only then, was the postponed first annual general meeting of Transvaal Gold Mining Estates held. G. Rouliot, an associate of Alfred Beit's, presided, Phillips, though he took the keenest interest in the affairs of the company to the end of his life, never resumed the chairmanship. But behind the scenes he remained its guiding genius, and he never lost his affection for the wild and rugged country in which the gold was to be found.

I have tried to show that the process by which this new mining venture was founded was anything but prosaic. The truth is that the mines which this company was formed to control have a romantic history that is unparalleled anywhere in the world. More than that — they are inextricably linked with the history of the Transvaal and South Africa, whose destiny they helped to shape.

To tell the full story I must go back many years . . .

CHAPTER II

THE OLD TYRANT

The great central plateau of the Transvaal, which men have always called the Highveld, is held aloft in its north-eastern corner by a spur of the Drakensberg range. On the road to the north-east the village of Machadodorp marks the edge of the plateau. Beyond this the descent begins.

Lydenburg, once the capital of a Voortrekker republic, stands above two mountainous shelves that may, in the beginning of time, have been the shores of the sea.

You climb the last ridge beyond Ohrigstad River and there, 2,000 feet below, lies the Blyde River valley — one of the most beautiful valleys anywhere in the world. Perhaps it is wrong to describe it as a valley, for that suggests gentle slopes and rounded hills. This is a deep rift between two mountain ranges. Here, long ago, Mother Earth smiled and this was the little wrinkle that the smile left upon her scarred face. Four generations of men have halted their journeys on the ridge above the valley, looked down and then, with a sharp intake of breath, remembered the days of their youth. To the Voortrekkers the valley must certainly have seemed a replica of the mountainous beauty of the Cape Colony on which they had turned their backs. To Scotsmen it looked like the Highlands with burns and braes complete. To Welshmen, many of whom were to settle there, it presented a perfect picture of the land of their fathers where the harps once sang . . . This is the valley that shelters the little town of Pilgrim's Rest. It was once a valley of gold.

The road drops sharply down Pilgrim's Hill, crosses the river and then, for about half a mile, becomes the main street of Pilgrim's Rest. Beyond the village it climbs again and then winds round the lower slopes of the mountains on its way down to Graskop. This, too, was a mining town in its day, originally planned as the "capital" of the gold fields. It stands on the edge of the escarpment and below lies the sheer precipice of the Drakensberg. A wide road now runs down through Kowyn's Pass, carved out of the face of the Berg, and as you stand at the top gazing out across the Lowveld to the distant Lebombo mountains you wonder how they ever brought wagons and oxen up and down this mountain side.

For this is the "Great Divide" that has had a profound effect on South Africa's history. It was once the wall that shut the Transvaal off from the sea.

From the very earliest days of the Great Trek from the Cape, the Voortrekkers were obsessed by the idea of finding a route to the sea. They would establish their republic far beyond the boundaries of British rule and then find a seaport to serve as an outlet for their trade. They could achieve true independence only when this dream came true. The thought dominated

"The Voortrekkers were obsessed by the idea of finding a route to the sea."

their lives from the day Natal became a Crown Colony.

There was only one other port available, and that was Delagoa Bay. In 1837 it was little more than a fever-stricken swamp, and the Portuguese would have been happy to sell it to anyone who paid them in cash. But the price they wanted was far beyond anything the first republics could afford. Nevertheless, a road that led to a Portuguese seaport was better than one that meant trafficking with the British in the land from which they had trekked.

It was only 175 miles from the edge of the Highveld to Delagoa Bay, but they were the most difficult 175 miles in Africa. The wagons had to climb up and down the Drakensberg, the barrier from which the early Portuguese explorers had turned back. But that was not the only difficulty. In the lowlands that lay at the foot of the mountains there was fever that laid low men who had faced every other peril in trekking up Africa. Then, too, there was a mysterious sickness that killed cattle (this was the tsetse fly, which flourished in the area between the Sabie River and the Lebombo Mountains) and there was yet another disease that meant death to horses.

Both Louis Trichardt and van Rensburg believed that somewhere in Portuguese territory they might find a paradise where they and their families could settle and establish farms somewhere near the coast. Both died in the search for the settlement of their dreams. Van Rensburg led a party of 29 men and women as far as the banks of the Olifants River near where Phalaborwa is today. There they were all massacred by savage tribes who were terrorising the outlying Portuguese settlements of those days. Louis Trichardt took his party across the Drakensberg in what was one of the most spectacular journeys ever achieved by men, wagons and oxen. But in the Lowveld they all contracted malaria and Trichardt, his wife and most of the party died in Delagoa Bay.

12

Hendrik Potgieter wanted a road to the coast. He and a party of his followers had made a journey to Lourenco Marques in 1840, leaving their wagons and the women and children behind somewhere near where Graskop stands today, and taking their horses down the mountain side through Kowyn's Pass. It was on this journey that Potgieter learned of Louis Trichardt's death. He returned to Delagoa Bay in 1843, this time to meet the emissary of a Dutch trader named George Ohrig, who had sent a ship there and planned to trade with the republics. Though Potgieter, then the only man living who had made the journey twice, knew the terrible hardships that would be involved, he welcomed the plan for trade through Delagoa Bay and assured Ohrig's representative that a road could be made from the Highveld to the coast. This plan, and his determination to live beyond the 25th parallel of latitude, to which limit British rule had now been extended by proclamation, dominated the rest of his life and shaped the history of the Transvaal.

The trekkers, who all came from different parts of the Cape, had never been a united party. They had followed their leaders across the Orange River and there they had camped while scouts explored the land to help them to decide where they were to settle. Far in advance of the main body were Louis Trichardt and van Rensburg, pushing their way to the north to meet their fate. Piet Retief and his party were making their way to Natal.

In the meantime the Matabele under Moselekatse, whose kraal was at Mosega, near where Zeerust is today, brought the wrath of the Voortrekkers down on his head by the brutal murder of two isolated parties of white men and their families. Potgieter led a commando in an attack on the "royal" kraal, killed 2,000 Matabele warriors without losing a man, and drove the whole tribe across the Limpopo to Rhodesia. The Transvaal was now safe for settlement and it was to the Transvaal that Potgieter wanted to lead the wagons.

It was at this point that dissension flared up among the Voortrekkers. Potgieter argued for the beautiful open grasslands that he had seen across the Vaal. But Pretorius and most of the main body had set their hearts on settling in Natal, of which the advance guard had sent back glowing reports. Others had decided to stay where they were, near Winburg in the Orange Free State.

Potgieter bowed to the will of the majority, but at the same time resolved at the first opportunity that he would break away and found his own settlement in the Transvaal. He thought that, since British settlers were already established in Natal, it would not be long before the British Government annexed the whole area. He also warned the trekkers that they would have to fight the Zulus. Both prophecies proved uncannily accurate.

Potgieter did not like Natal. But, more than that, he did not like Pretorius, who was the recognized leader of the larger group of Voortrekkers. The truth was that he was not prepared to take orders from any man, nor had he respect for any opinions but his own. Never was there a more stubborn, determined character. In any case he was never a member of the community. His life in those days consisted of long rides into the unknown, accompanied by a few of his followers. He would be away from the wagons for months on end, to return full of stories of the wonderful country that lay to the north.

Finally his dissatisfaction came to a head. He and his followers loaded their wagons and left. In 1838 they established the first settlement in the Transvaal, on the banks of the Mooi River, and called it Mooiriviersdorp. But this spot had been chosen in the dry weather. When the rains came the settlers were flooded out. They moved seven miles up the river and, in 1841, established a new town which they called Potchefstroom (literally, Chief Potgieter's Stream).

There cannot at this time have been more than 5,000 people in Northern Natal and the Transvaal. They had reached their promised land. There was as much land as anyone wanted. Their cattle flourished, their homesteads began to take shape, and the trees they had planted grew in size. Yet, because their leaders, Andries Pretorius and Andries Hendrik Potgieter could not agree, they were divided into two warring factions. The Natal Republic, established by Pretorius, claimed the right to govern the Transvalers. But Potgieter said: "No". He had established the Transvaal Republic, and he believed in one-man government — the one man being Hendrik Potgieter. And you could not argue with Potgieter because he was never at home. His whole life was spent in expeditions into the interior, and his thinking was governed by plans to get as far away from the British as he could. He might discuss matters with his friend Casper Kruger, Paul Kruger's father, but he took no one's advice and expected obedience from his followers.

Potchefstroom had barely been established when he set off on his first journey to Lourenco Marques. He and his aides-de-camp took their wives and families and their wagons with them on this trip, and they trekked right across the Transvaal to the valley where Lydenburg stands today. From there they went on and climbed the hills above the valley I have described, and thought for the moment that they would have to turn back, for there seemed no way of getting the wagons down the hills. But Casper Kruger rode along the hilltops and found a gap, still called Casper's Nek, which provided a route they could follow (the old road to Ohrigstad still runs that way). They crossed the valley, climbed the mountains on the other side and reached Graskop.

They stood at the top of the escarpment and looked down its almost sheer face, as you may do today. Ahead of them lay the great plain and the mountain range beyond which they knew was Delagoa Bay. But how to get there?

In the end they left their wives and families, wagons, servants and body-guard on the Graskop plain, mounted their horses and rode down a game path.

It was agreed that, if they did not return within a specified time, the

Potgieter and his men rejoin their wives and families on the banks of the Blyde River.

wagons were to go back without them. As week after week passed, the wives grew more and more anxious. It looked as though their husbands would never return. At last the time came for them to begin the homeward journey. The wagons were loaded up, the oxen inspanned, and they set off on a sorrowful trek. It might well be that they were now a party of widows and orphans. In this dark hour they named the river beside which they had camped the "Treur" (River of Sorrow). But they had barely crossed the valley when behind them they heard the sound of hooves, shots and joyful shouts. Potgieter and his men had climbed the Berg unscathed and followed the wagon tracks.

In their thankfulness at being reunited they called the river they had first sighted from the hills above the River of Joy (the Blyde River), and that is the name it has borne for nearly 140 years.

I cannot recount here all the events that followed — the re-occupation of Port Natal by the British, the intermittent quarrels between the Pretorius faction and the Potgieter clan, or the complicated enactments of the Volksraad of Natal by which it sought to harness Potgieter and the Transvalers to obedience to the wishes of the majority. There was a semblance of government in Natal, but in the Transvaal the word of Potgieter was the law and nobody supposed that he took any notice of such instructions as were sent to him from Natal.

However, in between expeditions to the interior, he consented to a conference with Pretorius which led to the formation of a Transvaal Council, which acknowledged the authority of the Natal Volksraad but recognized

Potgieter as its Head Commandant, who was entitled to take its advice or not as he pleased.

Potgieter believed that the Natal Republic could not last. He had always maintained that the British meant to "swallow it up". When that day came in 1844 with the collapse of the Natal Republic and the landing of British troops in Durban, he gave formal notice to the British Government and to the citizens of Natal that the Transvaal would henceforth be a free and independent republic, all ties with Natal having been severed. He formed a Citizens' Council, every man of which agreed with every word he said, and published a constitution.

The exodus from Natal now began, and grew in volume in 1845 when it was announced that Natal was to become a Crown Colony. The people who had all laughed at Potgieter now flocked to join the "wild men" across the Vaal. Potchefstroom was surrounded by the wagons and tents of the new arrivals.

In the meantime, Potgieter had been studying the proclamation of the Governor of the Cape Colony, proclaiming jurisdiction over all territory south of latitude 25°. He had this ruled off on a map, and found that it included part of the territory north of the Vaal, including Potchefstroom. It was as he had feared. British rule was creeping up on him again. He seems not to have considered the impossibility of giving effect to the proclamation. It was time for him and his faithful followers to move on.

He announced to a mass meeting of the burgers of Potchefstroom his intention of trekking off into the wilds again, to found a new capital north of latitude 25°. In June, 1845, he began the trek, heading for the fertile land far to the north which he had seen on his first trip to Delagoa Bay four years earlier. He wanted the new capital to be as near the coast as possible. There, he told himself, he would establish a new settlement, and with the promised aid of Ohrig, the Dutch merchant, establish trade with Europe. It meant a trek of 350 miles, it meant establishing a new town, it meant finding a road that would take him through the Drakensberg. But what were such trifles as these to the dauntless Hendrik Potgieter? His fellow countrymen could follow him or not, as they pleased. He would go alone if necessary.

There are times when, in reading of the never-ending journeys of this stubborn, tireless man I feel a twinge of sympathy for the members of the Potgieter family and his lieutenants. They were for ever being required to pack up, to wave good-bye to a place they had learned to love and to move off into the wilderness. He was on the move for the best part of 16 years. No less than five Mrs. Potgieters bore the brunt of his restlessness. Four of his wives died. The fifth survived him. Yet he was only 60 when his turn came.

On this trek to the north Potgieter followed the route he had taken in 1840. On that expedition a broad, well-watered valley had caught his eye, not far from the precipitous descent that led to the valley of the river they called the Blyde River. He knew where to find it, and after some six weeks

16

of travel in very cold weather they outspanned for the last time and began to lay out a town modelled, small though it was, on Potchefstroom. They gave it one of the oddest names a town has ever borne — Andries Ohrigstad. This was a combination of the leader's first name and the surname of the Dutch merchant who was to trade with the new settlement via Delagoa Bay.

Alas! Andries Ohrigstad was to prove a town of disaster. It was unbearably hot in summer and infested by mosquitoes. Among them were the anopheles, and men returning from hunting trips in the Lowveld brought the malarial infection with them. Soon almost the whole population had fever. Many of them died, for they had no idea how to treat it.

Malaria, particularly other people's malaria, Potgieter could have borne with equanimity. What he could not bear was a faction in the town that questioned his authority and demanded a form of democratic rule. These people set up a Volksraad and, always the first step in these disputes, published a constitution which laid it down that the Head Commandant should take orders from the Volksraad.

This was too much for the old warhorse. He did what he had always done in such a situation. He moved on. After two years of bitter quarrels he called his followers together and trekked to a new settlement in the Zoutpansberg, leaving the inhabitants of Ohrigstad to their fever and their feuds. They could have their Volksraad, but they would have to get along without a leader.

That was the end of Ohrigstad. Potgieter had founded the town. Potgieter destroyed it. The survivors asked themselves why they should endure fever and the paralysing heat of summer in a town that no longer had a meaning. They, too, climbed into their wagons and trekked to higher ground 25 miles further south. They called their new town Lydenburg, the town of suffering. The name was a memorial to the friends and relatives who had died of malaria. It might equally well have described the unhappiness of the younger generation, who had found the rule of the Old Tyrant of the Transvaal unbearable. Lydenburg, with his influence removed, was a much more cheerful place than Ohrigstad had ever been.

In the meantime Andries Pretorius had taken part in the battle of Boomplaats, had been defeated and now had a price of £2,000 placed upon his head by the British. This meant that he had to take refuge beyond the Vaal. Whether he liked it or not he was now a Transvaler.

You have now to picture the Transvaal as a state, if state it could be called, without a head, without a central government and without unity. The burgers of Potchefstroom recognized Pretorius as their leader. Far to the north, Hendrik Potgieter ruled the settlement in the Zoutpansberg, while Lydenburg hung as a sort of floating trophy between the two, the acknowledged leader of the community now being W.F. Joubert. The one law that everybody recognized was the decision of the Potchefstroom Volksraad that every burger over the age of 16 was entitled to take up two farms — surely the most generous provision ever made for the citizens of a new state.

Then the British government in the far-off Cape Colony suddenly changed its policy. It gave up all attempts to control the northern territories and to expand British rule. Hitherto the Voortrekkers had been outlaws. But in 1851 their independence was at last recognized. Pretorius was summoned to attend the Sand River Convention in 1852. There a treaty was signed which guaranteed the autonomy of the new state beyond the Vaal, and announced Britain's intention of establishing friendly relations. The nonsensical claim to the administration of all the land south of latitude 25° South was dropped.

To the Voortrekkers this was the lifting of a dark cloud. For 16 years they had lived in the wilderness as a protest at what they regarded as the injustices inflicted on them in the Cape, and always at the back of their minds had been the fear that British rule would catch up with them; by annexation, by war or other means. Now they had their charter, signed by the representatives of the British Government.

For Pretorius this was a triumph. He had been recognized as head of the new state. The treaty had been given into his hands, and the ground had been cut from under the feet of his old rival, Potgieter.

There ought to have been peace and unity after this, for the state that had been a state in name only now had its charter. But there was more trouble to come. Pretorius and Potgieter met at the new town of Rustenburg on March 15, 1852, and for the first time in all their troubled careers appeared to reach agreement. But in fact they both remained Commandants-General and made the disastrous decision that, when they had gone, their heirs should jointly hold this rank in perpetuity.

It has never been clearly explained why their followers accepted this principle of hereditary leadership, which ran contrary to the republican principles to which they owed allegiance. It must be supposed that, in their joy at the reconciliation of their leaders, they were prepared to agree to anything. The two old men were their heroes, venerated for the part they had played in leading the Great Trek. Neither of them had long to live. Their joint decision that their sons should inherit the leadership was not a subject for argument at the time. But it was to lead to 20 years of strife and culminate in civil war.

Andries Hendrik Potgieter died at his home in the Zoutpansberg on December 16, 1852. Andries Pretorius, who was then only 54, ought to have succeeded to the position that was rightly his as the last surviving leader of the Trek. He was a man of great ability who might have wisely governed the new state for another 20 years.

But he died only seven months after Potgieter had been buried. Thus the old feuds were perpetuated, for the people were left to choose between two new leaders, both young and untried, and the ship of state was still without a rudder.

CHAPTER III

A BANKRUPT REPUBLIC

The population of the South African Republic grew rapidly in the era between the founding of Potchefstroom and the advance of the Trekkers to Lydenburg and the Zoutpansberg. Nevertheless the entire population of the Transvaal at the time of which I am writing was no greater than that of a small town in Europe. There may have been 15,000 people within the borders of the Republic in 1850. In the next twenty years the total increased to 40,000. But it was still a poor country inhabited by poor people. From the President downwards everyone who lived there was on the verge of destitution. There were no industries. Every commodity required for civilised living had to be brought to Pretoria by wagon and the farmers' main source of income was by the barter of hides, ivory and biltong. There were rumours that the land was rich in minerals — gold, silver and iron. But the State did nothing to encourage prospecting.

Nearly all the difficulties and disasters the people had to endure at that time would have vanished if only they had stumbled on the gold that was there for the taking. Gold would have produced the capital that would have built their road to Lourenco Marques and given them railways much earlier in the day. They would almost certainly have owned the port of Delagoa Bay. They might have established a central capital, had a strong government, and been one of the most prosperous small countries in the world. But they never thought of looking for gold.

There were not many trained geologists in those days, and certainly there was none among the Voortrekkers. Nevertheless, it is astonishing that those sharp-eyed hunters failed to spot the visible gold in the river beds and on the hillsides of the Eastern Transvaal.

I have before me a map which shows the area of which I am writing. By drawing two parallel lines on it roughly three inches apart I can enclose an area from which well over R60,000,000 worth of gold has been taken in the past 100 years. And between the same lines I can plot the route that Hendrik Potgieter took on his first trip to Lourenco Marques in 1840. This was the road the hunters followed on their winter expeditions to the Lowveld. It led them straight across a gold field that was later to attract more than 2,000 diggers. The wheels of their wagons must have churned the gold-bearing gravel in the rivers. Again and again they must have walked past nuggets of solid gold lying exposed on the slopes they climbed. But they were not looking for gold, so they passed it by, their eyes on the road that lay ahead.

Probably had old Hendrik Potgieter known that there was gold in his beloved Transvaal he would have said: "We must inspan and trek. This will bring the British after us". Years afterwards Paul Kruger had much this

Building a water race at Pilgrim's Rest.

attitude to gold. Leo Weinthal, editor of the Pretoria Press in Republican days, recorded a statement of his that reads as follows:

"When, in 1885, the burgers of the lonely, fever-stricken De Kaap Valley came to their clannish old President (wrote Weinthal) announcing the discovery of a vast, auriferous Eldorado which would raise their country, threatened again with bankruptcy, to marvellous prosperity (Weinthal was speaking of Bray's Golden Quarry, the portal to the Sheba Mine at Barberton and he was rather given to long sentences), Oom Paul remained silent and was lost in deep thought for many minutes before replying as follows:

'Do not talk to me of gold, the element which brings more dissension, misfortune and unexpected plagues in its trail than benefits. Pray to God, as am doing, that the curse connected with its coming may not overshadow our dear land just after it has come again to us and our children. Pray and implore Him who has stood by us that He will continue to do so, for I tell you today that every ounce of gold taken from the bowels of our soil will yet have to be weighed up with rivers of tears, with the life-blood of thousands of our best in the defence of that soil the lust of others yearning for it solely because it has the yellow metal in abundance'.

So might Potgieter have spoken had he known. And yet how badly the Transvaal needed the revenue the gold was to bring it, and how gladly it welcomed its new-found prosperity. For the best part of 20 years it tottered on the very verge of bankruptcy, its currency inflated, its people living by exchanging the produce of their farms for the supplies they needed, and its credit exhausted. Indeed, there was a time when all the assets of the republic were in pledge to the banks. Gold saved it from disaster — and saved it in the nick of time.

After the death of the patriarchs their sons, Marthinus Wessel Pretorius and Pieter Potgieter, became joint Commandants-General. But Potgieter was killed in the campaign against Makapan. His son Andries, aged nine, became

20

heir to the title. Then Mrs. Potgieter married again and her husband, Stephanus Schoeman, as Andries's step-father, appointed himself as a sort of acting Commandant-General until the boy should come of age. Young Andries never came of age. He died. His step-father, who was an aggressive man with whom no one cared to argue, then assumed command, though he had no shadow of right to the hereditary rank.

Pretorius, who saw no hope of ever agreeing with Schoeman, left him severely alone. He appointed a commission to draft a constitution for a central government, and in 1856 called a conference in Potchefstroom to consider the plan. The commission produced a constitution largely modelled on the American one. This was discussed in detail and for days. Finally it was accepted.

It provided that the new state should be called the South African Republic, that it would have a President elected for five years, an executive council and volksraad elected for two years. Power would be almost completely in the hands of the volksraad. There would be only one recognized church, the Dutch Reformed Church, and no equality between white and black. Potchefstroom was to be the capital, although Pretorius already had a plan at the back of his mind for a more central capital.

Pretorius was elected the first President of the republic, and found himself with trouble on his hands.

As a sop to the Potgieter faction, who obviously were not going to be happy under a new government and a president who did not come from their ranks, Stephanus Schoeman had been elected Commandant-General. But, though this legitimized the title he had assumed, Schoeman refused the position. He was not going to serve under Pretorius.

Lydenburg reacted even more sharply. The burgers there had not been consulted, and they maintained that the conference ought to have been held in their town where, it had been agreed, the volksraad should meet from time to time. They were not going to take instructions from Potchefstroom.

They severed all ties with the new republic, ran up their own flag and declared the town and district "De Republiek Lydenburg en Zuid Afrika". This happened on March 11, 1857, and Lydenburg maintained its independence for three years.

Pretorius decided to ignore the mutineers in the north. It was undoubtedly his wisest course, for he had a number of irons in the fire at this time. One of his plans was for the unification of the Transvaal and the Orange Free State under his Presidency. Another was for a central town that would serve as the seat of the government and commemorate his father.

The Free Staters rejected Pretorius's overtures, and an attempt to make them change their minds almost led to a battle before the President grasped the fact that he was not wanted in the Free State and retired. His project for a town on the banks of the Aapies River was more successful and, in February 1857, with the building of a church and the appointment of a landdrost,

Pretoria was born, though its name was first "Pretoriusdorp" and then "Pretorium" before it finally became "Pretoria".

Pretorius, working hard for unity, succeeded in coming to terms with the Potgieter clan, though this meant that he had to accept the rebellious Schoeman as his Commandant-General. He achieved this agreement in 1859, and followed it up by getting the Lydenburg republic back into the fold, after negotiations that lasted almost 12 months. Both the Lydenburgers and the Zoutpansburgers thought that Potchefstroom was too far off to be the capital. Thus Pretoria, the republic's newest town, came into its own.

If Pretorius had stayed at home after this he might have welded the warring factions in the Transvaal into one people, and ushered in an era of peace and something approaching prosperity. But throughout the negotiations he had one eye on the Free State, and no sooner had the uneasy truce been reached than he was off across the Vaal to press his claims for the Presidency of the neighbouring state. Lydenburg officially merged itself into the South African Republic on April 3rd, 1860. But there was no President to welcome it into the fold. In January that year Pretorius had been elected President of the Orange Free State, and had applied for six months leave of absence from the Transvaal.

Although this happened over a hundred years ago, constitutional lawyers are still puzzled as to how the state secretaries and members of the two volksraads could have agreed to an arrangement by which one man was elected to rule two separate states. It was not merely unworkable, but probably illegal as well. It may well be that every document to which Pretorius put his hand in those days was without the force of law, not that it worried anyone then, or worries them now.

No one doubts today that Pretorius was full of good intentions. He was trying to carry out his father's dying command that he should work to bring about unity among the survivors of the Trek and their descendants. He sincerely believed that this was his mission in life. But he seems to have over-estimated the power of his personality and to have persuaded himself that he had but to give the command and the people of the Free State and the Transvaal would join hands.

No sooner had his leave from the Transvaal reached its term than he applied for leave from the Free State, and returned to Pretoria to begin the negotiations which he hoped would eventually lead to union.

But the Volksraad was in no mood to approve of anything its absentee President proposed. It bluntly told him that he must choose between the Transvaal and the Free State. He could not be President of both.

Pretorius was deeply wounded by the Volksraad's lack of faith in him, by its failure to understand the ideals for which he was working. He resigned the Presidency of the Transvaal and crossed the Vaal again.

But Potchefstroom, where every man was for Pretorius, refused to accept the Volksraad's ruling. A mass meeting was held which proceeded to declare the Volksraad dissolved, to reverse its decision and re-elect Pretorius, while appointing the Commandant-General Schoeman acting President in his absence.

The revolutionaries, if this is the name they deserve, made a mistake in appointing Schoeman, for this presented him with the opportunity he had always wanted. He called a meeting of the Volksraad and sat by without batting an eyelid while that muddled assembly ordered the arrest of the very men who, quite illegally, had appointed him.

This so enraged Pretorius's supporters that they took up arms and, with Paul Kruger at their head, marched on Pretoria to deal with Schoeman.

But before they reached the town a meeting was arranged at which Pretorius presided. It was agreed to wipe the slate clean, elect a new Volksraad and settle down to obey its commands. The election was held, and the new Volksraad's first action was to sack Schoeman and all the officials he had appointed.

It was at that point that the civil war began, for Schoeman flatly refused to accept the Volksraad's ruling and stayed on in Pretoria issuing commands in his capacity as acting President. Paul Kruger led his men back to Pretoria. Schoeman and his followers bolted for Potchefstroom.

There is no really accurate chronicle of what happened after this. Kruger and Schoeman chased one another about the Transvaal with occasional exchanges of shots but few casualties. Pretoria and Potchefstroom were "occupied" again and again by the opposing forces. Their stay in the town would give them just enough time to commandeer supplies, dismiss all the civil servants appointed by the other side and then march out because the "enemy" was approaching.

In the end government had virtually ceased, and no one was quite certain what the warring commandos were fighting over except that Kruger's forces represented the Government and the others were "rebels".

There were several abortive elections during this period, in which scarcely anyone voted. Then at last Pretorius, having resigned the Presidency of the Free State, returned in 1864 and acted as mediator between Kruger and Schoeman.

Another election was held in which only 2,600 votes were cast, and Pretorius was once more elected, by a majority of 400 votes. Paul Kruger became Commandant-General.

It was, of course, a comic little civil war in which many of the combatants were the first or second cousins of men on the other side, and all were really members of one large family. It is easy today to laugh at the whole affair and tell funny stories about the night riders and the commandos who fought on the principle that he who fights and runs away lives to fight another day. But the truth is that it was a period of anarchy which had the most disastrous consequences for years to come. It undermined the morale of the landdrosts, who were left wondering whose orders they should obey and whether their salaries would ever be paid. It brought the Republic to a state of bankruptcy and, worst of all, encouraged the native tribes to acts of lawlessness. The word soon went round that the white men were killing one another (though this was a gross exaggeration), and the cattle thieves went into action. The loss of face the republic suffered among the tribes during this upheaval was to involve them in the "kaffir wars" of the future.

One man, and one man only, emerged with credit from the fratricidal struggle. This was young Paul Kruger, the Rustenburg hunter who was the Oliver Cromwell of his day. Kruger had no doubts about the rights and wrongs of the situation. He was for law and order, the upholder of the "volkswil". The veneration that his fellow countrymen felt for him in after years began in these troublous times.

Marthinus Wessel Pretorius's life must have been a nightmare during this period. He was for ever dashing backwards and forwards between the Transvaal and the Free State, trying to settle the problems of the states he was supposed to govern. Indeed, the broad national road that runs between Bloemfontein and Pretoria today might well be named the "Pretorius Highway", for long stretches of it were hammered out by the hooves of his horses.

Theoretically, when he returned to Pretoria in 1864 and was re-elected President of the South African Republic, he had his second chance. In fact there was no second chance. It was too late. Even an administrative genius, backed by large quantities of hard cash, would have had difficulty in tidying up the appalling muddle into which the affairs of the republic had fallen. Pretorius had neither genius nor cash. He survived another election in 1869 in which only a fraction of the population voted. Then, after his inefficiency in presenting his case to the arbitration court cost the South African Republic its legitimate share of the newly discovered diamond field on the lower Vaal (in the Bloemhof district), the Volksraad turned against him. It asked him to leave and, in 1871, he went. With him went the hereditary principle that his father and Potgieter had sought to establish.

The people of the Transvaal now made a momentous decision. They decided to find a President outside the borders of their own state, a man who belonged to neither faction and to whom the quarrels of the past would have no meaning. I say the "people", but it was the elders of the Volksraad who came to this decision. They consulted President Brand of the Free State. Brand recommended one Thomas Francois Burgers, a Dutch Reformed predikant whose parsonage was at Hanover in the Cape Province.

Why Brand made this recommendation and why the Volksraad accepted it we shall never know for, in the light of subsequent history, it was an extraordinary proposal. Burgers had many of the qualities that the republic needed. He was young, vigorous, well-educated and had travelled widely. He also had some knowledge of economics and was certainly progressive. But he had had little administrative experience beyond that provided by his ministrations to his flock, and had been involved in a quarrel with the elders of his church. They had suspended him for expressing views contrary to the established doctrine. He had answered them by taking the matter to the Cape Supreme Court, having the decision of the Synod reversed and himself reinstated in his ministry. This had not endeared him to the church, which never ceased to use its influence against him.

In addition to this he was something of a romantic and full of "new-fangled" ideas. Anyone less like old Hendrik Potgieter, or more certain to clash with the old conservatives of the Transvaal Volksraad, it would have been hard to imagine. Nevertheless, he was the man they chose.

There was an election, in which just over 3,000 votes were cast. Thomas Francois Burgers, the unknown, secured 2,964 of them and, on June 27, 1872, arrived in Pretoria to be sworn in as President. He was 37 years of age — 16 years older than Cecil Rhodes, who at that time was building his fortune on the diamond fields. He was better educated than Paul Kruger, better educated than Rhodes, but he lacked their skill in handling men.

Burgers ought to have had no illusions about the awe-inspiring muddle that he was now expected to tidy up. News of what had been happening there had reached the Cape, and it had been freely prophesied that the republic's days were numbered, that it might even be necessary to send troops to help the burgers in their wars with the Venda and the Pedi.

Even so, there were shocks for the new President when he began to investigate the affairs of state. There was virtually no revenue, and what there was available had not been collected. The treasury had met every new financial crisis by printing bank notes. The republican £5 note, known as the "blueback", was worth about R6 in the outside world, and the only currencies that commanded any respect were the coins and notes of the Cape Colony and Natal. Anyone who was required to live on a salary, and this applied to all the public servants, was bankrupt unless he could supplement his income by other means. That meant, of course, that there was a great deal of corruption of petty theft.

Men who owned wagons and oxen lived by shooting game and making an annual pilgrimage to Potchefstroom or Pietermaritzburg, where they bartered the products of their farms — karosses, ivory and biltong — for things they needed and perhaps a little "foreign" cash. As far as they could, people clung on to this "real" money and paid their debts in republican bank notes. But the stage had been reached where, before a sale went through, the seller often stipulated that he must be paid in Cape notes or even in cattle rather than in the debased currency of the Republic. Merchants issued "good-fors" in the form of cardboard squares. There were even little tickets of this description issued for popping into the collection in lieu of cash at church services.

Burgers tackled the financial problem by persuading the Cape Commercial Bank to lend the state £66,000. He obtained this advance with difficulty, for no one regarded the South African Republic as a good risk, but the money sufficed to pay the salaries of the disgruntled civil servants and also enabled him to call in some of the worthless notes and stave off the crisis. But it was only a temporary despite. If the Republic was to survive it had to have more sources of revenue. It was spending a great deal more than it was getting in.

Burgers began to lay the foundations of his subsequent unpopularity by sacking corrupt officials, by insisting on proper book-keeping in all departments, and by trying to collect the accumulation of unpaid taxes.

Whether he could have saved the state and restored its credit, and what would have happened if he had failed, are open questions. Historians with some knowledge of accountancy who have attempted to investigate the public accounts of the day have emerged from their researches pale and shaken. The South African Republic was undoubtedly bankrupt in 1872, and heading for greater bankruptcy. It is to be doubted whether it was even justified in paying its President a salary.

Its proper course of action, the only remedy for its ills, would have been to apply to the government of Natal to be taken over as a protectorate in exchange for a loan that would have built the railway, the roads and the schools it needed.

Such a course was quite unthinkable to the people of the Transvaal. They would have torn to pieces anyone who suggested it. The spirit of Potgieter still lived in the land.

It was at this point that South Africa's fairy godmother, who stands perpetually in the wings waiting for just such a crisis as this, made her second appearance on the scene (she had already appeared at Kimberley in the Cape with diamonds). This time it was gold she brought — traces of gold that seemed to say: "Search and ye shall find".

The effect was miraculous. It was as though a dying man had risen from his bed and walked.

There was not much gold at first, only an ounce or two. But the South African Republic's credit improved overnight. The banks were still inclined to be cautious. There had been rumours and announcements in earlier days, but no gold. This, too, might prove to be a false alarm (as, indeed, it did). Let the chickens be hatched before they were counted. At the same time . . .

The fact was that the world was starved of gold at that time. There was no steady, uninterrupted supply of this most precious of commodities on which world trade depended. There had been finds in California and in Australia, but the banking houses of London, Paris and Berlin would have been happy to buy 10 times as much of it as they were getting. The mere fact that there might be gold in the Transvaal made the South African Republic important in their eyes.

New maps of Africa began to appear on the walls of offices in London. It was in a place called the Transvaal, 500 miles north of Kimberley. Might be worth watching . . . It was called the South African Republic . . . The

President was a fellow called Burgers, used to be a parson . . . that sounded promising . . . Nothing much so far, but we'll keep an eye on it.

The name of Thomas Burgers is for ever linked with the first discovery of gold. It was the only bit of luck he ever had, poor man!

CHAPTER IV

THE SEARCH FOR GOLD

The first geologist to visit the Transvaal was an Englishman named John Henry Davis. He arrived in 1851 — just after the independence of the republic had been recognized by Britain.

There are two quite separate stories about Davis's visit, neither of which can be confirmed. One is that he arrived independently, prospected and found gold, and was then hustled over the border and told never to return — because the republic feared that if it were known that he had found gold the British would forget their promises and annex the country.

The other story says that President Pretorius met him in Natal and invited him to visit the Transvaal to prospect for precious stones and metals, but that he found no trace of anything worth mining.

What I cannot understand about the first version of the facts is why, supposing that it is true that Davis was deported, the republican government did nothing about his discovery after he had gone. Undoubtedly they were worried about their somewhat tenuous title to the land in which they had established their state. Yet barely a year afterwards, when a second prospector appeared on the scene and, perhaps because he was not an Englishman, received official encouragement, they had no information to give him.

This second prospector started his career by finding traces of gold not far from where Johannesburg stands today. He was a man from the Cape Colony named Pieter Jacob Marais, who had worked on the Californian gold fields and was thus entitled to call himself a "Forty-Niner". He had had no luck in California, had travelled to Australia where he worked on the Bendigo field, but without success there either. He panned gravel in the Crocodile River and in the Yukskei, and was able to produce a microscopic "tail" of gold. He hurried to Potchefstroom with his find.

The members of the Volksraad studied his specks of gold and authorised him to continue prospecting. He was to have a reward of £500 if he found payable gold, was to be manager of any mine that might be found, and to have a share of the profits. He was sworn to secrecy on pain of death. Quite what the Volksraad meant to do if gold was found we do not know. But they wanted to be sure that there would be no announcements and no influx of settlers.

What was at the back of their minds is revealed by the clause in the agreement which said: "Should it happen that P.J. Marais divulges any information about the conditions of the discovered gold mines, or anything in connection therewith to any foreign power, government or any particular person, and by doing so causes the independence of the Republic to be disturbed or threatened in any way, such action shall be punished with the penalty of

28

death and no extenuating circumstances will be taken into consideration".

With this terrifying penalty hanging over his head Marais went prospecting all over the Transvaal, for two years. There was no secrecy about what he was doing. His few specks of gold had launched the wildest rumours, and though everybody said: "Marais's prospecting for gold. Keep it dark . . ." everybody told everybody else. Marais had informed the Volksraad that, in his opinion, there was more gold in South Africa than in America and Australia combined. It was a most remarkably accurate forecast of what was to come and, as he was the only man with mining experience available, it started a wave of optimism. Unfortunately he knew nothing about geology and very little about prospecting. He found no gold.

We know today that there was visible gold in the gravel of the rivers in the Pilgrim's Rest area, and that after heavy rain storms nuggets were exposed on the slopes of the mountains. The Voortrekkers found early workings in various parts of the country, and they noticed that some of the more comely native women wore ornaments of gold. How was it that, in spite of these indications, in spite of Marais's prospecting, it was 30 years before the first real find was made? The answer is that the Transvalers were a pastoral people who simply were not interested in minerals or mining.

As for Marais, the Witwatersrand outcrop meant nothing to him. He was looking for alluvial gold. He panned in the beds of hundreds of rivers but, such is the luck of the draw, he panned in the wrong places. It was perhaps fortunate for his peace of mind that he died without knowing what he had missed.

After the failure of Marais's expedition the Volksraad rather lost interest in gold. It was, of course, pre-occupied with affairs of state such as the new constitution, the secession of the Lydenburg and Zoutpansberg republics and the civil war. It thought it had heard the last of gold mines.

Then on to the scene, in 1866, strode a German schoolmaster named Karl Gottlieb Mauch with a passion for exploration, geology and botany. Mauch's motto was: "Go anywhere, do anything". He ranks as the most energetic explorer who ever visited Africa. For four years he trekked backwards and forwards across the nothern territories collecting rock specimens and panning in the beds of rivers.

He was like a badly trained pointer. He was always hot on the trail of gold, but as often as not he pointed in the wrong direction. Yet so impressive was his personality (and his collection of geological specimens), so obvious his sincerity that he lives in history as the "father" of South African gold mining. He died penniless, as did most of the early mining companies who followed his lead. But the fact remains that his reports started the boom in the Transvaal and, in the long run, led to the formation of the Chartered Company and the exploration of Rhodesia. One cannot point today to a single discovery made by Mauch that actually resulted in the opening up of a payable mine, though he did once point in a general direction east of Lyden-

29

burg and say: "Gold will be found there". Nevertheless he set the ball rolling.

He joined up with Henry Hartley, the hunter, and trekked with him to the wilds of Matabeleland. He visited the Zimbabwe ruins and toured the whole area north and south of the Limpopo.

He found gold in the Tati River in 1867, and when he returned to Potchefstroom at the end of this trip he gave a statement to the *Transvaal Argus* which was to be reproduced in newspapers throughout the world. Mauch combined the old workings that Hartley had shown him and the traces of gold he had found in the Tati River to build up a theory that Africa had once supported a great gold industry, and that in due course it would build another, even greater, chain of gold mines. He was, of course, absolutely wrong in his theory as to where the gold would be found. He honestly believed that somewhere in the area where he had prospected the fabled mines of King Solomon would be discovered.

Immediately, the Transvaal was "in the news" — not as a gold-bearing area, but as a jumping-off place for the legendary gold mines in the north. All sorts of strange characters began arriving in Potchefstroom, looking for guides who could lead them to the Tati River. Commandant Jan Viljoen was sent, at the head of a commando, to see Moselekatse and obtain concessions from him. On his return President Pretorius issued a proclamation claiming for the republic all the land to the north of where Mauch had said that gold would be found. No one outside the Transvaal took the least notice of this announcement. Both Britain and Portugal at this time expected the republic to collapse through lack of funds and maladministration. They were not perturbed by a claim that could not possibly be made good.

The first expedition left Potchefstroom on March 11, guided by Henry Hartley. It called the area in the Tati River the "New Victoria Gold Field", a title that was scarcely justified by the small quantity of gold it produced. Mauch returned with financial backing and set off to explore the region north-east of Lydenburg. He found a little gold in the Selati River and started another crop of rumours. But his only tangible reward was the naming of the Mauchberg which towered above the gold fields that he failed to find.

Potchefstroom by this time had begun to grow accustomed to seeing parties of prospectors heading north, full of optimism and armed with picks and spades. It cheerfully sold at a profit all the things the diggers wanted, and was kind to them when they returned broke and disillusioned.

Presently there hove into view an expedition such as no one had ever seen before. It was led by Sir John Swinburne, who was a relative of the poet, and brought with it a steam engine and mountains of gear. Swinburne was the representative of a company called the London and Limpopo Mining Company, which had been formed to investigate Mauch's discoveries and be first in the field. Swinburne bought a building in Potchefstroom. He offered to buy up the whole note issue of the Transvaal and all the land that was available, but the Volksraad said: "No". He could explore wherever he liked beyond the Limpopo, but the Transvaal wanted no British companies buying up its land.

Thomas Baines was among these early prospectors, and in his *Gold Regions of Africa* and his diaries you may find some description of those early days. But Baines was better as an artist than as a writer or prospector, and the treasure he left us had little to do with gold.

All the Tati expeditions failed. They left behind them as they beat a retreat, a number of prospectors who hadn't their passage money home but who had found that they could live in South Africa by shooting and trading with the natives, and so continue their search for gold. Mauch, still the prophet they followed, had declared that there was gold almost everywhere. The hope that springs eternal in the prospector's breast kept them going. They were soon scattered throughout the northern areas of the Transvaal, though the discovery of diamonds at the Cape thinned them out when the news came through.

It must be remembered that in those days prospectors always looked for gold in river beds. This was how it had been found in America and Australia, and how they thought it would be found in Africa. Every prospector's kit therefore included a shallow iron basin, known as a "pan", into which samples of the gravel were put and washed in the hope that, as the pebbles and the soil were sluiced away, there would be left a trace of gold. The maddening feature of the rivers of Africa was that such traces were often found, but they were false trails. Had you scooped out every cubic yard of gravel in the area where these traces were panned, and washed it thoroughly and carefully, there would have been at most an ounce or two of gold. The hills of Africa cling very firmly to their treasure.

Among the prospectors who tramped across the Transvaal in 1869 was a party from Natal led by Edward Button, who was accompanied by George Parsons and James Sutherland. Sutherland was the most experienced prospector in the group, for he had worked on the alluvial diggings in California and Australia. He had, in fact, spent the greater part of his life in the hunt for gold. All three of them had prospected in Natal without success.

They arrived just about the time that Mauch had visited the foothills of the Drakensberg beyond Lydenburg, and they were impressed by the claims he made for the district. So, instead of joining the rush to the Tati River, they made for Lydenburg and, using that town as a starting point, headed north-east. There another prospector named Tom McLachlan joined them. He knew the district.

Almost immediately they had some luck. In several of the streams beyond Lydenburg — the Spekboom River was certainly one — they found traces of gold. They moved farther on and split into two parties, Button and Sutherland pushing north as far as the Murchison Range (which they named), while McLachlan and Parsons fossicked round above the edge of the Berg where Graskop is today.

31

On one of his visits to Lydenburg for supplies, Button was told that traces of gold had been found on the farm "Eersteling", near Marabastad, and he was invited to prospect there. He went there in 1870.

There is very little information available about what Button, Parsons, Sutherland and McLachlan did between 1869 and the end of 1870. But the knowledge we have today makes it clear that the game of blind man's buff was almost at an end. These four experienced prospectors were now at work in an area where there was a great deal of free gold. I have a strong suspicion that they found it but decided to keep their mouths shut. They were "uitlanders" and, although the republic was now showing a more friendly attitude to prospectors, they had no guarantee that they would be allowed to continue working or, for that matter, to keep the gold they found. It had been the clear intention of the Volksraad to take over any payable gold that Marais found. Button and his partners had every reason to suspect that this would be the fate of any find they made.

If they sold their gold in the Transvaal they would be paid out in worthless bank notes. The sensible course would be to keep the gold and get the full price for it from the Bank of Natal.

On December 21, 1970, the Volksraad passed a resolution which read: "The Raad resolves to empower the Government to grant reasonable rewards for the finding of precious stones and precious minerals such as gold, silver, etc. This is to be acted on provisionally and to be made law at the next sitting".

Twelve days later, on January 2, 1871, Button wrote to the landdrost of Lydenburg claiming a reward for the discovery of gold made by himself, McLachlan and Sutherland on fields that were situated five days journey from Lydenburg.

Allowing for the necessary time for the news of the Volksraad's decision to reach him, he could hardly have acted more promptly.

Shortly afterwards he announced that he had found gold at "Eersteling", and sent samples to Pretoria for the Volksraad's inspection. He then visited Pretoria in person and described his find. The Volksraad appointed a commission to investigate the discovery, and its members looked with awe at the two ounces of gold which Button had produced. Every prospector in the country rushed to the area and started fossicking. But the Volksraad granted Button a concession and, armed with this, he went off to London where he floated the Transvaal Gold Mining Company with a capital of £50,000 — the first gold mining company in the country to work a mine.

The Eersteling mine produced some gold — enough at any rate to whet the appetite of the prospectors. But it is doubtful whether the mine did more than pay for the 12-stamp battery that Button imported. Nevertheless, it was the Transvaal's first gold mine, and as such has immortalised Button, its finder.

The Volksraad seems to have shared my suspicions for, shortly after the excitement of Eersteling, it clarified the mining law, laying down that:

Mining rights were the property of the State.

A discoverer who did not give immediate notice of his find to the nearest landdrost would forfeit his reward.

The Government would investigate all reported finds and, if they were payable, would appoint a commission to exercise control.

It also laid down the scale of rewards payable for the discovery of gold fields:

£500 if 500 ounces of gold were produced within 12 months.

£750 if 500 to 1,000 ounces of gold were produced within 12 months.

£1,000 if the amount exceeded 1,000 ounces.

This was amended after Burgers became President to a reward of £500 payable to anyone who discovered a field on which 3,000 licences were issued within 12 months.

No one ever succeeded in getting any of these rewards out of the government, though it is not to be doubted that they had the effect the Volksraad hoped they would have. Button's claim in respect of the discovery five days journey from Lydenburg was gazetted, but that was as far as it went. The events that led to the downfall of Pretorius and the election of Burgers were now taking shape.

It was to be the second President's task to deal with the first real gold rush in the Transvaal.

It started just as the other rumours had started. On February 5, 1873, A.F. Jansen, the landdrost of Lydenburg, wrote to the Executive Council in Pretoria to say:

"This will serve to bring to your notice that alluvial gold has been found by Messrs. G.R. Parsons, Thomas McLachlan and J.L. Valentine at a distance of six hours' ride on horseback to the east of the town of Lydenburg. In the two samples seen by me there was one nugget of about two dwt. and several fine pieces of gold, some about the size of small peas and some a little smaller. The abovenamed men have made application to register certain ground to enable them to claim an award in the event of sufficient quantities of gold being found in the future".

"The ground which they wish to register is situated to the east of the town of Lydenburg, between two breaks in the Drakensberg, to the east reckoned from here, i.e. from the two said ridges . . ."

The first find had actually been made at Hendriksdal, south of where Sabie is today. It was followed by a richer strike on the slopes of Spitzkop where the Malieveld Mine was established in the later years.

Jansen, the landdrost, visited the district and was left in no doubt that this was the real thing. ". . . I found that the results greatly exceeded those given by me in my report of February 5, 1873", he said. "With four mine natives after five days work I found myself in possession of between three and four ounces of pure alluvial gold containing some beautiful nuggets. Several people are already working there and not one has returned home empty-handed.

".... As a large crowd of people can be expected at any moment from Natal and elsewhere I think it advisable that the Government should take action of some sort . . ."

He reported that Abel Erasmus, who a short time before had acquired the farm Graskop, was there and had sold three-and-a-half ounces of gold to J.N.R. James for £8. Thus Abel Erasmus comes into the news as a digger. He was to become a famous character in the district.

The government, urging Jansen to send them frequent reports, watched the situation carefully and finally, when there was no doubt whatsoever that this was a gold field, proclaimed the diggings on May 14, 1873.

The geography of the officials in Pretoria was somewhat vague. There were no names on their maps beyond Lydenburg and Ohrigstad, so that the proclamation was worded thus:

"Whereas the Government of the South African Republic has received satisfactory evidence of the existence of payable gold fields in the area of Ohrigstad River, district Lydenburg, now therefore, I, Thomas Francois Burgers, President of the South African Republic, with the advice and consent of the Executive Council, declare and proclaim the area, Ohrigstad River, district Lydenburg, to be open for gold diggings under the existing laws and regulations for this country . . ."

The fact that the diggings were nowhere near the Ohrigstad River worried nobody in Pretoria. So the prospectors and diggers who immediately packed their swags and set out for Lydenburg got the shock of their lives when they reached the mountains and found the miniature Alps they had to climb up and down to get to the diggings. But it would have taken more than a mountain range or two to stop them. On they came, in such numbers that Jansen feared that, in the absence of any source of supplies, some of them might starve. Fortunately there was game to be had for the shooting, and Natives supplied grain, cattle and goats.

In the meantime McLachlan, the pioneer, had acquired the farm Geelhout-boom further up on the plateau above his first strike. He prospected there and found gold in the river that run through the farm. This was an area richer even than Spitzkop. They found gold in every stream. More and more diggers began to arrive. They were heading for Spitzkop, but the new finds saved them half the journey. They unloaded their packs, camped beside the stream on Geelhoutboom and pegged their claims. And almost without exception they found gold.

Among them were men from Australia and America who knew how law and order ought to be maintained on proclaimed diggings. They found that they were in wildest Africa without a register of claims, without officials to whom disputes could be referred, and without any amenities whatever. They turned on Jansen, the sole representative of the Government, and told him in the frankest terms what they thought of him and the South African Republic.

Poor Jansen! He must have missed his comfortable house in Lydenburg and the peaceful proceedings in his court there. However, he seems to have handled the situation well. He organised a diggers' committee to frame rules and regulations for the field, and appointed one Major W. MacDonald, an American who looked like a character from a Bret Harte story, as Gold Commissioner with power to register claims, collect the necessary fees and settle disputes.

In a letter to the State Secretary he reported that MacDonald was the diggers' own choice for the position and added ". . . as this gentleman knew how to make himself popular among the diggers, could handle difficult situations and maintain his position it appeared politic to leave him in that appointment".

MacDonald, his salary £29. 3s. 4d. a month, started his career with a flock of 250. It rapidly grew to over 1,000. He seems to have handled them with immense tact and yet managed to assert his authority. He deserves an honoured place in South African history as the first gold Commissioner and representative of law and order in a very "tough" community.

Jansen, who had difficulty in explaining to Pretoria what was happening, suggested that it would be a good idea if the President could visit the diggings. Burgers thought so too. He was worried about the effect that this gathering of "uitlanders" might have on the Republic, and so were the members of the Volksraad. It was what they had always feared would happen. There were a lot of Englishmen among the diggers, and where Englishmen settled the flag was apt to follow. They urged the President to go.

So in August, 1873, President Burgers set out for Lydenburg and then took the road that led to Spitzkop.

The diggers started off by being suspicious, but within two days they were all for Burgers. In the first place they found that he spoke excellent English (his wife was a Scotswoman), and that he seemed thoroughly sympathetic. Then he won their hearts with a neat bit of humour, the sort of joke they understood.

He visited MacDonald's camp, which was also his "office", and ran his eye over the list of claim holders.

"McDonald . . . MacDonald . . . two MacPhersons . . . MacTavish . . . MacAndrew. Why, it's all macs", he said, "I am going to call this place Mac Mac".

And Mac Mac it has remained to this day. The diggers loved the name. He christened the area "New Caledonia Gold Field", and this title appeared in official documents. But no one ever called it anything but the "Mac Mac Diggings".

He confirmed MacDonald's appointment as Gold Commissioner, describing him to the Volksraad later as an American and "a good republican", promised funds to improve the road from Lydenburg and appointed Messrs. Walter Compton, W. Cameron and one Wainwright as members of a roads committee which was to be responsible for seeing that the track that ran to Lourenco Marques was turned into a wagon road.

On MacDonald's recommendation he appointed Thomas Searle, Tom McLachlan, Herbert Rhodes and Captain Dietrich, a former German officer, as Justices of the Peace. Herbert Rhodes was Cecil Rhodes's brother, though there seems not to have been much brotherly love between them.

Claim licence fees were fixed at 5s. a month. Burgers at first held out for 10s., but found that the feeling of the meeting was against him. A trading licence, it was agreed, should cost £9 a quarter, but it included the right to sell liquor.

The diggers found Burgers a most likeable person. Burgers on his part was impressed by the orderly way in which the camp was run, and relieved to find that it was so far away from the rest of the Transvaal that it might have been in another country. It was true that it was an English-speaking community but, as he saw it, it was not remotely interested in anything but the hunt for gold.

One of Burgers's first acts on his return to Pretoria was to arrange for the purchase of Abel Erasmus's farm "Graskop" for the sum of £1,000 (R2,000). He planned to lay out a township there which would be the "capital" of the diggings.

But before this plan came to fulfilment the diggings moved away. There was more gold over the hills.

CHAPTER V

MAN WITH A WHEELBARROW

Gold had now been found in all sorts of places in an area that extended from Hendriksdal, south of the Sabie River, to McLachlan's camp, later to be named "Mac Mac", on the escarpment of the Drakensberg above Graskop. And the news had spread as the news of a gold strike always does spread. Would-be diggers were arriving every day in twos and threes. Virtually all of them had walked most of the way and their worn boots and tattered clothing cried out that it had been a long, hard, walk. Some had made their way down the mountain side on the rough track that ran from Lydenburg. Others had tramped the whole way from Lourenco Marques. That was a distance of only 150 odd miles but it was a perilous journey, to be undertaken only by those who were prepared to risk their lives in the hope of making a fortune. In the summer months the heat was appalling and at least two-thirds of the men who tried to walk across the area that today is largely occupied by the Kruger National Park contracted malaria. It depended on how long they had spent in Lourenco Marques whether this laid them low on the journey or began to show itself after they had climbed the escarpment. The period of incubation of the disease is about a fortnight so most of them got through before the symptoms showed themselves. The fate of those who became too weak to walk is almost too awful to contemplate — a slow and lonely death from starvation, with the hyenas waiting for the end.

It was not regarded as any part of the duty of the Portuguese colonial administration, or for that matter of the South African Republic, to assist these adventurers. There were no police camps or first-aid posts on the route. The Portuguese simply shook their heads sadly as they watched these heavily laden men marching confidently into the swamps that lay between the bay and the Komati River. There was no roll call before they left and no counting of heads after they crossed the Transvaal border so that we shall never know how many of them died on the way. Those who survived eventually arrived at Graskop and Mac Mac with hair-raising tales to tell of the wild animals they had seen and the other perils they had encountered on the way.

Where once there had been some twenty or thirty men working on scattered claims along the water courses there were now a hundred or more and new faces were seen every day. To one Alec Patterson, a slow-moving, taciturn man who was working at Mac Mac, the diggings were becoming over-crowded. He was a "loner" who could do without the company of other men. He had earned the nickname of "Wheelbarrow Alec" because he had arrived in the area with all his equipment loaded on to a wheelbarrow. He was believed to have come to the district from Kimberley but no one knew how he had got there or at what stage of the journey he had acquired his

"Wheelbarrow"
Patterson moves on.

wheelbarrow. Now he decided that it was time to move on. He worked his claim until sundown, made a final wash and then packed his pick, his shovels and his sluice box on to the wheelbarrow.

"I'm off", he said the next morning and headed for the hills.

No one is quite certain what route he took but somewhere beyond the camp at Mac Mac he must have swung off on a game trail to the north-east and pushed and pulled his wheelbarrow up a spur of the mountain that rose 2,000 feet. On the other side of this ridge, in a narrow cleft in the hills, he spotted a stream that zig-zagged its way through the valley to meet a river (the Blyde River, though he did not know this) that crossed the valley.

Patterson made his camp beside this stream, and noticed that there were peach trees growing on its banks.

He may have wondered where they came from.* Many have pondered over

* Peach trees were found in many other parts of the valley, particularly on the farm Frankfort and at a point on the Blyde River afterwards called Peach Tree Creek.

The earliest known picture of the village of Pilgrim's Rest. The Joubert Bridge over the Blyde River is on the right and on the hillside beyond it are the first mine buildings.

One of the few surviving photographs of a digger of the old school standing in the centre of his claim. The old gentleman with the white beard is George Lilley, discoverer of the Lilley Nugget and one of the pioneers of Pilgrim's Rest. His sluice box is in the foreground.

A group of diggers outside the European Hotel at the turn of the century. The hotel proprietor, Mr. W. Stein, is the shirt-sleeved figure, seventh from the left. The old building is still there and now serves as an annexe to the Royal Hotel.

A very early view of the village of Pilgrim's Rest.

this mystery since. The only possible explanation seems to be that hunting parties from Lydenburg had camped there in earlier years and scattered their peach stones on the banks of the stream. If that is the truth of the story there must have been many hunters and a large supply of peaches. The trees have survived a hundred years of neglect.

Peaches formed no part of Alec Patterson's diet. He lived on mealie meal and rhebok ribs. Gold, alluvial gold, was all that interested him.

And now at last, in this new "creek" he had found, his dreams came true. He dug out some of the river gravel, panned it and there, at the bottom of the pan, was a bright "tail" of gold. He panned again and there was even more gold. No doubt about it . . . he had "struck it rich".

He rigged up his sluice box and began to dig. And at that precise moment in September, 1873, he must have been the happiest man in the world. He had found gold. He was entirely alone in "his" valley. The weather was perfect, the surroundings indescribably beautiful. He had all the water he wanted for washing his gravel. What else was there in the world he could ask for?

Sooner or later he would have to make his way back to Mac Mac for supplies and to register his claim. He knew what that meant. As soon as he produced gold to pay his licence fees and to settle for what he needed the mob would be after him like a pack of beagles. They would "rush" this peaceful valley, and soon there would be claims pegged out all along the stream.

He put off the evil day and went on digging.

In the meantime another digger named William Trafford had left the Mac Mac diggings and climbed the ridge. He, too, spotted the stream and panned the gravel. When he saw the bright tail of gold in his pan he was deeply moved. He had found his Eldorado. This was the end of his pilgrimage.

The legend that has been handed down from father to son says that he shouted to the mountains: "The pilgrim is at rest", and the echo came back clear and loud: "Pilgrim's at rest . . . rest". And so the name he gave the valley was Pilgrim's Rest.

Why this emphasis on "pilgrims" and "pilgrimages"? Had Trafford read John Bunyan and been reminded of Christian and the Slough of Despond? Alas! The explanation is far more prosaic. One of the first expeditions to Mac Mac came from Maritzburg. There were 12 of them, including Herbert Rhodes and the marker from the billiard room of the Victoria Club. Their "luggage" included a wagon load of liquor.

They called themselves "the Pilgrims", and the name was adopted by the early diggers. There was a time when everyone at Mac Mac was a "pilgrim".

It was a happy choice as the name of the valley. Almost any other member of that adventurous band, having struck gold there, would have taken a swig from the bottle in his pack and named it "Whiskey Creek" or "Jones's Luck". Since the district was to carve its niche in the history of South

Africa it was fortunate that Trafford was there first to give it this romantic name.

Trafford did his duty. He hurried back to the Gold Commissioner's shack at Mac Mac, registered his claim and told everyone who was there what he had found.

The results exceeded Alec Patterson's gloomiest expectations. Some 200 diggers packed up their belongings and trekked over the mountains. They were soon spread out all along the stream, and almost without exception they began finding not merely alluvial gold but nuggets of all shapes and sizes, some of them so weathered that they looked like the filigreed gold that Indian jewellers design.

At first the "rush" was local. But the news spread to Lydenburg, to Lourenco Marques, to Kimberley and to Cape Town. Men who had hesitated when the first reports from the Transvaal came through now said: "This is the real thing!" and set out for the fields. Sailors deserted their ships in South African ports. Australian and American diggers, down on their luck, scraped together the passage money to Durban and Lourenco Marques. It was the Klondyke and California all over again, except that the journey to the field required some capital. Kimberley, where many claims had petered out, supplied about a third of the new diggers.

The farms on which the new discoveries were made were Ponieskrantz, Driekop and Grootfontein — three of the properties which Transvaal Gold Mining Estates were to buy from Benjamin's company 12 years later. These were names that were to become famous in Johannesburg and London in due course. But the diggers of 1873 did not pause to find out who owned the farms. That was the Gold Commissioner's business. All they had to do was to get in first, peg their claims and dig. Had they been interested they might have found that Ponieskrantz had been so named by the Mullers, who lived at Kruger's Post, on the other side of the mountains that tower above the valley. They had been hunting there one day and a knee-haltered horse had fallen over a krantz. They called the farm on which the accident happened "Ponieskrantz".

In his reminiscences H.W. Struben, the Rand pioneer, declared that he once owned Ponieskrantz and Driekop. He said that in 1872 his friend Piet Marais of Pretoria persuaded him to visit Lydenburg on a prospecting trip. He fossicked about on the banks of the Blyde River where he found a little gold and some evidence of ancient workings. Though the gold they found was not payable he and Marais decided to buy Ponieskrantz and Driekop. After getting back to Pretoria they drove straight to Rustenburg where the owners lived and bought the two farms for cash.

"Nothing much happened for some time", says Struben. "But shortly afterwards, while I was sitting in the Durban Club, a friend of mine came to tell me that rich gold had been found on our farms and that several hundred diggers were ground-sluicing for alluvial.

"I returned at once to Pretoria, persuaded President Burgers and Judge Buchanan (then Attorney-General) to go with us, see the diggers and arrange proceedings. I employed myself in collecting all the information I could from the works on the mining laws of Australia, New Zealand and California — which I had sent for some time previously — and drafted a set of laws which, I considered would suit South Africa.

"The Attorney-General did not like me having usurped his place but, as there were no Transvaal mining laws and he had made no attempt to frame any, Mr. Burgers agreed that he would discuss the laws that I had drawn up, clause by clause, and with a few slight alterations the law as drafted by me became the Transvaal Gold Law."

Presumably this was the Gold Law which was finally promulgated in 1875.

Struben's recollections of the President's second visit to the diggings were written 47 years after the event, but they remained extraordinarily clear. What he does not mention is the fact that there was a certain amount of unrest among the diggers, who felt that they were being neglected by Pretoria.

Major MacDonald, the Gold Commissioner, moved his "office" from Mac Mac to Pilgrim's Rest early in January, 1874, because the greater part of his flock were now hard at work there, and there was a steady demand for licences and registrations in the district.

He wrote from Pilgrim's Rest on January 12, saying that he was having trouble with new arrivals on the diggings who were not amenable to discipline. He also forwarded petitions from the diggers asking for representation in the Volksraad and nominating Tom McLachlan and F.P. Mansfield as their spokesmen. By almost the same post the President received a letter from McLachlan which said that he had been prospecting in the district known as "Die Kaap", and that he had found gold there on Government ground. He enclosed a sketch plan of the area which showed that, while "warm", he had not discovered the Barberton field. On his map Moodie's farms are marked "not gold-bearing".

These representations, combined with Struben's plan to visit the diggings, persuaded President Burgers that he must go there again. The State Secretary informed MacDonald that the President would arrive at Pilgrim's Rest on February 2, and most of the diggers decided to assemble there to meet him.

Struben gives a lively account of what happened when the President arrived.

"It rained incessantly that season and the rivers were high," he says. "We were warned on the way that the diggers were unruly and had threatened to assault Mr. Burgers if he came to the diggings to interfere with them. So, on reaching the swollen Blyde River, a camp was formed and a council of war was held. Some tried to persuade the President to return to Pretoria and not take any risks, but I pointed out how completely such a retreat would destroy the prestige of the Government, offered to swim the river and interview the

The owner of Ponieskrantz arrives stark naked on the east bank of the Blyde River.

diggers in the morning, and I prevailed.

"In the morning some hundreds of diggers assembled on the opposite bank. I swam across in a 'state of nature', introduced myself as the proprietor of the property, said I intended to make reasonable terms with them and that President Burgers, who was on the other side, wished to see them and discuss the matter.

"The good enough fellows cheered me, said they would treat Mr. Burgers with respect and, at my request, sent to the mining camp for a long rope to assist us through the rushing stream . . ."

It makes a nice picture. In the mind's eye one sees the owner of Ponies-krantz arriving stark naked on the east bank of the Blyde River to interview these temporary tenants. Struben says that he was unable to come to satis-factory terms with the Government and the diggers later (presumably this means that he could not work the property) and that he sold it to a "Port Elizabeth syndicate". This may have been Benjamin or his representative.

The diggers hauled the wagon, with the President on board, across the flooded river (an anxious moment for Burgers, who had confided to Struben that he could not swim). A conference followed at which the proposed new mining law was discussed, and then the diggers gave the President a dinner in the camp.

What a banquet that must have been! It was prepared by one Mathias Mocket, universally known as "The Bosun", who had been a seaman in his day and who knew something about cooking. The menu has not been preserved, but all the "old hands" remembered that the final course was plum pudding served with brandy sauce, and that the President asked for a second helping of the sauce. They also recalled that something went wrong with the Bosun's pastry, and that it required "a sledge-hammer to break it".

Another story says that Burgers was shocked by the amount of liquor he saw consumed. The Bosun, defending his fellow guests, explained that it was not their fault. Their mothers had taught them to drink.

Struben says that the diggers were quite satisfied with the new mining laws as outlined to them. They made one or two "slight alterations", but otherwise raised no protest. Since he was present at the meeting one cannot doubt his word. They must either have changed their minds at a later date, or else the law as he drafted it underwent considerable amendment, for all the evidence shows that there were certain sections of it to which they took strong exception. This was particularly true of the clauses that allowed concessions to individuals and companies such as that which Benjamin was granted in 1881.

The year 1874, which marked the President's second visit to the diggings, and the first eight months of 1875 saw the peak of prosperity for the alluvial diggers. It is an occupation in which prosperity comes suddenly, and never lasts very long.

In Pilgrim's Rest in those days there was room for all — and gold for all. No sooner was a claim worked out than the digger moved off to a new "strike", and with reasonable luck found gold there, too. But alluvial digging bears a strong resemblance to roulette, the game in which you must leave the table while you are winning. This was precisely what the average digger could never do. He had to go on looking for new fields to conquer, and this was his downfall. There were men at Spitzkop, Mac Mac and Pilgrim's Rest in 1874 who made enough money in the course of a few months to keep themselves in comfort for the rest of their lives. But they could never drag themselves away from their claims. One more wash . . . just one more fossick in the valley over the hill . . . just one more round of drinks! Of all the hundreds of men who staked their claims somewhere between Sabie and Vaalhoek not more than 20 left the fields with money. The majority died there or at Barberton, and lie buried in nameless graves.

What an amazing collection they were, these men, and how some of them have lived on in legend ever since! They came from every country in the world. Between them they spoke almost every known language. Soldiers, sailors, bank clerks, barmen, remittance men and gentlemen adventurers — they were all here. Some had surnames and occasionally were handed letters from "home". Others were known only by their nick-names and nobody asked them questions about their parents.

The very names ring with adventure. Tom McLachlan, Billy Dawkins, Bert Lilley, Herbert Rhodes, Alick Dempster, Alois Nellmapius, Len Baker, St. Leger-Smith, Ted Sievewright, Jimmie Bryson, Guy Dawney, Osborne,

Barrington, Farley, F.P. Mansfield, Ross, Charlie Roberts, Big McPherson, Dick Giles, W.A.B. Cameron, "Wild Bill" Leathern, James Armstrong, "Ikey" Sonnenberg and his brother. There is a story about every one of them.

And then add to the list the men with "shovel" names . . . The Bosun (best-known of all), French Bob, Sailor Harry, German George, Charlie the Reefer, Wally the Soldier, Black Sam, Bob Buck, Yorkie (who came from Yorkshire), Bismarck, American Knox, Artful Joe, Spanish Joe, Yankee Dan, and a host of others.

Nellmapius was a Hungarian who made money at Pilgrim's Rest and kept it. The diggers awarded him the title of "Count", and he became the Transvaal's first industrialist. Billy Dawkins built a long water race at Spitzkop which is there to this day. He took £20,000 from his claim and then vanished into thin air. Len Baker was a London dentist who had come to the Transvaal to set up practice. The "gold fever" caught him, and he spent his life on the diggings. A strip of ground on the map called "Baker's Bliss" is his memorial. There is at least one resident of Pilgrim's Rest today who can remember gazing with awe at the case of instruments he carried but rarely used.

Herbert Rhodes became a member of the Volksraad and died in Rhodesia when a cask of rum, which was part of his camp equipment, caught fire and exploded in his face. Ted Sievewright achieved immortality in "Jock of the Bushveld". Tom McLachlan's son became the most renowned surgeon of his day in Cape Town.

They all had a story to tell, but only one of them told it. This was W.C. Scully, author, poet, magistrate and pioneer. He made no money on the diggings, but he stored up memories. For the authentic atmosphere of those days read his description of the trek to Lourenco Marques which MacDonald, the Gold Commissioner, led. It gives you the picture of the hardships — the fever, the tsetse flies, the lions, the droughts — that the pioneers who took that road endured.

Percy FitzPatrick came later. He reached the diggings in 1884 and had a desperate struggle to make enough to give him three meals a day.

J.B. Taylor remembered going into a store in Pilgrim's Rest and finding behind an improvised counter "a typical rooinek, a youth of about twenty, red-haired, burnt, blistered and freckled by the sun, with eyes that tumbled with merriment and a smile that completely captivated us . . ."

This was the young FitzPatrick.

An Irish family, the Glynns, had settled at Kruger's Post on the other isde of the mountains. Glynn senior and his sons, Henry, Joe and Arthur, used to visit the diggings to sell their produce to the diggers and to buy gold. The family moved to Sabie in 1880, where Henry bought the farm Grootfontein for £600 (its first owner had paid £7 10s. 0d. for it), and his father settled on the other side of the river on a farm named Ceylon.

Henry Glynn's farm was afterwards mined by The Glynn's Lydenburg

Company and produced gold to the value of some £8,000,000, over the next 60 years. Jim Makokel, the wagon boy, lived on Glynn's property before he joined Percy FitzPatrick at Barberton and found his place in the pages of "Jock of the Bushveld".

The gold for which the diggers searched in those days was alluvial gold, which meant that it was free gold that could be recovered by washing the gravel from the beds and banks of streams. But there were nuggets, too — lumps of solid gold usually found under or wedged against the boulders in the streams.

Most of the nuggets found at Mac Mac and Spitzkop were comparatively small. But when the first claims were pegged at Pilgrim's Rest there were some astonishing finds.

The biggest of them all exists only as a legend. It was found under a very large boulder in the bed of the creek and is said to have weighed over 25 lbs. However, two members of the syndicate working the claim are alleged to have snatched it up and made a bee line for Lourenco Marques so that there is no record of this great lump of gold.

There is an authentic record of a find on one of "Count" Nellmapius's claims — a nugget that weighed 123 ozs. Nellmapius was regarded as the luckiest man on the diggings in those days, and his luck held for the rest of his life.

George Lilley then dug one out of the creek at almost precisely the spot where the village stands today. The Lilley nugget weighed 119 ozs. 2 dwt. Henry Glynn records that his father paid £750 for another nugget that weighed 208 ozs. The "Breda" nugget, found at a spot known as Peach Tree Creek, weighed 214 ozs.

These, of course, were the strawberries on top of the basket. Most of the nuggets weighed an ounce or two, but there were hundreds of them in the first claims pegged. Three diggers in a partnership, J.W.S. Barrington, Osborne and Farley, cleaned up 13 lbs. 8 ozs. of gold, mostly in nuggets, in one day's working — probably a record for the field if we except the "monster" nuggets.

William Scully in his reminiscences of Pilgrim's Rest says that four men who had worked three-and-a-half shallow claims (he does not give their names) authorised the bank manager to announce that they had taken £35,000 worth of gold out of the creek. But the story I like best is one about the "tidying up" that took place in R.T.W. James's store at Mac Mac. Joe Barret, who ran the store for James, had a bright idea. He was about to lay a new mud floor. He suggested to his boss that they should put the "old" floor through the sluice box. They did — and cleaned up gold to the value of £40!

The nuggets, of course, accounted for only a fraction of the gold found.

Most of it was gold dust extracted from the gravel. Pilgrim's Rest gold, when it came in nugget form, had a curious pale radiance. It was "ashblonde" gold, a colour given it by the high percentage of silver it contained in its raw state. Many of the smaller nuggets were mounted as brooches and were once very popular ornaments, and valuable ones.

There are no accurate records of how much gold was recovered during the years 1873 - 74 - 75. I have seen it stated somewhere that, in 1875, the Natal Bank and the Cape Commercial Bank handled raw gold to the value of £106,000, but that was certainly not the aggregate. At one time there were over 1,500 diggers at work, and over the whole three-year period there must have been an average of 800 scattered about the field. To make anything approaching a decent living a digger had to find an ounce of gold a week, for which he would receive approximately £3. 10s. 0d. This was the recognised wage for white men who worked on ohter men's claims. But we know that at Mac Mac the diggers averaged from 5 dwts. to as much as 8 ozs. a day, and that the Australians, the most expert of the diggers, set themselves a minimum of £8. 10s. 0d. a day. It seems certain, therefore, that the community could not have existed on the scale it did unless the diggings were producing at least £300,000 to £400,000 a year. Over the period of high prosperity more than £1,000,000 must have come from the claims.

The mystery that still remains unsolved is what became of all that gold. It certainly did not flow into the coffers of the South African Republic. MacDonald's accounts for 1874 - 75 have been preserved, and they are almost pathetic in their simplicity. This was his statement of revenue received:

Digger's Licences	£700
Registrations	25
Fees (for notarial work) . .	100
Trading Licences	1,150
Import duties	75
Toll	50
Fines	50
Stamps	15
Additional Income	35

Total £2,200

His own salary had increased to £450 a year and his police "expenses", which presumably included the upkeep of a wattle-and-daub jail, were £500. To this had to be added part of the cost of the landdrost's salary, and the pay of a clerk. So that it is clear that the Republic was getting virtually no profit out of the diggings. And most of the gold mined there was going out of the country.

President Burgers, who had expected a golden harvest from the diggings, began to worry about his vanishing gold.

CHAPTER VI

THE PRESIDENT'S GOLD POUND

Thomas Burgers's second visit to the diggings in February, 1874, was a visit with a purpose.

The young President had by that time begun to tackle the most pressing of all the problems that faced the young Republic he governed. This was the shortage of cash. Not to put too fine a point on it, the State was bankrupt. It owed the Cape Commercial Bank £60,000 and could not repay the loan. Its revenue scarcely sufficed to meet current expenses such as the salaries of public servants and, although the old bank notes were being called in, the new note issues was hardly more popular.

The diggings were the one new source of revenue in sight. For years officials had said: "If we find gold all will be well". Now gold had been found and was being produced at a most satisfactory rate, and the population of the Republic had increased by at least a thousand. But the results were disappointing. Where was all the money that ought now to be flowing in? What was happening was that, as fast as the diggers produced the gold, it passed over the counters of the stores and the bank and left the Transvaal for the Cape, Natal and Lourenco Marques. The gold buyers were making a profit of 10s. to 15s. an ounce on their transactions, and the shrewder diggers were hoarding their gold against the day when they would pack up and leave the diggings having "made their pile" (not that there were many who achieved this ambition). Any currency other than the despised Republican bank notes was acceptable to the diggers, but chiefly they preferred to exchange their nuggets for goods, an arrangement that suited the storekeepers, who made a two-way profit. Thus, though the Republic's notes were available, the community lived largely by barter — gold exchanged for food, clothing, tools and large quantities of liquor.

MacDonald, the Gold Commissioner, had been given £1,000 with which to buy gold, and had thus had practical experience of the distrust with which the republican currency was regarded. He wrote to Pretoria more than once pointing out the urgency of the need for coins on the diggings, and stressing the difficulties of dealing with the diggers entirely in paper currency. Pilgrim's Rest was, in fact, a community where no one ever had any change.

In the meantime, a Swiss named T. Perrin, who at an earlier date had been employed in the Swiss State Mint, had arrived in the Transvaal, applied for a licence as an assayer and, having obtained it, moved to Pilgrim's Rest, where his services were in demand. There, in his spare time, he sat down and produced a remarkable document advising the South African Republic to establish a mint.

This document, now preserved in the archives of the South African Mint,

Valuing a nugget.

is well worth quoting. It began on a very practical note.

"When the Californian gold diggings were opened", said Perrin, "our first French Financier, the late Baron Rothschild, sent over to San Francisco a young man of his family, M. Davidson, for the only purpose of buying gold. The richest man in Europe thought it was worth his trouble to monopolize the gold and create a new branch of his immense firm in the young and well promising country. The U.S. Government soon came into competition with the rich banker, but with one more chance of success, viz. the possibility of Coining.

"A mint was created and national coin began to abound in America. So did Australia. Both nations understood that it would be folly to leave undisputed to traders the profit of buying from diggers, folly to forfeit this grand privilege of a government — stamping and issuing coins.

"A mint established near the gold diggings could realise a large profit of which a liberal government would let the diggers have their share. Freight, loss of interest during the time of transport, insurance money, commission of the buyer who has to sell again to any European market, all these are as many expenses saved if gold is *'hic et nunc'* transformed into coins. Should the Government give to the digger the intermediary price between the real value of the finds and the amount offered to him by any other purchaser, the bargain would still be a vry remunerative one to both contractors. The price of gold increasing would soon prove an encouragement for all hands at work already, an effective allurement for many yet to come."

Mr. Perrin's literary style may not have been perfect, but he certainly knew all the tricks of the trade. He had, in fact, put his finger on the source of the Republic's financial difficulties, and the one possible solution.

"The question is to know whether buying all the gold found in the New Caledonia Field would not prove too large an enterprise for the Transvaal public finances," he continues (as indeed it would have proved at the time).

"We do not think it would require much money. Diggers do not as a rule sell large quantities of gold at once. Most of them have to get rid of their finds at the end of the week to pay the week's expenses and they do not care if the money they receive and have to give in payment is counted in notes or hard cash. To those only who should happen to sell in large quantities payment in gold would be prefereble.

"Even in this case, what else would it be for the Treasurer but a mere advance of a few hours for which the Mint, the next day, would pay him back with a large interest added to capital?"

The versatile Mr. Perrin then went on to outline in detail a plan for a mint to be established at Pilgrim's Rest. Accompanying the memorandum were careful drawings of a suitable building and all the equipment needed, and an estimate of the cost of the building — £600 (R1,200) — and of the plant — £362 (R724).

This document, 11 pages, all handwritten, was presented to Burgers on his arrival at Pilgrim's Rest in February, 1874.

It came at a time when the President was casting round desperately for a plan that would save the Republic from a fate that seemed inevitable — the collapse of its finances. He had been in office only 18 months, but he saw the writing on the wall. Unless money was found, the public service put on a proper footing and the bank loan repaid, there was no future for the youngest state in Africa. His mind was full of plans for railways, for a harbour in Delagoa Bay, for settlements and schools, but they were all frustrated. Where was the money to come from? How could a Treasury which had difficulty in paying the salaries of its landdrosts finance any scheme?

We shall never know what happened when Perrin presented his plan for a mint, but such evidence as is available seems to suggest that this impulsive, imaginative young President read it and decided then and there to adopt it. He would keep his country's gold and take the profit to be made from it by minting coins on the lines suggested by Perrin. But how to convince the Volksraad, conservative, suspicious of all new plans and already grumbling that the new President was spending too much money? How could he persuade these patriarchs that the Republic must follow the example of larger states, have its own coinage and use its gold to its own advantage?

I picture him sitting in his wagon at Pilgrim's Rest and reading and re-reading Perrin's memorandum. And then was born the bright idea. He would take gold from Pilgrim's Creek, genuine Transvaal gold, and have coins minted. Then, with these practical examples of what his plan would mean, he would face the Volksraad and say: "This is what we must do. We must have our own coinage and here are specimens to show what it will look like".

Once he had set his imagination to work the mint was practically built and the old, tattered notes replaced by shining new coins bearing the arms of the Republic. It was time to act. He could not wait until he returned to Pretoria. It was February, and the Volksraad met in May.

So, on February 9, 1874, a few days after he had received Perrin's memorandum, he wrote to J.J. Pratt, the South African Republic's Consul-General in London. The letter was headed "Pilgrim's Rest, New Caledonia", an address of which Pratt had never heard. But the signature was the authentic signature of T.F. Burgers, President of the South African Republic.

The letter said: ". . . the Government having resolved to get a few coins struck of the value of the English Sovereign I have bought 300 ozs. of our Native gold for that purpose which I shall remit to you immediately on my return to Pretoria.

"The Assembly will meet in May next and by that time I am anxious to have the money here. As the time is short I write you about the matter in time to make enquiries either at the Royal Mint in London or at some other mint in Belgium or elsewhere, whether there is a chance of getting the work executed in time."

Though the President says "the Government have resolved" I think we are entitled to read this as "I have resolved" for, had the Government come to this decision earlier, the first letter on the subject would certainly have been dispatched from Pretoria. All the evidence seems to show that Burgers had his bright idea on the banks of Pilgrim's Creek and acted, as he often did, on the impulse of the moment.

Eleven days later the State Secretary wrote to Pratt from Pretoria to say the gold was on the way and added:

"I also send you a portrait of His Honour the President and a sketch of the way in which the sovereigns are to be struck. They must have the exact value of the British £1 sterling. I enclose several copies of our Coat of Arms. By a mistake of the painter the word Transvaal has been put between the S.A. Republic. I have drawn a line through it as it must not be inserted but the words Zuid-Afrikaansche Republiek must be so divided that they just fill the circle round our Coat of Arms. The President is very anxious to have the coins here in Pretoria at the commencement of May, so no time must be lost. Please have the dies prepared at once so that when the gold has arrived you can have the coins struck at once."

The actual quantity of gold sent to Pratt in London was 22¼ lbs. It has been stated over and over again that President Burgers bought two nuggets while he was in Pilgrim's Rest in February, 1874, and that all the sovereigns that were subsequently minted came from these. But, though there is evidence that he did in fact buy nuggets, they certainly did not provide over 22 lbs. of gold, and it seems likely that he also took back to Pretoria some of the gold that MacDonald had bought from the diggers.

50

No one is quite certain as to what the President acquired. The story that seems most likely to be true is that recounted by Mr. B.J. Burgers, the President's nephew, in after years.

He said that a man named Potgieter, who was a member of the President's former congregation at Hanover in the Cape Province, had followed him when he moved to the Transvaal. The President helped to fit him out for an expedition to the diggings.

Potgieter pegged several claims and worked very hard to make a living, but without much luck. Finally he gave up and loaded his family and all his possessions on to his wagon to return to Pretoria.

Then, before beginning the long journey, though the oxen were actually inspanned, he went down into the creek "to say good-bye to his claim". He noticed a crack in a large boulder which he had not inspected before, brushed out the sand in the crack and found two large nuggets. He called them the "Emma" and the "Adelina", and they weighed 16½ ozs. and 22 ozs. 17½ dwts. respectively. These, Mr. Burgers believed, were the nuggets the President bought. But whether this is the true version of the story or not it is obvious that these nuggets did not provide all the gold that was required.

Mr. Pratt, the South African Republic's Consul-General in Britain, seems to have been a man whom nothing could surprise. He took the request for the minting of sovereigns very calmly, and set out to consult assayers and the Royal Mint itself.

He very soon found out that there was no hope of getting the sovereigns minted by May, when the session of the Volksraad began. However, he found an engraver to the Royal Mint named L.C. Wyon who was prepared to make the necessary dies and pouches for a mere £42 (R84).

Indeed, all through the proceedings one is struck by the extraordinary economy with which the whole operation was carried out. Messrs. Heaton & Son, "moneyers" of Birmingham (which meant that they were authorised manufacturers of coins and medals) offered to make the sovereigns at 3d. each, using dies, punches and gold supplied.

In the meantime Messrs. Johnson, Matthey & Co. of Hatton Garden had dealt with the gold and returned the following certificate: "We the undersigned, melters and assayers to the Bank of England and the Royal Mint, do hereby certify that we received from Mr. J.J. Pratt one parcel of African Gold Dust weighing 266.50 ozs. which, when melted, yielded a bar weighing 252.40 ozs. of quality 932 fine gold and 64 fine silver in every 1,000 parts.

". . . That the said bar was refined and produced 236.625 ozs. of gold of the quality 998⅓ which was subsequently alloyed to the quality of the British sovereign viz. 11/12 gold (916-2/3) and 1/12 copper, producing 256.275 ozs. of such British standard, returned to the above Mr. J.J. Pratt for coinage."

And so the process went slowly forward, with meticulous weighing and measuring by all concerned and with the President waiting impatiently for the

51

moment when he could spring his big surprise on the Volksraad.

There was a final delay caused by a "breakdown" of the dies, with the result that the experts today can recognize the difference between the "thick beard Burgers sovereign" and the "thin beard Burgers sovereign".

At long last Pratt was able to send off a first consignment of 695 sovereigns, followed by a further 138–833 in all. There were actually 837 sovereigns minted but, by special permission of the President, Pratt retained four.

The final account which Pratt presented to the Republic is worth quoting as a model of economy, undreamed of in our day:

To Expenses incurred in coining 833 coins:

Freight of gold dust	£5. 5. 0.
Johnson Matthey A/c refining	1. 19. 8.
Expenses to Birmingham	2. 11. 0.
Wyon, engraver to Royal Mint, for dies	42. 0. 0.
Messrs. Heaton, the Mint, Birmingham	20. 12. 5.
Telegram and messenger to Southampton with first parcel of coins per *African*	2. 6. 0.
Union Co. freight and charges	3. 12. 0.
Insurance £700 at ½% and duty	3. 11. 9.
Donald Currie & Co., freight and charges on 138 coins ...	1. 12. 6.
Insurance at ½% and duty	14. 6.
Expenses incurred, delivery of gold dust carriage to and from Birmingham of gold, coins and dies, Telegrams, postage etc.	5. 16. 0.
Total:	£90. 0. 10.

It was finally not until September 24, 1874, that the President was in a position to ask leave of the Volksraad to make a statement to its members. There were objections from some of those present who did not wish to deviate from the order paper. However, when the President said that he had planned to stage a surprise for the Raad in connection with the finances of the country, but if there were objections he would withdraw his request, he was allowed to proceed.

Burgers then said that, with the consent of his Executive Council, he had sent Transvaal gold to Britain and had coins to the value of £1,000 minted, and he was now about to hand £50 to the chairman as a sample of the new coinage.

The announcement was greeted with loud cheers.

He then pointed out that this was the first coinage ever specially minted for South Africa, and declared that it was an important step towards forming a nation. His likeness was engraved on the coins but this, he declared, was against his wishes.

The Volksraad sees the first Burgers sovereign.

The loud cheers which had greeted Burgers's first announcement rather died away after he had completed his speech, and his critics began to ask questions.

He ought, of course, to have been commended for his enterprise. But he was not a popular president, and in producing these coins he had committed two cardinal sins. He had not consulted the Volksraad, and he had caused a "graven image" of himself to be made and perpetuated on the coins. In their heart of hearts it was to the engraved portrait of the President that most of the members of the Volksraad objected most strongly. They suspected that this was another of his "tricks", that he was setting himself up as a king or emperor. But this was not what they said in the long debate that followed. Their objections were based on the fact that they had not given authorisation for the minting of the coins, that the security that had been given the Cape Commercial Bank might be affected, that they did not know what the coins had cost.

The debate lasted all the following day. Finally five motions were put to the Raad, four of which rejected the coinage as legal tender. They all had the disadvantage that, if they were accepted, the Republic would lose some £800 and some fine new gold coins.

In the end they accepted a motion which said: "The Raad resolves to accept the gold pieces which were laid before it by His Honour the State President and declared by His Honour to be of the exact and same value as one English pound sterling, as legal tender in this Republic".

The President, having been informed of this decision, thanked the

Volksraad, and assured its members that he had not had the coins struck to make a name for himself, but to make the burgers feel that they were a nation. There would be more coins minted, including coins of lesser value.

On the following day Burgers handed 24 of the gold coins to the chairman, and each member received one in payment of his first day's attendance in the session of the Volksraad for 1874. Burgers then declared that the official name of the new coins would be the "staatspond", because a "sovereign" did not exist in the Republic.

This produced a more genial frame of mind in the Raad, which passed a resolution that one staatspond should be sent to the head of each of the states that had acknowledged the independence of the Republic. It also instructed the Chairman to present one of the coins to the President as a momento of the solemn occasion.

That coin, Burgers's sole reward for a great deal of hard work, is now treasured by a Johannesburg man who counts it as one of the most precious objects he owns.

There were finally some 700 staatsponden available for distribution to the public, who bought them eagerly. Within a few days of the President's first announcement they were worth £2 apiece.

Whether any of them ever reached Pilgrim's Rest I cannot say. Probably most of them were snapped up in Pretoria and put away among the family treasures. But the fact remains that it was gold from Pilgrim's Creek that produced the first distinctive South African gold coins.

Today they are among the most valuable of all the gold pieces that collectors buy and sell. A Burgers "thick beard" pound, when it comes on the market, now fetches R1,000. But it is seldom seen.

Despite all the difficulties they encountered, Messrs. Heaton of Birmingham did a good job, and the coins have an air of distinction.

President Burgers's plan for a State mint went wrong, as did nearly all his plans for the Republic. Nevertheless, the idea was sound. Even the dispatch of those single coins to the heads of "friendly" States showed that he was thinking on the right lines, for a gold pound is a good public relations officer wherever it may go.

In due course, after the discovery of the Witwatersrand, the South African Republic established a State Mint, though it did this by encouraging the National Bank to build the necessary establishment and install the machinery. The mint then became the property of the State, which leased it to the bank at an annual rental of £50.

Mr. Perrin, who had written the original memorandum on the establishment of a mint, deserved rather better luck than came his way. For 16 years he pleaded for a mint that would produce the Transvaal's own "ponden" from its own gold. But it was not until 1899 that he became the Master of the Mint. He had held the appointment for barely 18 months when Pretoria was taken by the British, and the mint was no more.

This was the telephone unit in Pilgrim's Rest which kept the Boer forces in touch with Lydenburg and Kruger's Post. Holding the telephone to his ear is Mr. Izak Joubert of Sabie. Next to him is Mr. Barter, who, before the war had been the local policeman. Standing behind are P. Minnaar and K. Pienaar of the Pilgrim's Rest post office. Seated in front of them is Mr. Hamman. In front of him is Willie Byrne who manned the telephone at Kruger's Post.

A group of Pilgrim's Rest burghers under the command of Field Cornet J.H. de Beer (in white helmet).

The elderly man on the right of this group is Tommy Dennison, the man who held up the coach on Pilgrim's Hill and later ran the Highwayman's Garage in the village. This is the only known photograph of Dennison and is now in the Pilgrim's Rest Museum.

The Staats Munt te Velde (the State Mint in the Field) which made gold coins at Pilgrim's Rest, using a press found in the mine workshop and dies made by hand in the blacksmith's shop. The coins were inscribed "Een Pond, 1902" and "Z.A.R.". On the left of this group is Mr. P.J. Kloppers, a schoolmaster who ran this mint with great efficiency. Mr. Kloppers is holding a hammer. Next to him is W. Reid, the mechanic, handling the press, Dirk Graham with the crucible and Field-Cornet A. Pienaar is seated in front with a collection of coins.

CHAPTER VII

MISS ELIZABETH, THE DIGGER

The first annual general meeting of the Transvaal Gold Mining Estates Company must remain adjourned a little longer while we continue our survey of the properties that Alfred Beit and Lionel Phillips were to buy.

You ought, by this time, to have in your mind's eye a picture of a narrow, winding valley in which there is not anywhere as much as 20 square yards of level ground. In the "V" of the valley runs the creek, Pilgrim's Creek, and on either side tower the mountains rising steeply to peaks almost sheer above the stream. This is a gentle rivulet in winter but, drawing strength from hundreds of water courses on the mountain sides, it can become a roaring torrent after heavy rain. It flows north-west to join the Blyde River.

Observe that in this area there are few "krantzes", "spruits", or "dongas". The Americans and Australians who were among the first arrivals on the diggings knew a "creek" when they saw one. When there was water in a spruit it was a creek. When it was dry it became a gulch. So this small section of the map of South Africa is plastered with "creeks", "gulches", "ridges" and "gulleys". It even had a "Sacramento Creek", which runs close to a "Klondyke". And "Brown's Hill", "Columbia Hill", "Duke's Hill", "Walker's Hill" and "Black Hill" are to be found among the "kops" and "koppies".

Any picture of an early American mining camp fits the Pilgrim's Rest scene in 1875. Hundreds of tents lined the banks of the creek, and the diggers were quite content to sleep on a slope of one in three as long as they were near their claims. It was the position of the claims that mattered, and the placing of the pegs. The banks of the stream looked like a giant pin cushion, for there were pegs everywhere. (To the uninitiated it ought to be explained that diggers' pegs are long rods that project four feet above the ground claimed and bear a plate or a card on which the owner's name is written). Alluvial gold claims in those days were 150 by 150 Cape feet, and it was every digger's objective to get his claim across the stream with a bit of the bank on either side included. Once his claim was pegged that ground was his, to be worked by him and no one else for as long as he paid the monthly 50 cent fee. In the early days I believe there was for a time a diggers' regulation, imported from Australia, which said that if a man did not work his claim for three consecutive days it could be "jumped". But in a region where men often went down with malaria and supplies were difficult to obtain, this proved quite unworkable and was soon forgotten. To the diggers the invisible boundaries of a claim, as defined by the pegs, were as inviolate as they would have been had there been high steel fences all round the area. There were, of course, arguments about boundaries in some places, but in all the history of Pilgrim's Rest there were few cases of "claim jumping".

55

No digger thought of building himself a shack unless he started finding payable gold. If that happened, if it became clear that every cubic foot of gravel would have to be taken out and washed, he might pause in his labours for a day to level a ledge and build a rough wooden shelter. But he had to be sure that he was going to make money before he did that, for wood was one of the most expensive commodities on the diggings.

By and large, then, it was a tent town. There were three camps, "Upper", "Lower" and "Middle". On the track that ran some 75 yards above the creek, MacDonald, the Gold Commissioner, had his shack, and there the store-keepers pitched their tents. A general dealer's licence, as I have explained, included the right to sell liquor, and not to have sold liquor would have meant not selling anything. Digging for 10 hours a day was thirsty work, and the percentage of teetotallers in the camp was slightly lower than the percentage of parsons (the first Anglican parson was not to be included among the teetotallers).

It is often said that it was the men who sold liquor on the diggings who made fortunes. But I doubt if this is true. So fierce was the competition that in 1875 there were no less than 11 canteens in the camp, as near to the claims as their proprietors could get them. They divided the trade fairly evenly, and they had to keep the prices down or lose their customers. The "break-ages" were heavy as the bottles bumped their way down the perpendicular track on the slopes of the mountain. There were bad debts.

These "pubs" had whimsical names. Herbert Rhodes had a popular establishment at Mac Mac called "The Spotted Dog". Others were "Ye Digger's Bar", "Our House", "Tom Craddock's Bar", "The Halfways House" and "Stent's Cathedral". No one was expected to walk far for refreshment. If necessary there was always a "runner" ready to deliver a bottle to a claim.

In this tent town everything was measured in pennyweights of gold. The traders and the barmen all had scales on their counters. The customer had his gold dust in his pocket, usually in a bottle or a tin (the Colman's mustard tin made a useful container), and this was "money". The gold was tipped into the pan of the scales and carefully weighed. It was then, by tradition, the buyer's privilege to "blow" it, which meant that he pursed his lips and puffed to remove the dust that might add a fraction to the weight of the gold.

But the practice of measuring out and weighing a couple of pennyweights of gold was tedious, so that what many of the diggers did was to hand their takings over to the storekeeper and thus obtain a credit for their week's earnings on which they could draw in cash or kind. This was a disastrous procedure for those among them who had a permanent thirst. When they made a find they drank until their money gave out and then returned to their claims.

"The Bosun", some of whose reminiscences were published in a journal called the *Mines and Claim-Holders' Journal* at a much later date, estimated that in the years he spent on the diggings he had taken out £50,000 worth of gold "at the end of his own pick" — and spent the lot. However, as he was there for 43 years and lived to be 83 that was not quite the record that it sounds, though he should be remembered with reverence by the wine and spirit merchants.

An ounce of gold was then worth £3. 10s. 0d., and a pennyweight 3s. 6d. to 3s. 9d. This meant that a bottle of "squareface" gin retailed at a little less than two pennyweights, and a bottle of Cape brandy at slightly more. But, as prices went in those days, these were reasonable. The diggers had to pay 2s. 6d. for a tin of milk, 6d. for a box of matches, over £4 for a bag of Boer meal and as much as £3 for a bag of mealie meal.

When they were prosperous they lived on meat, Australian "dampers" made from Boer meal, and large quantities of tea. When times were bad they were reduced to mealie meal and water from the creek, backed up by borrowed tots of gin. To anyone who has studied the remnants of the old wagon track that led down Pilgrim's Hill from Lydenburg the cost of goods brought to the valley does not seem high.

The digger's day began at sunrise. He would crawl out of his blankets, pull on moleskin trousers and a flannel shirt and thrust his feet into damp hobnailed boots. He might then stroll down to the creek for a wash, but he would not shave. A beard was as much the digger's trade mark as his pick.

There would certainly not be bacon and eggs for breakfast. There might be meat and a billycan of tea. He needed a substantial meal at this hour of the morning, for 10 to 12 hours of hard work lay ahead of him.

The hour at which digging ceased in the evening, usually 5 or 6 p.m., was laid down by the diggers' committee, and this was one of the laws of the camp that had to be obeyed. There were many men who, having found gold, would happily have worked far into the night getting ready for the next day's wash. But if there was to be law and order in the camp this could not be allowed. In the dark hours it would be a simple matter for a thief to come "nosing round" someone else's claim or even to take away a load of gravel while pretending to be working his own claim. This would mean that each man would have perpetually to be on his guard beside his pegs. For everyone's peace of mind, therefore, it was essential that all work should end at sundown.

It was a sensible regulation, originally evolved in California. It meant that anyone found working at night was suspect and required to pay a fine of £5 or more, and there was no appeal once the digger's committee had found him guilty.

Sunday was a day of rest, on which all work ceased.

"The work in the Creek was very arduous," says an early account of the digger's day. "The top soil, consisting sometimes of as much as 18 feet of red soil, had first to be removed. All this had to be thrown up and conserved on the claim.

"Underneath this was the layer of wash and boulders which contained the gold. Frequently there were two layers of gold-bearing wash and boulders. The boulders in the wash were a source of infinite trouble and frequent accident. A hole had to be dug at the side of the boulder and the ground loosened underneath so that the stone would roll in. The Bosun says that, to give the first warning, a digger in his bare feet stood on top of the boulder. On the first tremor being conveyed by his naked feet he gave a shout of warning to those below and jumped . . . It may be within our reader's own experience that his feet have on occasion given him the first intimation of loss of equilibrium . . ."

The gold carried down by the stream had, over the ages, sunk through the soil and settled above the bed rock. Nuggets and pockets of coarse gold tended to be held up by the boulders and were, therefore, often found beneath them. When a boulder was moved from its bed there was always a careful search on the spot to see what might be there. The river bed gravel was all removed and washed.

Each claim in the early days had its own "water race", a narrow channel through which the water was led to the sluice box. This was a long, coffin-shaped construction of wood, 20 feet or more in length, 18 inches wide and 18 inches deep. At the bottom, slats of wood were nailed transversely across the "floor" plank to form what was known as a "Venetian ripple".

The gravel, earth and small stones taken from the claim were shovelled into this box and the water led through it with a good "head" on it. The "spoil" was washed straight through the box and out at the far end. The gold, being heavier than the surrounding gravel, sank to the bottom of the box and was caught by the slats that formed the "ripple". In areas where the gold was particularly fine, it was the custom to put a blanket, a sheep skin, or even an ox-hide, at the bottom of the sluice box so that the fine particles could be caught up in the hair.

The great moment of the digger's day came when he "cleaned up". The mud and fine particles at the bottom of the box were then carefully scraped out and panned, a skilful process of rocking and tilting the iron basin until finally all the mud and pebbles were tipped out and nothing left but the tail of gold — the day's takings. Nuggets were, of course, spotted earlier in the proceedings, picked out, washed and popped into tin or bottle. This final process produced the gold dust, which might weigh a couple of pennyweights or as much as eight ounces.

It was these "clean ups" that provided all the fascination of the occupation, that kept men digging all their lives. There was no pattern whatever about the finding of alluvial gold. One man might excavate and wash tons of earth without finding as much as an ounce of gold, while in a neighbouring claim they might be taking out £20-worth a day. It was the daily gamble that made the life worthwhile, and inspired men to 10 hours or more of back-breaking labour.

In the very early days every digger had his own water race, made simply by digging a furrow from the edge of the stream. But when the population grew, these furrows became co-operative efforts, and each digger took his turn in the use of the water.

The furrows are there to this day as a memorial to the pioneers. Many of them are extremely skilled jobs, carefully contoured and often cut through solid rock on the hillside. They led water great distances to places where gold had been deposited. A flow of water was as essential to these early claims as was the digger's pick — perhaps even more essential, for the men would have been prepared to scrabble the earth with their hands once they had found gold, but without water they could do nothing.

The most famous of these furrows is still pointed out to visitors at Sabie. It was called "Swann's Race" and was built, though never completed, by an old digger named Swann who had found gold in an inaccessible spot in the hills. Swann was determined that no one should ever know where his mine was. He could apparently work it with the resources he had for, from time to time, he appeared with quantities of gold to buy supplies. But to make the fortune he wanted he needed water, and he set to work to carve a furrow which, it has since been estimated, was 20 miles long. He told his acquaintances that he thought it would take him eight years to complete the race. And then he would be rich beyond the dreams of avarice. But that was all he said. He worked on and on . . . and finally he died. They traced the course of the furrow, but no one has ever found Swann's "mine".

There was no native labour on the diggings in the early days. It never occurred to the Americans and the Australians, who set the fashions on the field, that there was any other procedure but that of "mucking in". They pegged their claims and went to work, and the others followed their example. But Alois Nellmapius, having taken a great deal of gold out of his claims, saw no reason why he should do his own digging. One day he appeared at Pilgrim's Rest with a gang of natives whom he had persuaded to work for him. He proceeded to teach them to use pick and shovel, implements they had never handled before, and was soon working twice as quickly as anyone else.

After that "Kaffirs were lively" wherever there were claims. It cost an ounce of gold, or £3. 12s. 0d. a week, to employ a white man to dig, but wandering members of the Pedi tribe were prepared to work hard for a few shillings and a ration of mealie meal. The men from Kimberley, who had been accustomed to letting natives do the hard work of diamond digging, were astonished to find white men working "like Kaffirs" when they reached Pilgrim's Rest. It was not their way of doing things, and they soon had gangs at work on their claims.

Most of these Africans were making their first contact with civilization, if civilization it could be called. It took them some time to find out what it was all about, but once they learnt the value of the yellow "Mali" for which the white man was looking they began to bring in nuggets they had picked up, and their finds led many a prospector to new ground.

The value of gold was not all they learnt. The diggers specialized in strong language and it was said that, collectively, they had the finest vocabulary of swear words in the world. These were among the first words of English that the Africans learnt. Many a farmer in later years was impressed by the string of rich oaths his wagon boy could produce in a crisis, some of them delivered in what might have been an Australian accent. This was "Pilgrim's Rest English", a full-flavoured tongue.

One report on the diggings published by the Society for the Propagation of the Gospel in the early days said that there was a digger on the field who held special classes every Sunday "to teach the Kaffirs to swear". It seems more probable that the class was held on every claim throughout the week.

They drank and used foul language, these hard-bitten men. They had black paramours and fathered many coffee-coloured children. But they did not steal from one another.

The law of the camp was stern on this point. A man found robbing a claim or stealing from a tent would be brought before the diggers' committee and sentenced to 25 lashes. He would then have his head shaved, half his beard removed and be told to "get out". He had then to abandon his claim and walk either to Lydenburg or to Lourenco Marques, and dared not show his face on the diggings.

It happened once or twice in the early days, but not very often. One of the legends of the district concerns a man thus treated who, having been ordered to go, tried to sneak back. He was shot and buried where he lay on the hillside. The stony ground surrounding his grave became the first graveyard in Pilgrim's Rest. What today is described as "the thief's grave" lies north and south, while all the other graves face east. There certainly is such a grave in the old graveyard, for I have seen it. Today it is nothing more than a mound of stones.

There probably had to be rough justice such as this in the "earlies", to ensure that men would be able to leave their tents and their claims unguarded. Thanks to the examples that were made of the first thieves, the digger's tent became his castle, in which he could store the two most valuable commodities on the field — gold and brandy. In the palmy days many of them kept a bag of nuggets which they hoped one day to carry with them when they left, never to return. And even the poorest of them treasured one two-ounce nugget as a form of insurance. It was to pay for a "decent burial" if they met sudden death.

The Gold Commissioner and his one policeman (his name was Barter) could not have controlled the diggings had it not been for the discipline imposed by the diggers' committee. Their only symbols of authority were half-a-dozen pairs of handcuffs and a tent in which they could put male-factor in the stocks (this place of detention later became a wattle-and-daub hut). But on the whole it was a law-abiding community. Fist fights and wrestling matches there were aplenty, and a great deal of drunkenness. But I can find no record of murders or serious assaults. There was none of the brandishing of pistols and exchange of shots at short range that made diggings in other parts of the world notorious.

The diggers had a sense of comradeship. They were not very free with information for it was every man for himself when it came to pegging claims, but they helped one another in difficulties and were generous when a man was down on his luck.

There was one ghastly exception to this rule, a story of the man who let down a friend that is still quoted 80 years after it happened.

An Englishman named George Gray and his partner set out one day in 1873 to walk to Lourenco Marques, where they were to buy supplies and then tramp back to the diggings. Somewhere in the foothills of the Lebombo Mountains Gray developed malaria and was so ill that he could walk no further. His companion made a camp, put food and water and a loaded rifle beside the sick man and then made a dash for Lourenco Marques, intending to return with more food and medicine.

Instead he went into a canteen and had a drink, then another . . . He was drunk for 10 days. When at last he sobered up and walked back to the camp Gray was dead and the hyenas surrounded the remains of his body.

But that was the one case of its kind recorded. Partners quarrelled over where to peg claims, over the division of the profits and over meals and drinks. But they stood by one another in trouble. When men became friends on the diggings they were friends for life.

The scandal of the day was the importation of native women from Portuguese territory. Before the wagon road to Lourenco Marques was made, supplies were carried to the diggings by porters. Among them would be a bevy of buxom girls who thought nothing of walking 170 miles through lion country (it is today's Kruger National Park) with cases of gin balanced on their heads.

The Portuguese gentlemen who ran these caravans were not content with selling the gin. They sold the girls, too. Many of them never returned to Lourenco Marques but settled down as "housekeepers" in the diggers' tents.

The Reverend Gerald Herring, in his history of Pilgrim's Rest, described a Christmas Eve outside one of the pubs.

". . . A number of men came into camp to celebrate the festive season. A number of their dusky ladies had the temerity to wander in, too. But for this freedom they had to pay.

"A large barrel stood in the middle of the street. It was half full of water. Into it the men dropped coins for which the women struggled. The awkward and inelegant posture taken up of necessity by each competitor in turn furnished the diggers with their opportunity. The valley echoed with screams and laughter and the smack - smack - smack of hard and horny hands."

It was obviously time for the first white women to appear upon the scene, to turn the shacks and tents into homes and to re-shape the morals and

"The valley echoed to their screams of laughter and the smack-smack-smack of hard and horny hands."

manners of the community.

As far as I can discover, Mrs. Tom McLachlan, who lived in a stone house built for her by her husband at Mac Mac, was first on the scene. She was certainly there in 1872, and helped to nurse many a fever-stricken traveller who had crossed the Lowveld from Lourenco Marques only to collapse on the track that led up the mountainside to the diggings.

Mrs. Dietrich, wife of the German officer whom I have mentioned as an assistant to MacDonald, arrived with her husband in 1873. She was accompanied by two daughters, one of whom became Mrs. Elsa Smithers and set down her recollections of Pilgrim's Rest in a book called *March Hare*.

Among her memories is that of Miss Elizabeth Russell who lived in a tent on the diggings and worked a claim of her own, often standing knee-deep in water.

Most of those who wrote about the early days of the diggings seem to be under the impression that there were two Russell girls at Pilgrim's Rest in 1873*. However, I am assured by Mrs. D.W. Bosch, a grand-daughter of Elizabeth Russell whose married name was Cameron, that this was not so. There were two Russell girls, Elizabeth, whom her family called "Bessie", and Annie. They were the daughters of H.B. Russell, a well-known citizen of Heidelberg and Pretoria, in both of which towns he established businesses as a miller and merchant in the seventies. Mr. Russell forbade his daughters to go

* In the editions of *Valley of Gold* published in 1961 I accepted this statement as being correct. I was wrong.

62

to the diggings but Elizabeth defied him and she and her brother Alfred, who was always known as "Tucker" Russell, made their way there and acquired a claim in the creek. Their father was extremely angry when he found that he had been disobeyed and the rest of the family were forbidden to communicate with the runaways", who were warned that, if they failed to pay their way, they would get no help from their parents. Later Mr. Russell must have forgiven them because Elizabeth was married from the family home in Pretoria.

She certainly has her place in the history of the Transvaal for she not only went to the diggings, and worked a claim there at a time when such conduct by a young woman was regarded as scandalous, but she made a success of the venture. As a school teacher her salary had been R50 a year. One of her claims at Pilgrim's Rest is reputed to have earned her R400 a month profit for some considerable time.

All in all Elizabeth seems to have been a young woman well ahead of the women of her day. She had been born in London on May 29, 1850, but came to South Africa with her parents in 1855. They settled in Maritzburg Natal, where Mr. Russell ran the Boston Mills and the girls were sent to Cheltenham House school in Pinetown. There her best subject was always arithmetic but she found the school discipline irksome. She left school at the age of 16 to become a governess and later taught at Caversham in Natal.

Her father and the rest of the family settled at Heidelberg where Mr. Russell opened a store. But Elizabeth went to Harrismith where she ran a private school of sorts and took in music pupils as well. She worked her income up to about R50 a month and managed to buy a piano for R150. Then came news of the discovery of gold "in the Lydenburg district". She and her brother, Tucker, decided to try their luck on the diggings. She sold her piano, bought 30 bags of wheat, picks and shovels, blankets and food. Then she set to work to make herself a tent of heavy canvas. At length she and her brother set out with the reproaches and warnings of their parents ringing in their ears.

She had shown a sound business instinct in taking with her a cargo of wheat. She had this milled on the way down to Lydenburg and sold the flour at a very handsome profit.

The young Russells found to their surprise that there were quite a number of people they had known in Natal in Pilgrim's Rest. They pitched their tent near that of Captain Dietrich and wife who were old friends. Elizabeth was fortunate in finding that Yankee Dan, one of the best-known of the older diggers, was prepared to act as her adviser. He guided her round many pitfalls.

She and her brother had no luck at all in their first claim. They decided to move to the Middle Camp where she had pegged another claim. They were employing eight Bantu to do the hard labour and their funds were beginning to run out so Elizabeth set up a side-line, the manufacture of sausage rolls and ginger beer which sold remarkably well. But, while she was thus engaged, young Tucker started slacking. There was a family row and Tucker left in a huff.

Elizabeth then moved her tent to the Middle Camp and fired all the staff except one, an African named "Basket" whom she set to work under her supervision. One day, after much fruitless digging, he burst into a war dance and rushed to her tent where he handed her a nugget weighing four ounces. Basket had saved the day. The claim was a rich one and Elizabeth, joined by another brother named Harry, began to make substantial profits.

Working a claim near the Russells at this time was a young American named W.A.B. Cameron. Elizabeth liked his enterprise and his looks and soon they became engaged. They were married in St. Albans, Pretoria, in 1874. President Burgers attended the wedding and *Die Volkstem* described it as "a golden wedding", a subtle reference to the fact that both bride and groom were gold miners. The reporter on this occasion also said that Miss Russell was "the young lady genius of the diggings". The President proposed the health of the "bride and bridegroom".

Soon after this Cameron was elected to represent the Lydenburg diggers in the Volksraad. In 1876 he and his wife went to the United States to attend, as the official representatives of the South African Republic, an international exhibition that was being held in Philadelphia. They visited London en route to the United States. On this tour Elizabeth ate her first oyster and decided then and there that it would also be her last.

Eventually, after their return to South Africa, Elizabeth and her husband found that they were incompatible and parted. They never met again. She was left with five children and the story of her struggle to feed, clothe and educate this brood is almost a book in its own right. This fearless, forthright woman to whom Pilgrim's Rest must raise a monument one day, lived to be 80. She died in Volksrust in May, 1931.

She was one of South Africa's pioneers, her character shaped by the years she spent in the wilds of the old Transvaal.

CHAPTER VIII

THE PRESIDENT'S GOLD CROSS

One of the accepted legends of Pilgrim's Rest is that the Reverend Cawkill Barker, the not-too-sober Anglican parson, who is said to have been exiled to the diggings after he had behaved badly in Pretoria, frequently visited "the Russell girls" in their tent. Mr. Smithers says that when MacDonald, the Gold Commissioner, made some caustic remarks about these visits one of the Russell girls horse-whipped him. But we now have the evidence of a granddaughter that there was only one Russell girl on the diggings and I have always doubted the story that MacDonald was horsewhipped. I find it hard to believe that anyone, least of all a female, could have thrashed this tough customer. I fear that this legend must fall by the wayside.

On the other hand completely authentic extracts from an old manuscript diary do confirm some of the other legends. For example:

"October 20, 1873, Mac Mac, New Caledonia: Last Monday one, Pratt, a White man, was brought up and charged with stealing, found guilty, 25 lashes, then escorted five miles out of camp — banishment for life".

and

From *Die Volkstem* (copied out in the diarist's handwriting): "A miner, Hugh Cartwright, was brought into Pretoria under escort and in irons for the offences of defiance of the Gold Commissioner's authority, treason towards the State and assault on the Sheriff of the Gold Fields in the lawful execution of the Gold Commissioner's warrant.

The writer of this diary insisted that President Burgers had named the camp on Geelhoutboom "Mc Mc", not "Mac Mac" but, over the years, he seems to have been outvoted.

No doubt exists as to who was the first baby born at Pilgrim's Rest. She was the daughter of John and Mary Purcell who reached Mac Mac from Kimberley early in 1873. The Purcells moved to Pilgrim's Rest soon afterwards and, on the banks of the Blyde River, Mrs. Purcell gave birth to a girl who was christened Maud Mary. Dr. John Scoble, who was later to succeed MacDonald as Gold Commissioner, spread the news that John Purcell had "a 10-lb. nugget" and the diggers flocked to see the child. The whole camp adopted the baby who was soon in danger of becoming the most spoilt child in the Transvaal.

Maud Mary Purcell grew up and married Herbert Wilfred Charles Lilley, son of the discoverer of the Lilley Nugget. They had three children and Mrs. Sheila MacFarlane, her youngest daughter, still lives in Pilgrim's Rest where her mother spent nearly all her life.

There also lived in Pilgrim's Rest a most distinguished old lady, Mrs. Isabella Cornelia Joubert, a daughter of Diedrik Muller, who once owned the farms Ponieskrantz, Morgenzon and Doornhoek, and whose grandfather, Johannes Muller, owned and worked the farm Geelhoutboom on which Mac Mac stood. Mrs. Joubert's first husband was Johannes Hendrik de Beer, universally known as "Maboompie" de Beer, once the best-known and most respected citizen of Pilgrim's Rest, who was a mine owner, storekeeper, transport driver, miller and Good Samaritan to the whole district.

Mrs. Joubert, who was related to Schalk Burger, Vice President of the Republic, and Abel Erasmus, was born at Kruger's Post, half way between Pilgrim's Rest and Lydenburg, and she lived in the village all the years of her life after she married Mr. de Beer. When I first met her ten years ago her memories went back to the days when a procession of men passed the Muller homestead on their way to the diggings on the other side of the mountains. Her family, true to the hospitable tradition of the day, fed this horde of hungry men from the resources of the farm.

"Some of them came back carrying bags of nuggets, but not many of them," she said.

She was Pilgrim's Rest's link with the past, the Grand Old Lady of the district but she died four years ago.

To two of the pioneer women of the diggings President Burgers presented the Burgers Cross. They were Mrs. Tom McLachlan, who had nursed the diggers, and Mrs. D. Austin, who nursed the men wounded in the Sekukuni war. These crosses are among the most valuable decorations in the world, for they are made of solid gold (it came from the Pilgrim's Rest diggings) and are beautifully designed.

A copy of the letter that the President sent to the recipients of the cross shows that he wrote in English and in his own hand. The letter reads:

"My dear Madam,

In handing you over the accompanying Burgers Cross as a token of sincere respect and acknowledgement on behalf of myself and the public of the goldfields for your kind and devoted services to those who were in distress I feel sure that I express the feeling of all when I say: May God reward you for your noble self-denial.

Trusting you may be spared for many years to enjoy the fruits of a noble work nobly performed.

I remain, my dear madam,
Your obedient servant,
Thomas Burgers."

If the truth were told, there probably was not a single white woman on the diggings in those days who did not deserve a decoration.

The trouble about alluvial gold is that, in the phrase the diggers were fond of using: "It comes and it goes . . ."

The deposits in the creek at Pilgrim's Rest were rich, probably as rich as any found in the world to that date, but they could not last for long. At the height of the boom there were 1,400 men in the district, each turning over a ton or two of ground a day. It was mining with a very fine sieve. In the spots where good finds were made they crowded together and without doubt they took out every ounce of gold they could get at.

The bed of the creek looked as though it had been bombarded with high explosives. Every square yard of earth had been excavated and large boulders rolled down its banks. Modern miners never cease to marvel at the miraculous way in which the diggers moved those enormous rocks without using dynamite.

They scratched the gravel from the bed of the stream, they tunnelled into the banks and pulled the debris down from the mountain side. It all went through the sluice boxes.

Some years ago Mr. W.J.L. Guest, who then owned the Royal Hotel in Pilgrim's Rest, gave a nartjie tree in his garden a thorough watering. Suddenly the ground below the tree fell in, and investigation showed that a tunnel ran right under his house. Some 90 years ago a digger had patiently burrowed into the hillside here, moving great boulders and building his narrow adit over 70 yards into the bank of the stream. Mr. Guest's house, now owned by his daughter, was one of the few buildings on the left-hand side of the Main Street. It stands on the site of a well-known landmark of the early days known as "Jack Hjul's House". Not far above this site Alois Nellmapius had his claims, and it proved the richest part of the creek.

By the end of 1874 the lesser claims in Pilgrim's Creek had been scraped bare and the diggers were fanning out over the countryside looking for new deposits. Peach Tree Creek, just "round the corner" from the village, on the banks of the Blyde River, produced some very rich deposits. The gold was of such high grade in these claims that the diggers who owned them were paid what was then considered the ',wonderful" price of £4. 2s. 6d. an ounce for their finds. Then a digger named Nolan found two small nuggets at a place which he called Waterfall Creek, on the farm Berlyn, and there was an immediate rush to the new find in which 60 or 70 diggers took part.

The field was now beginning to take its final shape, with the main body of diggers concentrated at Pilgrim's Rest and scattered groups making a living at Graskop, Spitzkop, Mac Mac, Elandsdrift, the Blyde River bank, Peach Tree Creek and Waterfall.

It had begun to be obvious to everyone that the alluvial gold was giving out and that the day of the "big finds" was over. However, there was so much gold scattered over a wide area that it was still possible to make a good living, and even the laziest men on the field could earn their keep. They said in those days that you could pan ground anywhere on the track that ran between Graskop and Pilgrim's Rest and find traces of gold.

Men began to turn their attention to the leader reefs. These were close to

67

the surface and, in their decomposed shales, there were often very rich patches of gold which could be removed by washing — if only water could be led to the claim. But as often as not it was impossible to build a water race to the places where the "leaders" were found. And in any case it was obvious that the proper way to treat the ground was by crushing the ore. Where once the conversation on the diggings had been all about claims in the creek and improved methods of using sluice boxes, it now turned to the problem of working "reefs" and to the cost of five-stamp mills. There was many a digger who knew, or thought he knew, where there was rich leader reef. But how was he to get at it, how to work the ground? The smallest battery, imported from Britain and transported from Durban to Lydenburg, cost about R3,000. They could only dream of the day when they might be able to afford one. But suppose they could, suppose they had the machinery hauled from Lydenburg, then dragged up a mountainside and installed, what would happen if the gold petered out? This was the problem that faced even those who had made money and saved it. They needed capital. They had to spread the risks. No longer was it every man for himself.

It was the dawn of a new era. Though most of the old diggers remained individualists to the end, there were those among them who began to form groups and partnerships, to pool their knowledge of the district and to plan methods of working the exposed portion of the reef they had discovered. Some of them took the risk and ordered stamps. It was capital they needed most, and thus the way was paved for the companies which were eventually to put mining on a proper basis.

In the meantime, Pilgrim's Rest had become the social centre, if that is the right word, of the community. There the diggers assembled for their meetings and their drinks. There they elected the two members of the Volksraad whom Burgers had promised should represent them (Herbert Rhodes was one of the men they chose).

John Purcell, supported by The Bosun, vouched for the story of a duel which took place in the town in those days, between Jimmy Bryson and a digger named Smith. This was fully recounted in *Mines and Claim-Holders' Journal* 30 years later.

The trouble began when Bryson and Smith were wooing "two attractive and well-built sisters who assisted in a relative's store up the Creek".

"In the romantic interior of the store Love's young dream stirred the sleeping passion of their souls. The sardine tins beamed a bright approval, the bags of coffee offered aromatic incense, the tins of salmon blushed a deeper pink at little love episodes. Here were two bachelors of equal degree and two maidens of very equal charms. Surely on this occasion the course of true love might have run smooth?"

But it didn't. A group of diggers who entered the store one afternoon found Bryson and Smith in "an almighty tussle" on the floor. They were separated and someone suggested a duel.

The duel between Bryson and Smith.

"... The two men were game, and early next morning Enfield rifles for two (at a hundred paces) and coffee for one were provided by an appreciative group of spectators in a secluded corner of Pilgrim's Creek.

"The signal was given, two shots rang out simultaneously and the un-unfortunate Smith fell in a welter of blood.

"Bryson's second rushed forward, rapidly examined the victim then shouted to Bryson: 'For God's sake clear, Bryson. He's done for.'

"Bryson, with an agonised wave of the hand, disappeared into the bush. Smith was carried to a neighbouring hut in a dead faint and the arch-conspirator MacDonald, with his confederates, waited for his recovery to inform him that the Enfields had been loaded with blank cartridges and that the blood had been conveyed by a sheep's bladder dashed down on his head by McDonald.

"It was a long and anxious time before Smith recovered from his swoon, and even then it took quite a time to convince him that he was not fatally wounded and that his kind-hearted mates had not invented the tale to ease his approaching dissolution. With painful ingratitude he stuck to his bed for 14 days, during which time his confederates had to look after him and work his claim.

"Meanwhile Bryson was known to be haunting the hills in the vicinity of Pilgrim's Rest and the repentant MacDonald made several efforts to get in touch with him ..."

There you have another of the authentic legends of Pilgrim's Rest. It is wonderful how a funny story lingers on long after the more prosaic details of life have been forgotten. The Bosun, who was present when the "duel" took place, as he was present at everything that happened in the camp, certified this as the correct version of the story as late as 1917.

Now clouds appeared on the horizon. President Burgers, who had the confidence of the diggers, was in Europe trying to raise a loan for his cherished dream of a railway between Pretoria and Lourenco Marques. While he was away a three-cornered row developed between the diggers, the officials in Pretoria and MacDonald, the Gold Commissioner. It centred round the new gold laws that were to be presented to the Volksraad.

Almost all the diggers objected to a proposal to increase the licence fee for claims from 50 cents to R1. MacDonald told Pretoria bluntly that he thought this clause would lead to trouble. On the question of granting blocks of claims to companies which would have exclusive rights to the ground the diggers were divided. Nellmapius, busy at that time trying to amalgamate a number of claims, led a faction that favoured this proposal as the only means by which the fields could be developed. The individualists objected vehemently. They said that the clause took away the rights the President had granted the diggers and would favour the companies, though at that stage of the proceedings the companies were no more than associations of diggers – the first of them being the "Pilgrim's Rest Gold Fields Company" which apparently was never registered.

MacDonald was suspected by the "free enterprise" party of favouring the "capitalists", and petitions for his removal from office were received in Pretoria, where he was already in disfavour because his accounts were somewhat sketchy and his administrative methods too unorthodox.

There was a prolonged exchange of acrimonious letters and a positive flood of petitions. But the more conservative members of the Volksraad had already made up their minds that the "Engelse" (the Englishmen) as they called the diggers needed discipline. The new gold law was promulgated virtually without amendment on June 21, 1875.

The diggers flatly refused to pay the 10s. claim licence fee, and MacDonald was forced to place 110 of them under arrest. It would probably be more accurately described as "house arrest".

There was further argument and exchange of correspondence, and then Pretoria climbed down. The regulation was altered and the licence fee became 50 cents once again.

By this time MacDonald had had enough. He resigned the post of Gold Commissioner, was given a farewell banquet by the diggers and set off for Lourenco Marques. It was afterwards alleged that there was a discrepancy of £240 in his books, but the Republic had had ample time to find this out before he left. Considering that he had been a chance appointment Pretoria ought to have been grateful for the services he had rendered the state. He was succeeded by Dr. John Scoble.

The news that the diggers were "in revolt" against the Government reached Britain and Europe in exaggerated form just as Burgers was negotiating for his £300,000 railway loan. It scarcely helped.

The whole business was unfortunate for it left a legacy of distrust among the diggers and persuaded the Volksraad that the President had been too "liberal" in his dealings with the uitlanders beyond Lydenburg. The people of Johannesburg and the mining industry were to pay for this in after years.

The South African Republic's slide to ruin now gained momentum. Sekukuni, chief of the Pedi, and his half-brother, Johannes Dinkoyane, became aggressive and the settlers in the Lydenburg-Ohrigstad district were in fear of their lives. The Republic could not afford a war against the tribes. On the other hand it could not afford a rising at a time when the fate of its first loan hung in the balance.

Burgers assembled a commando, which had no confidence in his leadership, and marched into Sekukuniland. It was a disastrous campaign. After two minor successes the commando was repulsed in an attack on Sekukuni's stronghold. Its members cried "huis toe" and melted away. The President was left in no doubt as to his own unpopularity and the impossibility of raising an adequate force to fight Sekukuni. He compromised by building a chain of forts on the border and raising a paid force of irregulars called the Lydenburg Volunteers. To meet the costs of the expedition he had led, and these new defence measures, he imposed a "war tax" which lost him what little popularity he had left. The citizens of the Republic simply refused to pay it.

During the campaign the diggers in the Pilgrim's Rest area were left largely to their own devices. The transport service from Lourenco Marques ceased, and wagons in the Lydenburg area were commandeered for active service. The result was that work on the diggings came to a standstill.

A rough-and-ready defence organisation was formed and women and children slept in a laager at night. The first brush with the Pedi occurred on Henry Glynn's farm at Kruger's Post, only 10 miles away. It caused a scare in Pilgrim's Rest and heightened resentment against the government which, it was felt, was leaving the population of the diggings to its fate.

The *Gold Fields Mercury,* a newspaper published in Pilgrim's Rest, owned and edited by an Irishman named M.V. Phelan, went into almost open revolt againt the republican government.

Phelan declared in an editorial that those who had been for the Republic had turned against it . . . they could not serve a state which forced its laws on its subjects. They had to pay taxes, but the state refused to give them any protection in the time of danger.

According to a later issue of the *Gold Fields Mercury,* on August 28, 1876, the diggers had held a meeting to discuss possible terms of friendship between Sekukuni and themselves. The meeting decided that the diggers would not pay taxes for expenditure occurred in the war, and that they would give their support to a plan for inviting the British Government to settle matters between Sekukuni and the South African Republic. The diggers also suggested that the Republic should agree to a federation with the British colonies in South Africa.

Though there is no evidence that these resolutions appeared anywhere except in the *Mercury* there is no doubt that they breathed the spirit of the times – open revolt. The same comments were being voiced in Pretoria, but not quite so openly.

In November, 1876, Phelan went too far. He published a criticism of Dr. John Scoble, the Gold Commissioner, which that official thought brought him into contempt. He had Phelan brought before him, fined him £27. 10s. 0d., and imposed a sentence of two weeks' imprisonment.

The diggers promptly held a meeting, marched to the jail and released Phelan, defying Scoble and his policemen.

Scoble retired to Lydenburg and a detachment of the Lydenburg Volunteers – 25 men and a cannon – under the commanding officer of the regiment, an Irishman named Aylward, was sent to deal with the diggers.

Had Aylward marched his troops into Pilgrim's Rest there might have been serious trouble. But he had been "agin the Government" too often himself to take this disturbance seriously. He rode into the camp alone and held a conference with the diggers.

The upshot was that every man-jack of them, including the commanding officer of the Lydenburg Volunteers, got drunk, and 18 of the ringleaders voluntarily surrendered on a charge of disturbing the peace. They appeared on this charge, were released on bail, and never came to trial – for reasons that will be apparent later.

Thus ended the one incident in which the diggers of Pilgrim's Rest, in spite of all their grumblings, actually defied the authority of the Republic. It might have been worse.

In the meantime a number of letters had been sent from Pilgrim's Rest to Sir Henry Bulwer, Governor of Natal, and Sir Henry Barkly, Governor of the Cape Colony, asking for protection and suggestion that the British Government should take over the Transvaal.

These petitions received fairly non-commital replies from the two Governors to whom they were addressed. But as these replies were sent through normal postal channels, which meant that they would be opened and read by Republican officials, that was only to be expected. There were undoubtedly similar appeals from some of the leading citizens of Pretoria, whose names have never been revealed.

The British Government acted. In January, 1877, Sir Theophilus Shepstone, accompaneid by an escort of Natal police, rode into Pretoria. Three months later he announced the annexation of the Transvaal and declared it a British Colony. So desperate was the plight of the Republic, so divided its people, that there was no protest. By reading a proclamation and hoisting the Union Jack, Shepstone was able to take over an independent state.

That was the end of Burgers and of his plans for a "new deal". He left Pretoria, broken in spirit and penniless, never to return. His mission had failed.

We know today that the British occupation of the Transvaal was precisely the tonic the Transvalers needed. As their indignation grew their quarrels were forgotten. Four years later, when Kruger sounded the call to arms, they rose as one man and fought for their independence. And after the defeat of General Sir George Colley at Majuba, and his death on the mountain side, they won it back. Public opinion in Britain veered in their favour. A Royal Commission produced an agreement which both sides signed, and from August 8, 1881, the South African Republic was a self-governing state once more, its boundaries guaranteed by Britain. The Volksraad met again on August 10, with the Triumvirate, Paul Kruger, Piet Joubert and Marthinus Wessel Pretorius, at the head of affairs until such time as a Presidential election could be held.

What had happened to the diggers while all this was going on? They had been wildly excited when the news of the annexation reached them, had hauled up the Union Jack and held a celebration in the canteens that had almost used up the entire available stock of liquor.

But when Shepstone visited Pilgrim's Rest in 1879 the enthusiasm had worn off. They met him with a deputation asking for help in prospecting and developing the country. They wanted to know when the Delagoa Bay Railway would be built. They found him unsympathetic. He told them that the railway would never be built and practically said that they must fend for themselves.

Shepstone had meant to spend the night, but the scenes that followed made him change his mind. The diggers plied the troopers of his escort with brandy until they could no longer sit their horses. Grass fires broke out, the horses stampeded and the oxen were lost. The party withdrew in disorder with most of the escort flat on their backs in the wagons.

The stark fact that the diggers had to face was that not even the hoisting of the Union Jack could revive the alluvial diggings. There was not enough gold to go round. The easy-to-get-at deposits had all been worked out, and although there were new finds here and there none of them proved as rich as Pilgrim's Creek. There were still claims that were producing gold, and men who had succeeded in pegging the "leaders" were making money fast. But there was no longer a living for 1,500 diggers.

They began to drift away from the field — some to prospect in other areas, others to return to the towns to find run-of-the-mill jobs and dream of might have been's. It looked as though the Transvaal's first gold boom was petering out.

The British occupation and the prospect of a stable government had encouraged investors abroad to invest in "Transvaal gold". Quite a number of companies were floated on entirely imaginary reports of new fields that were to be explored and old mines that were to be developed. But the war of 1881 and the subsequent handing back of the territory to the Boers frightened the British investor, who sold out if he could find anyone to buy his shares.

The Republic's provisional government found itself back where it had started. The British had settled the debts of the Burgers administration and put the financial affairs of the Transvaal on an even keel. But the moment they withdrew the old difficulties began again. The problem was the same as ever. There was no trade. The country could not pay for its imports and therefore could not balance its budget.

The Triumvirate there and then decided on a policy that Paul Kruger was to continue when he became President in 1883. They began to hand out concessions to anyone who succeeded in convincing them that he could establish an industry and pay for the privilege.

Nellmapius, with the astute Sammy Marks behind him, obtained the sole right to refine sugar and distil spirits, and forthwith began bottling Hatherley gin (named after a farm he acquired in the Pretoria district). Adolph Gates obtained exclusive rights to navigation on the Vaal River and to mine in various areas. And then, in November, 1881, David Benjamin "of Cape Town in the colony of the Cape of Good Hope" (but really of London in the county of Middlesex, England), obtained his concession to work the farms in the Pilgrim's Rest district.

Some say that Abe Bailey did the talking for Benjamin and obtained the concession on his behalf, but I have not been able to confirm this. He most certainly had a representative in Pretoria to put the case for him, and it may have been Bailey. The fact that he was prepared to pay £1,000 a year for the concession and compensate the diggers must have carried great weight with the Volksraad. It offered a neat solution to the problem of dealing with the pocket of unrest at Pilgrim's Rest. If Benjamin took over the diggers would have to go.

Benjamin certainly had courage as well as cash. He was gambling on his theory that there was far more gold at Pilgrim's Rest than ever came out of the creek. At a time when other investors abroad developed cold feet he alone stood firm, a financial Casabianca who was to reap a rich reward.

For at this precise moment South Africa's fairy godmother made another entrance from the wings, bearing her third gift. It was gold again.

Prospectors wandering through the wild and desolate valley known as "De Kaap", which Tom McLachlan had prophesied would produce gold, began to get results. They pegged claims in the "Duivel's Kantoor", found patches of gold here, there and everywhere and then struck the Pioneer Reef.

There were unemployed diggers all over the Transvaal at this time waiting for the signal they hoped would come. They rushed to the new field and pegged as near to the discoveries as they could get. They would hardly have put

A lion in the path at Barberton.

in their pegs when a new discovery would be announced and off they'd go again.

French Bob's Reef, Concession Creek, Pioneer's Reef, Moodie's, Barberton . . . the discoveries came one after the other. And then Bray found his Golden Quarry and began developing the Sheba Reef. The first 13,000 tons of ore the company milled produced 50,000 ozs. of gold. The shares soared to over £100 each.

There followed one of the shortest, wildest gold booms the world has ever known. Anybody who owned a claim or two, and some who had no ground at all, could float a company. Barberton had a stock exchange which worked all day and half the night. The shares fluctuated wildly as reefs pinched out and rich patches gave up the ghost. But as the market sagged new finds and rumours of finds would lift it up again.

In the end there were probably five shares sold for every ounce of gold produced, and the vendors shares in hundreds of companies proved to be worth less than the paper they were printed on. But when the boom collapsed and the dust settled there remained mines which really were working gold-bearing reef, and paying good dividends.

The Barberton bubble was a shady chapter in the early history of the South African mining industry in which a great many investors were "taken for a ride". But it served to advertise the fact that the gold was there.

All over the world men said: "First at Pilgrim's Rest . . . then at Barberton. It will turn up again somewhere." They little knew how right they were.

In the meantime David Benjamin got out his surf board and neatly caught the wave of investment. It mattered little that the farms he owned were miles from Barberton. After settling the claims of the diggers with the assistance of Mr. E.J. Jorissen, the State Attorney, he floated the Transvaal Gold Exploration Company in 1885.

Its chairman was Mr. G. Maynard Farmer of Cape Town, but most of its shares were held in London. It sent to Pilgrim's Rest as manager of its properties a young American mining engineer named Gardner Williams.

And in 1886 it was able to announce that it had recovered gold to the value of £1,576.

CHAPTER IX

1886 — MEMORABLE YEAR

The Barberton boom caught the eye of the wealthy men of Kimberley.

The amalgamation of the diamond mines was beginning. As Rhodes and Barnato bought up syndicates and acquired claims, more and more of the smaller men found themselves unemployed, but with money to burn. Off they went to Barberton to join the fun. The reports they sent back whetted Kimberley's appetite. It sounded just the sort of gamble they had enjoyed in the early days of diamond mining.

Alfred Beit and Lionel Phillips both inspected the field and bought an interest in one or two companies. J.B. Robinson looked at it wistfully, but had no money to spare in those days. J.B. Taylor, whom both Rhodes and Beit knew and trusted, set up as a broker on the Barberton exchange. Abe Bailey was here, there and everywhere, buying and selling shares, taking up options on property and making a neat profit on almost everything he touched. Percy FitzPatrick, his transport undertaking having cost him every penny he owned, was in partnership with Messrs Graumann and Hirschel Cohen. They owned a hotel or two, some miscellaneous properties which included a newspaper called the *Barberton Herald*, and shares in various mining ventures.

FitzPatrick wrote for the *Herald* and believed that Barberton had a great future. It was there that he married Lillian Cubitt, whom he had first met at Lydenburg. He was still there when the crash came.

Gardner Williams inspected the Barberton field for Rhodes and damned it with faint praise. He gave it a year or two, he said, and then it would be played out. He had come to the Transvaal to manage the Transvaal Gold and Exploration Company's property at Pilgrim's Rest and he hadn't a very high opinion of that either. The word went round that Gardner Williams had given Barberton the thumbs down signal, and after that investors were more cautious. Rhodes and Beit said "No" to all the propositions that were put to them.

Lionel Phillips was not satisfied simply with an inspection of Barberton. He obtained leave from the French and d'Esterre Diamond Mining Company, of which he was then manager in Kimberley, and explored the Lowveld.

"Prior to leaving Kimberley I had formed a little syndicate in which Rhodes, Beit, Oats (afterwards general manager of de Beers) and one or two other friends and supporters who had confidence in my judgement had taken a share," he says in the course of his reminiscences. But beyond adding: "I took up some claims . . ." he fails to tell us what he bought for this syndicate. It seems probable, however, that some of Eckstein's interests in the Lowveld with which he started Lydenburg Mining Estates were acquired on this trip.

The only other interest that Kimberley had in the Eastern Transvaal gold fields, as far as I can discover, was that in 1878 a syndicate, which was represented by Bob Jameson, Dr. Jameson's brother, had bought Tom McLachlan's properties round Mac Mac and Graskop.

The firm of Jules Porges, Julius Wernher and Alfred Beit dominated the diamond market in those days, and they backed Rhodes in his plan to amalgamate the diamond mines. Alfred Beit, the representative of the firm in Kimberley, was far more than a mere backer. He was Rhodes's full partner in the enterprise, and without the capital he found Rhodes might never have achieved his dream.

The amalgamation of the mines and the formation of de Beers left Rhodes, Wernher and Beit at the top of the financial pyramid, and eventually gave them an income beyond the dreams of avarice. But diamonds were their business, and the formation of de Beers was the greatest coup of their careers. They were utterly absorbed in this transaction in 1886 when W.P. Taylor, J.B. Taylor's brother, sent Beit samples of gold that had been found in outcrops on the Witwatersrand, where the Struben brothers had been hard at work prospecting.

The samples were almost as impressive as some that had been found at Barberton. Beit was attracted by the prospect of being first in the field, but he found Rhodes uninterested. He decided to act on his own.

In the meantime J.B. Robinson had also got wind of the new strike. He needed money, and when you needed money in Kimberley in those days you turned to Alfred Beit. It was to Beit that he came for aid.

Thus was formed, rather hastily, the "Robinson Syndicate" — Beit, Robinson and M. Marcus — and with R50,000 on which to draw and instructions to keep his mouth shut (these were quite unnecessary!)* Robinson, who spoke Dutch and had "connections" In Pretoria, was despatched to the Rand. He was to buy farms and secure options in his own name.

The year was 1886 ... What happened after Robinson met the widow Oosthuizen is a matter of history. The Rand, across which the early prospectors had tramped and tramped again, had been discovered. It was to prove the greatest gold field in the world.

At first they thought it was another Barberton. But gradually, as claims were pegged along the outcrop for 20 miles, the significance of the discovery began to dawn on the men who crowded into the camp. This was no place for the alluvial digger and his pan. It was the sort of mining that called for capital and machinery.

Beit, despite the burden he bore in Kimberley, seems to have found time to study the possibilities and to act. He chose Hermann Eckstein, then managing a diamond mine in Kimberley, to represent him on the Rand with

* See *The Corner House* (Purnell) for a full account of the operations of this syndicate.

J.B. Taylor to assist him. They were to establish the firm of H. Eckstein & Co., which would take over at cost the third share of the Robinson syndicate which Beit owned. They could draw on Jules Porges, Wernher, Beit & Co., for any funds they required for new enterprises.

If ever two young men were given a handsome start in the mining business they were Eckstein and Taylor!

In 1889 Lionel Phillips was offered the position of adviser in mining matters to the new firm. He blithely accepted it and left Kimberley for Johannesburg. In the same year the eminent American mining engineer Hennen Jennings was engaged as consultant.

Just before this happened, however, the Rand, which had boomed to the sky in 1888, experienced its first, and possibly its worst, slump. The shafts ran into ore that defied the existing processes of gold extraction. The story spread that the mines were "done for" and, as FitzPatrick was later to tell Joseph Chamberlain, "grass grew in the streets of Johannesburg". The grass did not have long to grow. The MacArthur-Forrest cyanide process solved the problem of treating pyritic ore and the shares soared to new heights.

FitzPatrick, who had just recovered from his setback at Barberton, went "broke" again. He was saved by his friend, J.B. Taylor, who arranged that he should act as transport manager of an expedition that was to take Lord Randolph Churchill to Mashonaland and also to guide Beit there on a visit to inspection. This led to a job in H. Eckstein & Company, and eventually to directorship.

The opinion that Kimberley held of gold mining ventures in those days is well illustrated by the terms of Phillip's appointment in Johannesburg. He was to supervise and control the company's operations on the Rand, to act as manager of Eckstein's interests in Randfontein Estate and also to handle affairs in the Lowveld — then five to six days' journey from Johannesburg.

It was, of course, an impossible assignment. Phillips, almost from the day he arrived on the Rand, was busy pegging claims for his company and darting up and down the Reef inspecting properties. Those who knew him only in later life would have found it hard to believe that this small, slight frame could contain the energy he displayed in the early days. He has left a vivid description of his inspections of the "rabbit warren" of holes and tunnels which the amateur miners made. He often had to descend a shaft by jamming his back against one wall and his feet against the other wall.

"By sliding one's back down, say, a foot, and then similarly dropping one foot at a time (always maintaining a grip to prevent suddenly falling to the bottom), one got down, weary and torn. These early explorers revelled in making it very inconvenient, and even dangerous, to inspect their workings . . ."

Then, on January 26, 1893, a little over three years after he had been appointed, Hermann Eckstein died suddenly while on a visit to Britain. Phillips was summoned to London and informed that he would be made a

Lionel Phillips and Alfred Beit visit the Lowveld.

partner and become head of the firm in Johannesburg. J.B. Taylor retired, and was succeeded by Georges Rouliot, a Frenchman.

Busy as he was, Phillips always had the Lowveld and its possibilities at the back of his mind. He was a great nature lover, and his visits to the Eastern Transvaal had made a profound impression upon him. He had spent 14 years in Kimberley in the ugliest surroundings imaginable, and for all his "toughness" and eagerness in pursuit of profits there was an aesthetic streak in his nature that made him long for beauty. He was to satisfy it in later life with music, pictures and the lovely surroundings of his house "Vergelegen" at Somerset West. But in these, his early years, there can be no doubt that he fell in love with the beauty of the escarpment of the Drakensberg, as have three successive generations of mining men since that day.

When he was less busy, when the first Corner House mines had all been floated as companies and the profits were flowing in, he was for ever trying to persuade Beit to join him on expeditions to the district. They went there together more than once and thoroughly enjoyed themselves camping out, fossicking around in old claims and adits and even panning samples.

Henry Glynn describes how they came over to his farm at Sabie from Pilgrim's Rest to inspect the work on the reef he had uncovered "and were astonished at the pannings". In due course they were to float Glynn's Lydenburg Estates and produce gold from this farm for the next 70 years.

The charm of a district is scarcely sufficient reason for floating a mining company. Impressed as Beit and Phillips were by the scenic beauty of Pilgrim's Rest, they were probably even more impressed by the achievements of Benjamin's company which, over the eight years of its existence, had shown a steady increase in production. The value of its gold had risen from R3,152 in 1886 to R96,108 in 1891, and was to soar to R139,706 in 1894. These figures seemed to indicate that there were tremendous possibilities in the district if the mines had the resources of a Rand company behind them.

There is no record of when Phillips opened negotiations with Benjamin, of what part Bailey played or when it was decided to form the new company. The minutes of the first meetings of the directors of Lydenburg Estates are regrettably terse. But as I have said, it is as plain as a pikestaff that it was the intention of The Corner House to absorb the older company and to take over the Pilgrim's Rest farms, and this plan could only have been made if Benjamin agreed. Obviously since he had a seat on the board, he did agree.

Thus was born the Transvaal Gold Mining Estates Ltd. (alias Lydenburg Mining Estates). Neither its directors nor its shareholders could guess at the storms that lay ahead, though at least three of them knew of one little trouble that was on its way.

Percy FitzPatrick, as he took his place at the board meeting, may have reflected on the change that had come about in his fortunes. Ten years earlier Teddy Blacklaw, once of Ballarat, had taken pity on him and given him work on a claim in this very district to save him from starvation. And now he was a director of the company that had acquired the ground that was once the diggers' paradise. The secretary of the company, at £30 a month, was none other than his former partner in Barberton, Hirschel Cohen, now down on his luck.

Some of the shareholders in London also indulged in reflections. By simple mental arithmetic they worked out that it was not their company that had been absorbed but they who had in fact absorbed the Johannesburg company. With the 300,000 shares that had been allotted them for their holdings in the Transvaal Gold Exploration and Land Company, and their shares for their rights in the Jubilee Mines and New Clewer Company, they held the majority of the new company's 640,000 shares. And what, they asked, is the value of properties with such weird names as "Blijfstaanhoogte" and "Olifantsgeraamte", whatever that may mean?

They were to worry their directors with questions such as these, and requests that the annual meeting should be held in London, for many years to come. But before the first annual meeting was held, before they could frame their first questions, they received their first shock. Their chairman and two of their directors had been arrested on a charge of high treason. Worse news followed. Their chairman has been sentenced to death by the high court of the Transvaal.

To shareholders in the City of London, who knew nothing about the affairs of the Transvaal in those days, high treason was a very serious offence. They had been told before the amalgamation took place that the great advantage that would follow would be that the men of The Corner House, the men on the spot, would apply their "know-how" to the company's mines. This was a pretty example of how that know-how worked!

This is not the place to tell again the story of how Dr. Leander Starr Jameson took the bit between his teeth and invaded the Transvaal before his fellow conspirators were ready, and of how the whole muddled plot fell to pieces.

How far was the House of Eckstein involved? There can be no doubt that they were in it up to their ears.

Phillips had early come to the conclusion that a collision between the people of Johannesburg and the government of the South African Republic, as represented by President Kruger, was inevitable. He used to visit Pretoria once a fortnight and had many long talks with Kruger. He formed the opinion that the old President would rather die than give way an inch to the demands of the "uitlanders" in Johannesburg.

"Frankly, he hated all the uitlanders and their restless energy. His ideal was a patriarchal state with himself as Patriarch," says Phillips. He was sure that events were leading up to what he called a "civil commotion".

"In 1895 one of my senior partners, Alfred Beit, came out to the Transvaal," adds Phillips in his reminiscences. "On his way he had stayed with Cecil Rhodes at Groote Schuur. Beit, although a German by birth, was a keen imperialist. To my surprise I found that he thoroughly shared my opinion that revolution was coming. He told me that Rhodes held the same view, and thought we should take a hand to ensure success if possible.

"Generally speaking I was invited to co-operate, and after Beit's return to England I went down to the Cape to stay with Rhodes."

It is perfectly clear, therefore, that The Corner House was in the plot. But, though Phillips stoutly defended the Reformers' plan to the end of his life, it must be confessed that it did not bear the hallmark of efficiency for which the house was famous even in those early days.

Phillips and Jameson met in Johannesburg in November, 1895, to discuss the plan, and thoroughly misunderstood one another. Phillips was under the impression that Jameson was to take his orders from the Reformers, while Jameson thought that he was in charge of the whole operation.

Jameson returned to Cape Town to report to Rhodes who, having heard what he had to say, sent the following telegram to Rutherford Harris:

"Dr. Jameson back from Johannesburg everything right my judgment it is certainty we think A. Beit must come with you on November 29 on score of health you will be just in time. A. Beit to stay with me here and to come up with us and Governor. A. Beit must not consult Phillips who is all right but anxious to do everything himself and he does not wish to play second fiddle. Inform A. Beit from me he must come C.J. Rhodes."

Phillips was afterwards to maintain that he had never at any time meant to take the leadership of the revolt, but that it was thrust upon him by the

ABE BAILEY

PERCY FITZPATRICK

events that followed. The mystery that remains unsolved to this day is how anyone could have expected success with such complete lack of liaison between Jameson "in the field" and the Reform Committee in Johannesburg. Up to the very last minute they were even in disagreement about whether the rising was to take place under the flag of the South African Republic or the Union Jack.

The subsequent trial and the death sentence imposed on the four leaders subjected Phillips to very severe mental strain. It is not everyone who has sat in the condemned cell and heard "sawing and knocking going on outside which we were told was due to the erection of a scaffold".

But the period of imprisonment in the Pretoria jail had its comic side. Under pressure from this gathering of important and, in some cases, very wealthy prisoners the jail discipline collapsed. The prison yard became an unofficial stock exchange and place of business.

I have already described how Lionel Phillips and Alfred Beit visited Henry Glynn's farm at Sabie and decided to exploit the reef there. These discussions were well under way and the plan for the company formed when Phillips and FitzPatrick went to jail.

"I went to Johannesburg a few days after the Jameson Raid," says Henry Glynn, "and went to Eckstein & Co. to get a settlement. But the Johannesburg firm could not deal with the matter as Mr. Lionel Phillips and Mr. Percy FitzPatrick were in jail in Pretoria.

"I went over there the day before their trial, and got a permit to see Mr. FitzPatrick. I was admitted, and he and I had a conversation about the matter.

"He said: 'At 6 o'clock tonight you will find a letter in the rack of the

83

Grand Hotel which will explain to my people all that is necessary for a settlement.'

"At 6 p.m. I found the letter in the rack. This letter I took to Johannesburg, and it enabled me to close my business."

Thus was Glynn's Lydenburg established in the shadow of Pretoria jail. It seems to have been a good augury for, on a capital of R350,000, the company was to pay R2,378,732 in dividends over the years to come.

All the companies of which the prisoners were directors had interdicts served on them on the application of the State Attorney of the Republic. These orders restrained them from disposing of the shares held by the Reformers.

The significance of this move was apparent to the lawyers when they looked up the law.

A section of the Gold Law of 1885 read:

"Everyone within the boundaries of a proclaimed field who commits the crime of insurrection, rebellion, or any unlawful resistance against the Government or the lawful authority upon the fields shall, over and above the punishment fixed by law for such a crime, forfeit all his rights and property situate upon the said fields in favour of the State."

At the end of the trial the State Attorney asked that this provision of the law should be applied to the prisoners' property.

However, Mr. Justice Reinhold Gregorowski, the Free State judge who, it was claimed by lawyers afterwards, wrongly interpreted the law of the Transvaal in sentencing the leaders to death, was in their favour on this point.

He refused the application for the confiscation of their property on the grounds that the State's claim should have been included in the indictment presented to the Court.

Lawyers have since declared that he was wrong on this point, too. All the necessary details were in the indictment.

If the judge had upheld this application the South African Republic would have found itself in possession of some very valuable mining shares.

In the end Phillips, Frank Rhodes, Hays Hammond and George Farrar paid a fine of £25,000 each and, with the exception of Rhodes who was banished from the Transvaal, gave an undertaking that they would not directly or indirectly meddle in the internal or external politics of the South African Republic.

They kept their word, though it meant walking a tight rope for the next three years.

CHAPTER X

GREEK ALPHABET PUZZLE

Phillips and FitzPatrick sidestepped a Select Committee of the Cape Parliament which was appointed to inquire into the causes of the Raid. They both felt that they could not give evidence until Jameson had stood his trial in Britain. They were certain that anything said would prejudice his case.

To avoid passing through Cape Town on their way to England, for this would have involved a summons to appear before the Select Committee, they were transferred from the ship that had brought them from Durban to a Castle liner off Cape Point. Their friendship with Donald Currie helped to bring this about. The Castle ship hove to while they crossed a rather choppy stretch of water in a whaler and then climbed a rope ladder to her deck.

They left Johannesburg for Durban just before the first annual meeting of the Transvaal Gold Mining Estates, the company they had founded.

Phillips's letter book had been seized by the Republican police, and on his return to South Africa he was asked to give evidence on certain expenditures which was revealed.

"On the same day a few of the more progressive members of the Raad called on me with the information that the evidence sought had reference to money I had paid to assist in their election," he says. "They begged me to refuse. The object was to find an excuse for expelling them."

He refused on the grounds that the letter book had been seized for the purpose of incriminating him, and had been used for that purpose. He had been tried and punished. He now demanded the return of the book.

He got it back, but his lawyers advised him that he had probably not heard the end of the matter. If the Republican Government was determined to make things uncomfortable for him it was possible that they might arrest him again on one pretext or another. He decided to leave the Transvaal.

In London, after reading an article in the *Nineteenth Century* which he thought misrepresented the facts about the Raid, he wrote a letter to that journal correcting the misstatements. The State Attorney of the South African Republic announced that this was a breach of his undertaking not to meddle in the affairs of the Transvaal, and brought into force the suspended order of banishment imposed on him at the trial.

Phillips was most distressed to think that this implied that he had broken his word of honour. He took the opinion of two eminent Q.C.'s in Britain, both of whom said that his letter to the *Nineteenth Century* could not be regarded as an attempt to meddle in the politics of the Transvaal.

However, as he had agreed that the opinion of the Executive Council of the Republic should decide whether or not he had committed a breach of the agreement, he had no redress in law.

He was banished from the Transvaal for ever — or so he thought at the time. Actually he returned to Johannesburg and The Corner House in 1906.

As may be imagined, the directors and shareholders of the new company met for the first time on July 15, 1896, under a distinct cloud. The London shareholders, and those in Paris and Berlin, were particularly worried. They fairly bombarded the board with letters, all of which were answered with reassuring statements to the effect that recent events in the Transvaal had not in any way affected the company's prospects, and that a London committee was to be appointed for the special purpose of looking after the interests of overseas shareholders, and to give them all necessary information.

Fortunately, in Mr. Georges Rouliot, who had succeeded Lionel Phillips, the company had found an ideal chairman. He was a Frenchman of great charm and quite exceptional ability. One of his gifts was that, despite the number of meetings over which he had to preside, he always had the facts at his finger tips and his manner gave the impression that this company, above all others, was the one in which he was most interested. He had visited Pilgrim's Rest and studied the work done by the Transvaal Gold Exploration and Lands Company. Like everyone else who had visited the district he had fallen under its spell.

The only member of the original board who had survived the Raid was H.W. Glenny. Benjamin was now represented by J.P. Faure, and Abe Bailey by J.H. Ryan. Otto Beit, Alfred's brother, had taken Percy FitzPatrick's place.

The directors had appointed E. Hoefer as manager of their property, and G. Wertheman as consulting engineer. These two were already at work at Pilgrim's Rest.

To most of the shareholders the allotment of shares they were asked to authorise can have meant very little indeed. Gentlemen named Mark Lowinsky, Henry Cohen, F. Watkins, S. Brangham and E.F. Bourke, a member of the Pretoria family, were to receive shares for their claims. And the Ross Hill Syndicate, the Olifantsgeraamte Syndicate, the Jubilee and New Clewer mines were to be taken over. The significant "buys", as far as most of those connected with the company were concerned, were the Pilgrim's Rest concession farms and Hendriksdal, where the first gold in the district had been found.

But the old diggers who knew every one of the properties listed — and there were far more than I have mentioned — were impressed. They said that Phillips and Beit had "picked the eyes out of the district" and that the company would make money. In their mind's eye they could visualise the ground that had become the property of T.G.M.E., and could make some estimate of its possibilities. Their plan of campaign was now to fossick about in the areas near these holdings, find gold and then hope that the company would buy them out — at a price.

Burgher Wolhuter of the Rand Commando, who had vowed not to cut his hair until the war was over, looks like many of the young men of our day.

This photograph, taken in Pilgrim's Rest in 1900, shows President Steyn of the Orange Free State who was then passing through the district on his way back to the Free State after conferring with the Transvaal military leaders. Advocate de Villiers is on his right. General Cronje is the figure on the left of the group wearing a bandolier. General Wessels of the Orange Free State army is standing in front of but below General Cronje.

A pound note printed by the Staatsdrukkery te Velde (the State Printing Works in the Field) in Pilgrim's Rest. These notes were printed on sheets from ledgers and school exercise books.

The old electric tramway which pulled cocopans of ore to the central mill at Pilgrim's Rest. It was installed in 1897 and solved the mines' transport problems. Standing next to his cab is Gert Maritz who drove this tram for some 40 years.

Included in the company's holdings were a number of workings on Ponieskrantz which had been named with the letters of the Greek alphabet. They appeared on the list as the "Alpha Mine", the "Beta Mine", the "Eta Mine", the "Theta Mine", the "Iota Mine", the "Kappa Mine". There were even a "Chi Mine" and a "Nu Mine". Most of them, at that stage of development, were not really mines but open cast workings or adits on a hillside. They certainly gave the property an air of distinction. Nobody knew then, or knows to this day, who sprinkled the Greek alphabet about this corner of the Eastern Transvaal. It may have been Gardner Williams or Benjamin himself. But this touch of classical scholarship bore fruit, for two of those mines, Beta and Theta, have become famous in South African mining history for what they have achieved since those days. The Beta Mine was still producing gold in 1971, 85 years after it was discovered.

The whole venture was a gamble, but how great a gamble neither the directors nor the shareholders knew. Gold had been found on or near the surface in so many places in the district that the expert opinion of the day was that the reefs must be there in much the same formations as on the Rand. They pictured vertical shafts that would find something like the South Reef and the Main Reef Leader, and provide consistent values and steady returns.

All they had to do, they thought, was to find the reef and follow it down, as they were doing in Johannesburg. Had they known what lay ahead, and added to the sum total of their difficulties the cost of hauling every nut, bolt and sheet of iron they wanted by wagon from Machadodorp, they might have hesitated.

The prospects of the company, as seen by the directors, were admirably summed up by Georges Rouliot at one of the very early meetings in Johannesburg.

"If you bear in mind that your property covers about 300 square miles, and that the line of contact where the reef is to be found is traced over the property for upwards of 20 miles, you will come to the conclusion that there are vast possibilities," he said.

"Only, as I have pointed out before, there is nothing to guide us as to the localities where a new mine may be opened. It is only by vigorous prospecting that we can do so. And if we remember what has already taken place in some of the mines now being worked, the same thing may repeat iself, and we may at any moment strike new and extensive patches of reef."

That statement was often quoted by his successors. It was true in 1895, and it remained true for the next 60 years.

Once the Witwatersrand mines settled down to the steady pattern of production that has made them the world's biggest and most reliable source of gold, shareholders became accustomed to consistent output and profits year after year. The T.G.M.E. shareholders in Britain could never understand why "their" mines did not follow the same pattern, and loud were their grumbles when reefs "pinched out" and profits fell off.

In vain did the directors explain that the mines in the Eastern Transvaal were like all the gold mines of history that had preceded the discovery of the exceptionally consistent reefs of the Witwatersrand. The Robinson mine and Crown Reef had set an example which the shareholder, studying the returns from the depth of his easy chair, expected all mines to follow.

He was happy enough when the profits of the T.G.M.E. soared to £300,000 in later years and the dividend was 27 per cent, but he never understood why the production graph zig-zagged as wildly as it did.

The managers of the T.G.M.E. mines always had to watch this graph and to keep it as steady as possible. There were years when they were drawing ore from as many as 12 separate mines, carefully balancing development against crushings from rich "patches".

The whole area presented a series of never-ending problems for the mining engineer. But there is something to be said for mining in a district where a prospecting party may pan a sample and find a tail of gold that extends half-way round the base of the pan, or produce a nugget of solid gold. And that happened over and over again in the Pilgrim's Rest workings. One of the oldest documents in the mine office shows that they had their problems. This is a drawing of Brown's Hill on the banks of the Blyde River with a manuscript note, dated 1885, appended, which says:

"Mr. O'Donoghue says if the hydraulicing is commenced at the point marked X in red, and if the operations go on in the bed rock, the alluvial as well as the fine gold in the body of the hill will be got. The operation should be followed up the gulley marked in red B., C., D., keeping to the bed rock. When the point marked is reached two courses to be considered: Whether to keep on round back of hill or proceed along course marked in red E., F., G . . ."

Many a mine manager since those days has sympathised with Mr. O'Donoghue of 1885!

I found an amusing passage in a manager's report for the year 1899. Commenting on the work done on the Theta Mine he said: "I regret to report that the good rich reef you saw in the top drive off the opencast has pinched out . . . I may remark that mining proper at the Theta Mine is practically finished. The operations which are being carried on at present are more of a prospecting nature than mining."

How could he know, poor man, that he was writing of a mine that was to prove one of the richest small properties in the Transvaal, with patches of ore that almost equalled the discoveries in Brays's Golden Quarry at Barberton?

The valley is an area of heavy rainfall — as much as 80 inches a year. When there are storms the mountain sides become torrents, pouring water into the valleys below. Over millions of years the action of these streams of water, of high winds and hot weather ate into the overburden and eroded it. The erosion bit down to gold-bearing rock, decomposed it, exposed the gold and left it to be swept down into the streams by torrential rains, leaving nuggets of almost pure gold near the surface. And there the gold lay for hundreds of thousands of years, until at last the prospectors found it.

Only when the alluvial gold had all been collected from the valleys did men turn their attention to the reefs. At first it looked simple. You prospected, sampled, and, where the values were high, drove an adit into the hillside following the reef. But within a few years they found that they had run into a geological jigsaw puzzle of the first order. The so-called reef would suddenly swell out into a pocket of gold and then vanish altogether. If you drove 10 or 20 yards further into the hillside you might pick it up again, or you might simply waste your time. There were spots where all gold-bearing ground seemed to have been scooped out as the pith is scooped from a granadilla. Beyond such barren patches might lie more gold — or might not.In theory, if you surveyed across a valley from the known position of the reef on one mountain you ought to have been able to pick it up again on the other side. But in practice it was found that it might not be there at all, or might be 200 feet above or below the spot where it ought to have been.

The reefs in the Pilgrim's Rest area are known technically as "flat" reefs which means that, were it not for faults, dykes, areas where rivers have carved out the strata and other geological disturbances, they would be interbedded in the normal rock formation. But the tremendous pressures and upheavals to which they were subjected in the days when the Earth's crust was cooling caused them to twist like wounded snakes, and in some cases blew them clean out of their bed rock. The geological formation of the areas has a dip to the West of from five to seven degrees. It consists of the Pretoria, Dolomite and Black Reef series of the Transvaal system, resting on older granite. From the lower shales of the Pretoria series down to the older granite about 20 separate interbedded reefs exist, of which eight have provided most of the gold. The gold-bearing leaders which were once such a feature of the district are found at the base of the Pretoria series and in the dolomites and sandstones.

It was probably the use of the word "reef" that misled the London shareholders. To them a reef was a ribbon of gold stretching on and on for ever, which had simply to be brought to the surface and treated to produce dividends that went on and on for ever, too. Such was the influence of the consistent Rand mines, though they were barely 10 years old in those days.

If the truth were told, gold mining in the early days at Pilgrim's Rest was no more than an extension of the game of blind man's buff which the early diggers played, but on a larger and much more profitable scale.

Mr. Wertheman, the company's first consulting engineer, was undoubtedly a man of genius. He seems also to have had second sight. He studied the positions of the various workings from which ore was being recovered, and decided at once that there must be a central mill that would serve all the existing mines and those that were to come. There were a number of small and dilapidated mills all over the property. He scrapped all but two, the old mill on the Transvaal Gold Exploration Company's property and a 20-stamp mill at Kameel's Creek, in a picturesque setting among the hills to the West, which was crushing ore from Theta, Chi, Duke's Hill and other mines.

He advised the company to erect an up-to-date 60-stamp battery in a central position where the ore from the producing mines, Jubilee, Clewer, Beta and Theta could be treated in one process. To get it to the mill he decided to build seven miles of electric tramway (gauge 30 inches), with branch lines to each of the mines.

His main problem, of course, was power. There was no coal in the district, and no possibility of running steam engines. But Benjamin's company had established a small hydro-electric plant at the foot of Brown's Hill, on the banks of the Blyde River. When the river was running well, this power station gave enough power to run a small mill. In winter, when the river shrank, it often went out to action altogether.

Wertheman solved his problem by enlarging the power station and then building a water race which ran from a point higher up on the river to Brown's Hill. This race was two-and-a-half miles long, and its dimensions were six feet by four feet deep. What is more, it was lined throughout its length by iron plates rivetted together so that the bottom and the sides of the furrow were virtually waterproof. This could deliver 2,400 cubic feet of water a minute and, with a fall of 114 feet, generated 369 horse power. It was a very neat engineering job, and was built to last. The remains of the furrow and the plates that lined it are there to this day.

The miniature electric tramway was also a stroke of genius, for it ran in almost all weathers and permitted extensions of the line to new workings as they were developed. The cocopans ran up and down the hillsides to the various adits, and delivered the ore to the tram termini. Electric locomotives then hauled "trains" of trucks to the mill. And the Blyde River did all the work required to produce the power. One of these trains even took the children to school in the morning.

Thus Pilgrim's Rest had its electric tramway, admittedly a miniature one, not long after Johannesburg "electrified" its horse-trams. The tramway was a never-ceasing source of wonder to the Africans on the mine, who could not understand how anything could move unless it was pulled by horses or oxen.

Wertheman estimated that the existing system by which contractors hauled the ore to the mills in ox-carts was costing 7s. 6d. a ton, while his electric tramway would reduce this to 1s. a ton (in practice it worked out at 1s. 8d. a ton). He also estimated that he could have the whole installation in position, and the mill in running order, within 12 months of being told to go ahead. But in this plan he was defeated by the rinderpest epidemic of 1896 - 97.

The disease killed at least 60 per cent of all the cattle in the Transvaal. To Pilgrim's Rest, utterly dependent on ox wagons for the necessities of life, it was a disaster. Transport costs, already high, soared, and the cost of living

Getting the ore to the mill.

rose proportionately. The mines came to a standstill. Mr. Wertheman, waiting for equipment that never arrived, tore his hair.

Gradually all the difficulties were ironed out. The mill went up, the rails
were laid and the Eastern Transvaal saw its first electric tramway, the trucks
shuttling backwards and forwards over those seven miles of line. Old Hendrik
Potgieter must certainly have turned in his grave. In later years the memorials
to Wertheman's enterprise and skill were a few graceful, Victorian tram
standards, their arms still extended to hold a non-existent power cable over a
forgotten track. The greater part of the electric tramway was scrapped after
30 years of faithful service but the line served the Beta mine almost to the
end.

The cost of the new 60-stamp mill, of the electric tramway, of the water
race, of widening mine drives so that mules and cars could be used, of new
buildings and many other improvements was £117,000. By modern standards
this was a miracle of economy, particularly when one remembered the long
haul over the mountains from Machadodorp. But it was far and away the
largest sum that had ever been spent on mining in the Pilgrim's Rest district.

There was additional and very necessary expenditure for a plant to treat
slimes. At that time Hoefer, the general manager, said that ore from Theta
and Beta assayed 23 to 24 dwts. a ton, but the average extraction was only
13 to 14 dwts. a ton. Sampling showed that the slimes assayed 10 dwts. to
the ton!

In response to pressure from London shareholders, the first general meeting
of the company increased the number of directors to nine, to admit three
nominees of the former Transvaal Gold Exploration and Lands Company.

They were Messrs. Nicol Browne, W.A. Farmer and T.A. Sommers Scott. They formed a London committee which had power to convene an annual meeting of what were called "the European shareholders", and it was agreed that recommendations forwarded from this meeting would be considered at general meetings in Johannesburg.

It was, of course, a thoroughly ineffective arrangement, which served only to cause misunderstandings and a certain amount of friction. The "European shareholders" felt that their interests were being neglected because the general meetings were held in far-off Johannesburg. The firm of Eckstein & Co., which ran the company as they ran all their other companies, simply could not understand these complaints. They were not used to dissatisfied shareholders.

Percy FitzPatrick took the chair at the third annual meeting in 1898, and made some rather caustic remarks about the delays caused by the London meetings, which had to be held before the general meeting could take place. He questioned whether these London meetings served any useful purpose.

There was at that time considerable criticism of T.G.M.E.'s production costs. It came from shareholders who had never seen the road that led down the mountains to Pilgrim's Rest.

FitzPatrick met these criticisms wtih a detailed statement.

"The development of flat reef is much more expensive than that of a vertical reef or one where there is a good incline," he said.

"The timbering and maintenance of a mine in soft country is also considerable. Then we have seven miles of tramway on several systems and steep gradients for which reason our tramming costs figure at 1s. 8d. a ton against about 3d. a ton, the highest cost on the Rand.

"Our shipping charges for gold, cased bullion, etc. amount to 1s. 3d. a ton. Our royalty to the Government is 1s. 1d. a ton. The character of our ore necessitates the consumption of three or four times as much cyanide as is required on the Rand, and this adds 1s. 6d. a ton milled to the costs over and above what they would be here (Johannesburg).

"Then we contribute to the support of the Dynamite Monopoly to the tune of £6 a case of No. 1 dynamite instead of 75s. as it is on the Rand, 50s. in Swaziland and 35s. in Bulawayo."

But, after this recital of woe, he had a pleasant surprise for the shareholders which he saved for the end of his speech.

"At the London meeting of shareholders a recommendation was made to the board that a dividend should be paid," he continues.

"The suggestion was made shortly after the chairman had explained that we were sometimes embarrased by the reefs being too rich *(he was talking of the London Committee).* I am bound to say we have received no complaint from the manager on the score of over-richness of the reef. Managers are not so hard to please as all that! Nevertheless, we are in a position to meet the wishes of the London shareholders . . ."

92

And he then announced a dividend of 10 per cent.

The outlook for the company at this date seemed bright. The average monthly gold output was moving up towards the R40,000 mark. There had been important discoveries at Elandsdrift, south of Sabie, which were being developed, and there were still vast areas to be explored.

On August 11, 1899, another dividend of 10 per cent was declared. It was obvious that there were bigger profits in the offing.

Then, on October 10, 1899, the South African Republic sent its ultimatum to the British Government, and two days later the Boer forces crossed the Natal border. It was war!

CHAPTER XI

THE BOERS TAKE OVER

Pilgrim's Rest and the surrounding district were in the hands of the Boer forces throughout the South African War, save for a short period when General Sir Redvers Buller appeared on the scene in fruitless pursuit of his old enemy, Louis Botha.

All the mines shut down and, with the exception of two men who stayed on as caretakers and a couple of miners who were kept for maintenance, the white employees of T.G.M.E. were ordered over the border. They were forced to leave behind them a certain amount of gold and lead bullion, but they managed to put the power station out of action before they left.

One or two of the older diggers, to whom the search for gold was far more important than any war, went on working their claims in far-off places. But most of them made a bolt for Lourenco Marques. A few, who were burgers, waved good-bye to their friends and joined their commandos to fight for the Republic. Not since 1871 had the district been so thinly populated.

At the beginning of the war Pilgrim's Rest was a good 500 miles from the firing line. But when Pretoria fell to Roberts in 1900 the struggle was carried into the heart of the Transvaal. Kitchener eventually established his head-quarters at Middelburg, only 150 miles to the south. He pushed his forces along the railway line and eventually captured Komatipoort. The redoubtable Colonel Steinacker's irregulars then patrolled the Lowveld.

However, to the British, the rugged country beyond Lydenburg was of no strategic importance, and they made no further attempts to raid it. As a result, the whole area became a rallying point and a resting place for the commandos who would retreat there after a skirmish on the Highveld.

President Kruger and his Government-in-exile shuttled about the north-eastern Transvaal, with the Presidential train at Machadodorp as a main base, until such time as it was decided that the President should leave for Europe via Lourenco Marques.

To the period of guerilla warfare that followed belongs the story of the *Staatsmunt te Velde* (the State Mint in the Field) and the *Staatsdrukkery te Velde* (the State Printing Press in the Field), both of which were set up at Pilgrim's Rest.

The Boers' need of cash at that stage of the war was desperate. The commandos were living largely on such supplies as they could buy from the Bantu, and they were finding it difficult to persuade them to take the notes which were the only form of payment they could offer. On the other hand, the mere sight of a gold coin produced the mealies and the meat. They still had, at that date, some of the bar gold that had been removed from the Pretoria Mint and the banks by General Smuts in June, 1900, just before Lord Roberts marched in. General Ben Viljoen, who commanded the district, had also sent his men round all the reduction works on the mines in the Pilgrim's Rest area, and they had scraped the plates and carried off the amalgam.

But the gold reserve thus acquired was virtually useless for the purpose of buying supplies. It was coins they needed. So it was decided to set up a small mint and experiment with the gold.

Pilgrim's Rest was the obvious place for the experiment. There was no danger of a surprise attack by the British, since the valley was a natural fortress. And the T.G.M.E. mine workshop had a useful range of tools and equipment. A wagon carried the gold there from Machadodorp and it was stored in the mine office.

The proceedings opened with the utmost formality. A Mint Commission was set up which sent a message to the Government in the field asking for permission to mint sovereigns. This was received in due course and the State Mint in the Field was declared officially established. Mr. P.J. Kloppers, formerly headmaster of a school at Barberton, was appointed Head of the Mint.

Mr. Kloppers lived to become an Inspector of Schools in the Transvaal and died only in 1960, so that the story of his achievements is well documented. He will live in history as the man who made the South African Republic's "veld-ponde", now among the world's rarest and most valuable gold coins. The officials of mints throughout the world, having studied the means by which he produced these coins, have never ceased to raise their hats to him.

His first plan was to refine the gold, roll it, and then cut it up into squares which would be more valuable than sovereigns and might, he thought, be used to persuade the burgers to hand over their gold coins.

The Mint Commission turned this idea down. If he was to mint coins they must look like coins, they said.

Mr. Kloppers then examined his resources. He found in the mine workshop a hand punching machine used for striking rivet holes in sheet metal. It worked on the screw and press principle, and could be used, once he had made a punch, to cut the "blanks" (which would be slightly less than the diameter of a sovereign) from which the coins would finally be struck.

But finding the punch was only half the battle. He had to melt his gold, anneal it and roll it out in sheets of the required thickness. He had great difficulty in doing this until he found that a drop or two of sublimate of mercury, taken from the mine's first aid chest, worked wonders in making the gold more malleable. Then he had to make steel dies for engraving the "blanks". This meant turning steel bars on a lathe until they were the required shape, then softening them sufficiently to enable him to engrave "Z.A.R. 1902" on one side and "Een Pond" on the other. The steel had then to be hardened again, so that the engraved dies would stand the pressure to be put on them.

All these processes the miracle worker carried out, even to making the

95

chisels with which the dies were engraved. Then, just as it looked as though he were ready to begin, he struck another snag.

Under pressure from the upper die a gold "blank" tended to expand to a greater width than that of a normal pound, and also developed a ridge round the circle where the die bit home. There was nothing for it but to sit down and make a collar that would fit round the lower die and contain the "blank". And to allow for the expansion of the gold under pressure it had to have a grooved edge. He cut out the grooves with a file, and thus gave them something like the conventional milled edge.

This is an abbreviated description of an exceptionally clever bit of metal working by amateurs who had to do everything by hand. They minted their first pounds, one at a time, by applying the strength of their arms to the hand press. They weighed and measured each coin as it was taken out of the machine. In the mornings the Mint Commission weighed the gold, and handed it over to the Mint Master. At the end of the day they weighed the coins received and the scrap handed back to them.

Professor E.H.D. Arndt, of the University of Pretoria, who has written a detailed account of the minting of these coins, says that, so conscientiously did everyone concerned shoulder his responsibilities, during the whole period of the existence of the Field Mint that not two ounces of gold were lost.

They produced in all 986 veldponde. As they had some gold left on May 31, 1902, when the Peace of Vereeniging was signed, they continued minting until June 7, 1902. There was then a residue of gold worth precisely 5s., which was entered in the books as "in the possession of Mr. P.J. Kloppers". Mr. Kloppers kept that tiny piece of gold for the rest of his life, and many a Transvaal schoolboy saw this last relic of the "Staats Munt te Velde".

The Republic rewarded him with a medal which was a veldpond disc with "Z.A.R. 1902" on one side and his name and title "Muntmeester, Staats Munt te Velde" inscribed on the other.

The Pilgrim's Rest Mint gave good value for money. Its pounds, slightly thicker than the Kruger sovereign, contained gold of an average value of 22s. Today those sovereigns are worth R200 apiece, and are treasured by collectors throughout the world. At least half of them were made of Pilgrim's Rest gold, and they represented the Transvaal Gold Mining Estates Company's involuntary contribution to the Boer campaign funds. After the war was over the company claimed the value of the gold commandeered by General Ben Viljoen, but the claim was never met. The company's estimate of the total value of gold and stores commandeered was £113,396. 10s. 10d., of which the gold lost accounted for £96,444. 6s. 5d.

Not all the gold in the district fell into Boer hands, however. A laconic note from one of the investigators after the war informed the company that: "It is common rumour in Lydenburg that –, when he left Lydenburg for Delagoa Bay on clearing out, took the last clean-up from the Nooitgedacht Mine with him."

Nooitgedacht was worked at that time by a private company which paid a percentage of its profits to T.G.M.E.

The State Printing Press in the Field used the printing plant in Pilgrim's Rest — presumably the press that had once printed Phelan's *Gold Fields Mercury*. Its job was just as urgent as the Mint's. A landdrost in the district had surrendered to the British with the entire available stock of unsigned republican notes. A fresh supply was needed, and needed at once.

The ingenious Mr. Kloppers produced a copper plate of the Republican coat-of-arms, and also some of the type required (what a forger the man would have made had he not chosen to be a schoolmaster!), and he also manufactured a special Kloppers brand of ink. There was no suitable paper available, so they used pages cut from T.G.M.E. ledgers and a stock of school exercise books that were at hand.

With these raw materials they printed notes in denominations of £10, £5 and £1. Many of these crude notes have stood the test of time and are valued by collectors. For years after the war they kept turning up in Pretoria, and great was the sorrow and indignation of the people who presented them when they learnt that their hoarded wealth was valueless.

There was another form of currency in circulation at this time. This was a smooth, blank disc of gold, the shape and weight of a pound, but without Kruger's head or any form of incription. Some of these coins are still to be seen in collections and museums. They are known as the "kaal pond" (literally the "naked pound"), and are very valuable, so much so that in recent years forgeries have been produced. The collectors can tell the difference between a genuine "kaal pond" and a forgery. But even a forgery is worth £15 today, which gives you some idea of the value of the "Kaal pond" in genuine form.

It has often been stated that these blank gold coins were produced by the Mint at Pilgrim's Rest. But Professor Arndt's careful investigation has shown that this is not the case. Every coin issued there bore the officially approved engraving. The "blanks" were among the consignment of coins removed from the Pretoria Mint in 1900 before the British occupation. No one is quite certain how they got into circulation, but they were certainly not issued from Pilgrim's Rest.

The larger of the two presses that were used to mint the "veld ponde" continued to work in the T.G.M.E. blacksmiths' shop until 1959. The company finally presented it to the Mint where it stands as a memorial to the ingenious Mr. Kloppers.

One of the two caretakers of the mine property during the war was a man named Alex Marshall, who was an excellent photographer. He persuaded the staff of the Pilgrim's Rest Mint to sit for him. The result was a most interesting group photograph showing members of the Mint Commission and Mr. Kloppers the Mint Master, sitting out in the open air holding some of the machinery they used and examples of the "veld ponde" — and looking very

Digging for the Kruger Millions in the Sabi Game Reserve.

pleased with themselves, as they had a right to be.

Marshall also photographed the staff of the "Staatsdrukkery", many of the commandos stationed in the district and President Steyn and his staff during a visit they paid to Pilgrim's Rest. He managed to have blocks made of these photographs and printed a booklet entitled *Photos of the Boer Commandos at Pilgrim's Rest during the War,* which is one of the best of all souvenirs of the war. I do not know how many copies of this booklet have survived, but if you ever come across one buy it and guard it with your life, for it is a valuable item of Africana.

The presence of the bullion at the republican headquarters and the minting of gold coins at Pilgrim's Rest set up a chain reaction that has lasted to our day. This is the legend of the "Kruger Millions".

The most persistent of all the stories about this horde of gold is that it lies buried somewhere in the Lowveld. Colonel James Stevenson-Hamilton, who was first appointed warden of the Sabi Game Reserve in 1902, became an authority on this particular version of the legend. Once or twice a year an expedition would reach the boundaries of the reserve and produce a police permit to dig in the area. Then Colonel Stevenson-Hamilton and his rangers would be sworn to the deepest secrecy and the party, consulting a hand-drawn map, would move into the reserve and dig and dig for days on end. None of them ever found a sixpence, but they had much fresh air and exercise.

The warden came to the conclusion that there was at least one wily gentleman in Pretoria who made a living by supplying "secret" information as to where the gold was buried.

On the eve of the war The Corner House companies all moved to Cape Town, taking with them their minute books and ledgers. This meant that there was virtually no communication between the caretakers on the T.G.M.E. property and their head office, 1,200 miles away. Occasionally, however, a letter was smuggled out of Pilgrim's Rest and eventually reached the company's secretary in Cape Town.

One such letter has been preserved, and it is well worth quoting. It is dated April 8, 1901, and says:

"We are forwarding you inventory of stock. This was taken on 20th December, since when we have had no reliable means of sending it to you. We do not feel justified in trusting to natives as any failure would mean our being put over the border which, we think, the company do not desire. If you wish to communicate with us before there is a legitimate means kindly do not mention the fact of having received any letters from us as they may be received by others.

"Since taking this inventory we have lost about 300 cases of candles and about 60 tins of soda, besides some other smaller items that will not materially affect the inventory.

"If the company remain in the same position as at Present there will not be anything left on the property that will be of benefit to the Boers . . ."

They then describe how clothing, boots and blankets are being commandeered, and continue:

". . . All dwelling houses and other buildings that are fit to be inhabited are occupied by refugees from all parts of the Transvaal. We think it our duty to inform you that the property is threatened with destruction by sundry parties. We have direct information against three district officials that they have been and are still thinking about this matter. We hardly think they will go so far as they must know that there will be a hereafter and the fact of their destroying the property will not propitiate matters.

"You may rest assured we will do everything in our power to prevent such a catastrophe. About an hour ago the Boksburg commando arrived with instructions to place certain undesirables across the border, also to confiscate any property of same to the Government.

"We do not know how far this will affect us but there is little left with us without they take the clothes off our backs and the little food we have left.

"All these little worries added to the lack of everything but the absolute necessities of life and the lack of knowledge of the outside world make life almost unbearable. You certainly can understand the continual hourly annoyance we are subject to and we must smile while they whip us round the post.

"Things are very critical with us and we do not want anything to happen that will in any way jeopardize our position.

"Above all things you can do is to stop our friends on the other side (your side) from writing letters to us. Signed: Adams and Marshall."

They reported inter alia that A. Poulson, a miner in charge of maintenance, had fallen from a chute and broken his neck.

This letter seems to have been written in a moment of deep gloom. In fact none of the disasters of forecast came to pass, and the company's property was let off very lightly. The Boers were desperately short of supplies and they commandeered food, clothing and blankets, as they were fully entitled to do, but they treated the mine employees well and left all the machinery intact. In due course Alex Marshall, one of the signatories of this letter, was to become the mines' semi-official photographer.

The first official of the company to inspect the property after the signing of the peace treaty was Hugh Hughes, who had been appointed General Manager in succession to E. Hoefer, who had died.

His report, written at Pilgrim's Rest on July 14, 1902, said:

"I spent two days on the property but had to return to Lydenburg through lack of food. I think I should be able to get 40 stamps going within four months.

"The machinery in the workshop is in splendid order. The Boers used our punching machines for the minting of a few hundred 1902 sovereigns . . .

"I resurrected the safe containing all our documents. They are in exactly the same state as when buried. The three large safes inside the strong room were not touched in any way. The cash balance of £137 0s. 10d. was intact."

What was astonishing was the fact that the lead bullion, containing gold to the value of R34,000, lay there throughout the two-and-a-half years of the war and the Boers ignored it. Nor did they take all the gold that was available.

When the reduction works started up again in September, 1902, there was enough gold in the plant and still adhering to the plates to produce a bar of gold weighing 349.295 ounces.

When the Boers withdrew from the Witwatersrand in May, 1900, there was a plan among some of the commandos to destroy the gold mines, letting the shafts flood. In an order issued on May 23, the Commandant-General, Louis Botha, forbade this course of action. He ordered Dr. F.E.T. Krause, special commandant of the Witwatersrand, to protect the mines until such time as he handed the town over to the British. His order seems to have taken effect throughout the Transvaal, for even mines in such remote district as Pilgrim's Rest were left undamaged.

At the first annual general meeting of Transvaal Gold Mining Estates after the war, held in Johannesburg in 1902, the chairman paid a tribute to the republican forces for their restraint.

"The action of the Boer authorities in the Lydenburg district in connection with the mines under their control has been highly creditable to them." he said. "Of course they commandeered all stores and material of which they could make any use, but they avoided wanton destruction.

"It must be remembered in this connection that our property, which is scattered over a great area, was under the control of the Boers throughout the whole period of the war excepting for a few days when General Buller's forces passed through Pilgrim's Rest.

"Our manager, on his return, found all the Company's safes, books, documents and plans as he had left them in the strong room. He found unlocked in our store room the lead bullion for September and part of October, 1899 and above all he found practically intact the whole of the buildings, plant and machinery, valued at £200,000."

Much the same thing happened at Glynn's Lydenburg, the mine on Henry Glynn's farm 20 miles south of Pilgrim's Rest. This had been floated as a separate company late in 1895 with Phillips, Bailey, Benjamin, FitzPatrick and Henry Glynn on the board, and began paying dividends in 1897. In March, 1899, it declared a dividend of 15 per cent, and with working costs at less than 30s. a ton it obviously had a bright future.

The war closed it down. From October 1899 to September, 1902 it stood idle. A German storekeeper named Schmidt was left as caretaker, but he was expelled and sent over the border in December, 1901.

The Boers "worked" the mine for a few days, which really means that they crushed such ore as was available and took the amalgam from the plates. This minor operation gave them gold to the value of £4,828.

For some unexplained reason the republican government sent M. Preumant, a French mining engineer, to inspect this property in the early days of the war, (it may have been their intention to get the mine in working order and use the gold). M. Preumant was greatly impressed by the high values he obtained in sampling, and put in a most favourable report.

Mr. Leggett Neale, the manager, found the property much as it had been left in 1899. Nevertheless R38,000 had to be written off the value of building and plant because there had been no care and maintenance.

Theoretically the mines of the Eastern Transvaal had come through the war virtually unscathed. They ought to have been able to get production going very rapidly, but it turned out to be a very long and difficult process.

Native labour had vanished from the district and had to be coaxed back to work. There was a shortage of transport throughout the Transvaal, and the company was obliged to pay 15s. to £1 a hundredweight for the supplies it brought from the railhead at Machadodorp to the mine.

These were difficulties which the impatient shareholders abroad could not be expected to appreciate. They had gone without dividends for three years, and they soon began to clamour for a return on their investment.

They had to wait for it until 1906.

CHAPTER XII

DIFFICULT YEARS

Hugh Hughes, general manager of the Transvaal Gold Mining Estates company's properties at Pilgrim's Rest, used more strong language in 1903 than he'd had to use in the whole course of his mining career to that date.

He was being pressed to "get things going", and had to admit that he was making very slow progress.

He reported despairingly that, of the 1,500 Bantu mine workers he needed to resume full production, he had found only 336. Hundreds of tons of stores were piling up at Machadodorp, and the transport men were charging him a king's ransom to haul machinery and spares to Pilgrim's Rest. Timber, which he urgently needed to get the mine drives in working order, was costing him almost as much as good mahogany.

The transport riders were the aristocrats of the Transvaal in those days — those of them who had managed to keep their oxen alive in the wave of pestilence that swept the countryside after the war. Their services were needed wherever there was reconstruction under way, and they coined money. Why, they asked, should they risk their wagons and their oxen in the "slide" down Pilgrim's Hill, with wheels locked and brake blocks smoking, when there was work for them wherever they wanted it! They put Pilgrim's Rest at the bottom of the roster, and the mines had to wait for the stores they so desperately needed.

"For these ever-recurring transport difficulties there is only one effective remedy and that is a railway," said Mr. Samuel Evans, chairman of the company, at the annual meeting in Johannesburg in 1902. "As long as the Lydenburg gold fields have to depend for their supplies on the ox wagon it will be impossible to inaugurate a vigorous policy of development."

There were at that time, three tentative plans for railway lines to the district, each of which had its supporters.

The first was for a line from Belfast to Lydenburg, and eventually, in a round-about way, to Pilgrim's Rest, a distance of 118 miles. The new management of the railways was prepared to listen sympathetically to anyone who talked of a line between Belfast and Lydenburg, but when it came to the continuation over the mountains to Pilgrim's Rest they simply raised their eyebrows.

The second proposal was that the long-abandoned Selati Railway Company's line, which had come to an abrupt end on the banks of the Sabie River, 47 miles from Komatipoort, should be continued to Pilgrim's Rest. This meant laying about 40 miles of track, but would have involved climbing the Berg, and was considered an impossible engineering project.

The third, and most feasible, proposal was a branch line from Alkmaar or

The Lydenburg coach about to draw up in the main street of Pilgrim's Rest outside the post office, as it was some 60 years ago.

Transporting the ore from an adit on the mountain side. A photograph that illustrates some of the difficulties of gold mining at Pilgrim's Rest.

This is a picnic party at Pilgrim's Rest in the days when everybody rode. Note that the women are all riding side-saddle.

An old photograph shows one of the first motor cars in the district being towed up Pilgrim's Hill.

Wagons crash and oxen die on Pilgrim's Hill.

Nelspruit, on the main line, to Graskop, a distance of about 48 miles (though it involved laying 77 miles of track). This was the plan the company favoured and for which it pressed. But many years were to elapse before the line was built, and in the meantime the heavily laden wagons crawled across the mountains just as they had done in the good old days when there was no urgency about their mission. In the rainy season the roads often became impassable, and the delays ran into weeks.

For passengers there was the Zeederberg coach service, which changed mule teams every 15 miles and made remarkably good time between Pilgrim's Rest, Lydenburg and Machadodorp. But that was of no use to the general manager of the mines, who needed hundreds of tons of supplies.

"Transport is our problem . . . we are still waiting for stores," he said in every report he wrote. "Nothing can be done until this or that arrive . . ."

As we have seen, there had been no sabotage on the mines at Pilgrim's Rest, and comparatively little deterioration in the company's property during the war. Nevertheless, those two years, when all work came to a standstill, had cost the shareholders a fortune. In 1899 the mines had produced gold valued at R584,216. Now there was virtually no production to set against the heavy costs that were being incurred. It was not until 1904 that operations began to show a profit again, and even then it was so small as to offer no prospect of a dividend.

Though the difficulties of getting the mines going again were carefully explained to the London shareholders, some of them were not satisfied.

On the Rand the mines were in full production within a few months of the British occupation of Johannesburg. It seemed extraordinary to the shareholders 6,000 miles away that the Pilgrim's Rest mines (which, after all, were also in the Transvaal and now also under British rule) could not follow their example. Five years had elapsed since the payment of their last dividend, and there was no sign of any further return. There must be something wrong with the management of the company.

The only effective answer to these complaints would have been to invite a committee of shareholders to visit the Transvaal, then to have taken them to Lydenburg and on by wagon. At the top of Pilgrim's Hill their guide would have had to halt and point to the valley below and to the track leading down the mountain side, littered with the remains of shattered wagons and the bones of oxen that had died while the yokes were still on their necks.

"This," he would have said, "is the road by which all supplies reach our mines." It would have been a particularly impressive picture in summer, with the rain pelting down and the torrents pouring across the slippery track.

In the absence of any such demonstration, and in their ignorance of the conditions under which mining was carried out, these overseas shareholders, conscious of the fact that they held the majority of the shares, began to nag the Johannesburg directors. They formed a special committee whose sole duty was to ask what they regarded as "awkward" questions. They criticised the management, they asked that the directors should meet in London and, above all, they pressed for the payment of a dividend, though the accounts clearly showed that the cash in hand would not cover such a payment. It was a small internecine war which gave the directors a headache. Year after year they carefully explained the working of their mines, but few of the dissidents took the least notice of what they said.

At the annual meeting of the company in 1905, Mr. Samuel Evans commented somewhat acidly on the proceedings at the London meeting held two months earlier.

"At the meeting in London one gentleman who expatiated on the shortcomings of the Johannesburg directors contrasted our poor achievements with the splended accomplishments of the directors of Glynn's Lydenburg," he said. "As most of you here know, the boards of the two companies are almost identical, and I suppose I ought, in my capacity as chairman of that company, to take his remarks as a compliment."

At this meeting a Mr. E.R. Smith (note the name) read a letter from Mr. E.F. Bourke, an important shareholder, proposing the abolition of the London board and the practice of holding meetings in London. These, he said, involved the company in a great deal of unnecessary expense and, far from helping it, seemed to be hindering.

The chairman pointed out that he could not use the proxies he held from shareholders abroad to vote for a proposal of which they would certainly disapprove. He ruled that formal notice of the proposal must be given.

Nevertheless there was no doubt whatever that the meeting was unanimously in favour of abolishing the London board.

But this evidence of their unpopularity quite failed to subdue the London shareholders. After all, they held the majority of the shares (that is, if one counted shareholdings in France and Germany), and they felt they were entitled to be awkward.

At their annual meeting in 1906 they fairly badgered Mr. Nicol Browne, the chairman of the London directors, whom they accused of being under the influence of the Johannesburg directors. Mr. E.R. Smith, now apparently battling for the other side, made an inordinately long speech in which he outlined their grievances and the difficulty he alleged they had encountered in getting satisfactory answers from Mr. Browne. After Mr. Smith had been on his feet for over an hour, a shareholder interrupted to say that they were all busy men and would Mr. Smith mind coming to the point of his argument.

How important this point was may be judged from Mr. Smith's final statement. ". . . Now, gentlemen, why should we not be able to see the directors or their representatives from Johannesburg at least once in three years? Of course some persons wish the meeting to be held always in London. As a committee "(he was referring to the committee of dissident shareholders)" we never thought so. Some thought every other meeting. "Well, we are beggars and of course we can only ask for what Johannesburg will grant us . . ."

A shareholder: "Why are we beggars?"

Mr. Smith: "Because the Johannesburg board has the power, and unless there is an alteration of the articles of association they can hold their meeting where they wish."

A shareholder: "I always thought the directors were the servants of the shareholders . . ." (A voice: "Alter the articles!").

After this rather fruitless discussion had continued for some time, Mr. Charles Pakeman said a few decisive words.

Mr. Pakeman: "It is not workable. Here you have a Transvaal company, with a mine in the Transvaal, with directors resident in the Transvaal and with the secretary, the books and the offices in the Transvaal. And for a certain purpose you have got to transfer the whole company — body, brains and breeches — bodily to London. For what good? It does not seem to me to be businesslike, and I am not quite sure whether, under company law in the Transvaal, we are not compelled to hold our meetings in the Transvaal."

Mr. Nicol Browne, the chairman, who had been associated with the old Transvaal Gold Exploration and Lands Company, smoothed the ruffled feelings of the shareholders by explaining to them what the re-opening of work on the Theta Reef might mean to them.

"From my old and interesting acquaintance with this Theta Reef, I have notwithstanding all these troubles, prepared a few notes," he said. "It is a point on which I can speak much more easily than I can with regard to these

numerous interviews and committees which always harp on one string.

"This Theta Reef is a very remarkable reef indeed. I should think it is probably the richest reef in South Africa. The whole future depends on what the quality of it is. We had a very large quantity of it in the old days — such a large quantity of it that the working went on for many years. It was discovered in December, 1888. The first ore produced from it had an average milling value of 32 dwts. per ton and the average thickness of it was about five feet.

"Now it is a remarkable thing that the average thickness of this reef here" (he was speaking of a new discovery) "is about the same. It must be nearly five feet because some of it is 67 inches and some 42 inches thick and what is the greatest ore body, 90 feet, carried 11 ozs. to the ton . . ."

He urged the shareholders to exercise patience a little longer and not to press for a payment of dividends.

"I have seen splendid companies ruined by paying away a dividend before it has been earned," he said.

A shareholder: "That will not happen to us." (Laughter).

But Nicol Browne was quite right. The re-opening of the workings on the Theta Reef and the very high values in the new drives completely altered the appearance of the balance sheet. The production of gold increased, ore reserves were doubled and the company paid a dividend of 10 per cent that year. As rumours of new discoveries spread the shares began to move up. Soon they were to soar.

The storm in a teacup which these dissatisfied London shareholders had raised died suddenly away.

For the next 10 years even the dissident few were more than satisfied with the results shown in their annual reports. The day came when one of them, getting to his feet at the annual meeting, proposed a resolution congratulating the board on the efficient way it had developed the company's properties. It was carried unanimously. Who wanted meetings in London now? Who thought the directors' policy was too conservative? The fact was that over the next few years the dividends declared repaid investors all the capital they had subscribed.

A great deal of the credit for fhe company's success in these years must go to the man who succeeded Hughes as general manager, when the latter resigned in 1905 to take up an appointment on the Rand.

His name was Arthur Leggett Neale, and his wife was a daughter of ex-President Steyn. He had been manager of Glynn's Lydenburg Estates at Sabie, and had made a conspicuous success of that mine, which was the most consistent producer in the whole area. He was not only a good mining man but a strong personality. No one was ever in any doubt as to who was in charge on any property that Neale managed.

He was also well-known among the natives who lived just below the Berg as a man who took an interest in their welfare, and was a good "baas". The immediate result of his appointment was a marked improvement in the supply of labour on the mines in the Pilgrim's Rest district, for where Neale went the men who knew him were prepared to go, too.

Neale was a man of immense energy and drive, who was deeply interested in the geology of the district. Such spare time as he had was spent in the saddle exploring the mountain sides. He had the instincts of a prospector and he was never happier than when fossicking about in areas where there were traces of gold. He was particularly interested in the workings of the old diggers and knew the history of the field and where every find had been made.

There is reason to believe that even before he was appointed general manager of the company he had formed the theory that, so far, the mining operation at Pilgrim's Rest had merely scratched the outcrop of the deposits, and that the Theta Reef, supposedly worked out, would be found again if vigorous prospecting and development were done.

Within a few weeks of his appointment he set to work. His method of prospecting, based on his knowledge of the district, was to sink pits in promising areas and then to put in cross-cuts that followed up any traces of gold-bearing ore.

It is not too much to say that he staked his reputation and his future on his prospecting programme. The amount of prospecting and development done in those days was left largely to the discretion of the general manager, who had to keep an eye on the returns from the central mill and see that expenditure did not soar far beyond the profit margin of the producing mines, Clewer, Jubilee and Beta.

Neale's operations trebled the expenditure without at first showing any improvements in the rate of production. He was eating into the profits at what seemed an alarming rate.

But not for long. Within six months of his appointment he began to prove that his theories were right. He found gold in the hill above Peach Tree Creek. He produced samples assaying 18,3 dwts. over a wide section of the farm Vaalhoek. But, most important of all, he re-opened the Theta Mine, and found extensions of the reef that were to prove incomparably richer than anything that had yet been found. As early as 1906 he was able to announce that he had developed 6,500 tons of ore assaying 40,4 dwts., and a further extension of the reef he had discovered on Brown's Hill showed over 4,000 tons of ore in sight at 19 dwts.

He then began a drive in the eastern section of the old mine which located the lode in its true position and was to continue right through the hill to connect up with the southern section, a distance from outcrop to outcrop of some 2,000 feet. These workings, though they did not produce the spectacular values of the south section of the mine, opened up a very large body of payable ore — enough at least to remove all worries about keeping the mill supplied for some time to come.

Neale's moment of triumph came when, early in 1907, he was able to report to The Corner House that "in the two sections of the mine combined a total tonnage has been developed of 40,513 tons of an assay value unsurpassed by any mine in the Transvaal."

In fact, the body of ore developed was far greater than this, and the Theta reef was to be the company's most profitable asset for many years to come.

These developements brought about a remarkable improvement in the affairs of T.G.M.E. Not only had the company now a large body of good, payable ore in sight, but it also had a new mine in the making at Vaalhoek, 12 miles north of Pilgrim's Rest. In addition to this, Elandsdrift, to the south, which had been let to a tributor, was beginning to show good returns just as the agreement on which it was let lapsed. In 1906 it produced 2,738 ozs. of gold, and in that year the company took over.

At the annual meeting in 1907 the chairman was able to announce that the total receipts from all sources were £215,431, of which gold production accounted for R209,540. Only once in the history of the company — and that was in the year ended March 31, 1899, just before the South African War — had this figure been exceeded.

Out of the nett profit of £55,343 that year a dividend of 10 per cent was paid. The dividend was soon to increase, and increase again, as the gold profits jumped upwards.

The problem that had worried the directors up to this time was what would take the place of the Clewer and Jubilee mines once they had been worked out. Their new general manager had found the answer.

In a tribute to his enterprise at the annual meeting in 1908 Mr. Samuel Evans said:

"When Mr. Neale assumed charge of our affairs about three years ago the prospects were not particularly bright, and he is entitled to the lion's share of the credit for the remarkable improvement that has taken place.

"I believe that it was his decision to make another try at opening up the old Theta mine that proved the turning point."

They called him "Lucky Neale" in the district, but there was far less luck than good judgment in his prospecting. He made an intensive study of the gold reefs on the company's property, based on his intimate knowledge of Glynn's Reef and the pockets of gold in the Sabie area. And he had the courage to put his theories to the test.

The re-opening of the Theta mine, rumours of the richness of the ore there, the discoveries at Vaalhoek and Elandsdrift, and the knowledge that some of these finds were on Government ground, touched off another "gold boom" in the district in 1908. Some of the diggers who had retired to less exciting occupations returned to Pilgrim's Rest, ready to start all over again. The "Old-timers", who had gone on scratching for a living all these years, prepared to peg new claims. The Department of Mines, in response to requests from many small syndicates and individual diggers, decided to cancel the concession on the farm Graskop and proclaim the area as a gold field where anyone might peg a claim. Good values had been found in the north-eastern corner of the property, close to the Jubilee Mine and not far from Pilgrim's Rest.

To give everyone a fair chance the proclamation was carried out in much the same way as the proclamation of diamond diggings in later years. At sunrise Mr. W.F. Wagner, the District Registrar of Mining Titles, took up his position on the border between Graskop and Driekop and read the proclamation. The police fired a volley of blank cartridges as the starting signal for the rush. Five hundred men, some on horseback, some on foot, raced to peg the best claims.

Soon the whole area was pegged, with the area nearest the Jubilee Mine carrying the heaviest crop of pegs. There was a reasonable prospect that the company, which had pegged 37 claims in the area, would buy out the owners of the others nearby, so that there was a possible profit to be made without moving a cubic foot of ground.

This was really the last "rush" in the Pilgrim's Rest district, though Vaalhoek, Willemsoord, Buffelsfontein and Doornhoek were later proclaimed. It brought about the last assemblage of the diggers of the old school. The Bosun was there, and so was Bismarck, whose real name was John Hoyer, formerly a sergeant in the Prussian Guards. Spanish Joe, now nearly at the end of his career, turned out for the rush, as did Bill Spinner, George Bates, Harry Hill and "Engine Bill", a colourful character who had once driven the London-Glasgow express.

Some of them did well out of their claims.

"It is hard to estimate the value of the gold won from the claims worked

The rush to peg claims on Graskop in 1908.

and mined during the five or six years that followed the proclamation," says H.P. Valintine, who was Claims Inspector at the time. "But it was freely stated that a million sterling would hardly cover it, quite apart from the gold extracted from the Jubilee Hill by the Transvaal Gold Mining Estates Company."

It was the diggers' final fling.

CHAPTER XIII

THE STORM

When Transvaal Gold Mining Estates took over the concession farms at Pilgrim's Rest the company continued to pay the annual fee of R2,000, which David Benjamin had agreed to give the South African Republic from 1882 onwards.

But it will be remembered that the Government had reserved the right to vary this agreement and take, instead of the annual R2,000 concession rantal, a royalty of two and a half per cent on all gold recovered.

In 1896, when Phillips, FitzPatrick and Bailey were in hot water, the Government exercised this right. It was clear that they intended to penalize the absentee shareholders for the political activities of their directors. However, when a five per cent profits tax was imposed on the Rand mines in 1898, just before the South African War, it was not claimed from the company, the two and a half per cent royalty being considered a sufficiently heavy tax.

One of the first acts of the Milner administration after the war was to seize upon virtually the only source of revenue in the Transvaal and impose a ten per cent profits tax on the gold mines. The Treasury ruled that the Transvaal Gold Mining Estates Company must pay not only the royalty on gold won, but also the tax on its profits. It thus was proportionately more heavily taxed than some of the Rand companies which were producing vast profits.

The Board protested strongly against this unfairness, and eventually succeeded in persuading the Treasury to accept a compromise. It was agreed that the Government should take either the profits tax, plus the concession rent, or the royalty — whichever produced the larger amount.

"I think the Government might have been more generous to a company that is struggling — so far without benefit to its shareholders — to develop a mining industry in a district that would be ruined if we stopped operations," said Mr. Samuel Evans sadly.

But this was not the company's chief grievance. What it wanted above everything else was that 50 mile railway line from Nelspruit, which would solve at least half its problems and be of inestimable value to the whole area. There were, at that time, over 30,000 claims registered in the Pilgrim's Rest district, and they brought the Government of the Transvaal a considerable sum in revenue. The company itself was spending about R200,000 a year in wages, stores, timber and other requirements that could be bought locally. This was a lot of money in those days, and it certainly warranted a branch line. But, as always after a war, there was a shortage of both materials and engineers, and there were at least fifty other districts in the Transvaal that

111

were clamouring for railway lines. It was not until 1910 that the money was finally voted for the line, and even then four exasperating years passed before the first train puffed into Sabie station. Later that year the line to Graskop was opened.

Thus for twelve years mining operations at Pilgrim's Rest continued at the pace of the ox. The day came when the mines were crushing over 100,000 tons of ore a year, and showing a profit of well over R400,000, but their supplies still came down the mountain side in wagons, it was still a day's journey to Lydenburg, and the miners still galloped into the village on horseback.

A.L. Neale, the General Manager, protested as loudly as anyone else, but there were those who believed that secretly he was not unhappy about the delay. The railway, when it came, would mark the end of an era. Neale loved the valley, and he was its uncrowned king. Wherever he went in the district his word was law, and that was the way he liked "his" mines run. Other managers lived and worked within a few miles of their companies' head offices. They were constantly visited by directors and consulting engineers, but visits to Pilgrim's Rest entailed a long absence from Johannesburg and some hard travelling. They were comparatively rare.

Besides this his reputation in Johannesburg stood very high, for he had made a great success of his job. "Leave it to Neale," they said in The Corner House. It was a policy that was certainly producing results. Neale was in every respect the captain of his ship.

His first problem at Pilgrim's Rest had been to develop enough ore to keep the central mill busy. So successful had his prospecting been that, by 1908, the problem was reversed. He began to worry as to whether he had sufficient stamps to deal with the ore that was now reaching the mill. He recommended that two tube mills should be installed to bring the crushing capacity of the plant up to 11,000 tons a month. That represented the limit of the output of the company's power station. It was Neale's opinion that the company would soon need more power than this. As though to prove him right, on July 9, 1908, the night sky to the west of the village showed a red glow and a man on a lathered horse galloped down the main street crying: "Kameel's Creek is on fire . . . the mill's burning!"

The ancient 20-stamp battery on the other side of the hill, which had faithfully served the Chi and Theta mines for so many years, was completely destroyed.

The crushing capacity of the plant was reduced by 2,000 tons a month at a time when all the stamps were hard at work.

This was a blow, but it was as nothing to the disaster that was to come. On January 20, 1909, great banks of cloud formed over the Transvaal. They extended from the borders of the Kalahari Desert to Lourenco Marques. They were solid-looking clouds, thick, black and menacing.

"It's going to be quite a downpour," said the weather experts of the day,

112

looking anxiously at the sky.

The rain began to fall that evening. There were no "scattered showers" about this storm. Upon the whole of the Transvaal fell a solid blanket of water, a deluge that went on hour after hour. It rained without ceasing for seven hours. There was a pause, and then it started again. This time it continued for eight hours, and ever afterwards people on the Rand were to say they had "two solid days" of rain.

It was by far the worst flood the Transvaal had ever known. In Johannesburg houses collapsed, gardens were washed away and the street drainage failed so that the town was under water. Rivers rose overnight and flooded the farms on their banks. Dams began to overflow and add to the destruction.

Suddenly Johannesburg heard to its horror that the May Consolidated Dam at Knights had collapsed, and that the Witwatersrand Gold Mine was flooded. Then came the ghastly news that 152 men had been trapped in the workings and that there was no hope for them. A shift boss named W. White and six other white miners were among the men underground at the time, and there were at least 145 native mine workers below the level to which the water had risen.

This was the worst disaster since the dynamite explosion at Kazerne in 1896. The town went into mourning for the lost mine workers.

Then came a dramatic announcement in *The Star*. A study of the mine plan had convinced Mr. Prout, manager of the Witwatersrand Gold Mine, that there might be hope for some of the men. There was a chance that they might have been able to make their way up to the worked-out stopes on the eighth level which, measurements showed, were above the flood water. If they had survived the shock and the cold, if they had not been overwhelmed by the inrush of water, if there was sufficient air in the stopes . . . there was just a chance they might still be alive.

Every pump that could be brought to bear was set to work. The level of the water in the main shaft began to sink, the rescue parties stood by and the whole Rand waited, watched and prayed.

Five days went by, and still the water was above the level on which the rescuers hoped to enter the mine. Six days . . . seven days . . . it began to look as though there was no chance.

And then, on the morning of the eighth day, *The Star* came out with one of the most joyful announcements it has ever made. Some of the men had been found – and they were alive!

One by one they were brought to the surface – twenty-three of them in all. They had spent eight days huddled in the stope above the flood water, listening to the hideous sounds of a mine breaking up, until at last there was no sound but the lapping of the water in the drive below them. But they breathed and lived.

The epic story of the rescue of these men seemed to Johannesburg to mitigate to some extent the tragedy of the bursting of the May Dam. For weeks there was no other topic of conversation in the town.

As may be imagined, the Rand had very little sympathy to spare for the disasters that had befallen other districts. Tales of havoc poured in for the next ten days.

On January 25, *The Star* published this report from the secretary of the Transvaal Gold Mining Estates Company:

"The secretary writes: I have received the following telegram from the General Manager at Pilgrim's Rest: 'Terrific storm last night . . . River rose approximately 30 feet. All bridges over the Blyde River swept away. Jubilee station swept away. Main station intact. Heavy damage to Farmer's Race. Main drives at various mines mostly fallen in at the mouth. Cannot tell damage to mines until I can get in. Will report later on this but do not anticipate is so serious as the transport. Fortunately no accidents in mines. Central cyanide compound washed away. Six natives drowned at Clewer. Three boys killed and four injured by landslip overwhelming huts. River came down about 1 a.m. on 21st bringing immense amount of debris which caused successive collapse of bridges. Sending this by special runner to Lydenburg. Heaviest flood ever known by oldest inhabitant.' "

So preoccupied was Johannesburg when this telegram was published that there was almost no reaction on the Stock Exchange. The shares declined by five cents!

Behind this terse statement lay the story of a night of terror, for it is doubtful whether any district in the Transvaal had a greater rainfall than Pilgrim's Rest during the storm that began there during the evening of January 20.

Eventually, when there was time to look at the rain gauges, it was found that they had registered 8½ inches — and then run over!

"Four of us were playing bridge at Jack Secull's house that night," says a former resident of Pilgrim's Rest who remembers the storm.

"About 10.30 p.m., when our conversation was raised to shouting level because the noise of the heavy rain beating down on the corrugated iron roof made this the only way we could hear what anyone said, Mrs. Secull suddenly burst into the room with her baby in her arms. 'The water is pouring down on our bed,' she said. 'I'm sure the creek is overflowing and the water will soon reach the house.'

"The clash of big boulders colliding with one another in the creek could be heard above the din of the rain on the roof. Had there been any thunder we could not possibly have heard it. Nor could we hear any sound from the baby, though we could see it was yelling its head off. Undoubtedly there were five very frightened people sitting in that room, wondering if and when the thundering waters of Pilgrim's Creek about 25 yards below us would come pouring in."

As there was no sign of the storm subsiding this man fought his way through the torrents of water to his house, higher up on the hillside.

The great flood of 1909 — the bridge across the Blyde River
is washed away.

"Upon reaching it I found the water pouring out from under the front door and after slushing down the passage saw my poor wife sitting up in bed under an umbrella, crooning to the baby in his cot, over which a mackintosh was spread. On this the drip, drip could be seen but not heard above the noise on the roof.

" 'Isn't it terrible,' " she said. " 'I'm sure that some of the people living near the creek must have been drowned, poor things . . . it's not the water coming through the roof I mind so much but the water rushing down the hillside which is pouring through the doors.' "

For the people of Pilgrim's Rest it was the worst night of their lives. They sat cowering in their houses hoping that the foundation would hold, while the usually placid creek just below the main road through the village roared like the Victoria Falls.

And what a scene of desolation they saw when they put their heads out next morning!

The first thing that caught their eyes was the scarred face of Jubilee Hill on the other side of the creek. There had been a landslide that had brought down thousands of tons of rock and earth. It looked as though the crest of the hill had been dynamited in some gigantic mining operation.

Worst disaster of all — the bridge across the Blyde River had been swept away, and forty yards of roaring torrent lay between the village and the road to Lydenburg. Not that this mattered a great deal, for it was clear that the coach from Lydenburg would never get down the hill until the road was re-made.

Such was the force of the water at the height of the storm that two of the heavy stone and concrete piers had vanished altogether. Pieces of the heavy

115

steel H-girders were found more than a mile down the river, bent and twisted as though they were copper wire.

The power station at the Jubilee Mine had vanished into thin air, and only a few pieces of heavy machinery were ever recovered. As for the electric tramway, there was scarcely one of its seven miles of track that had not been dislocated by the storm. There were places where search parties had to be sent out to find the missing rails.

Eight hundred feet of Farmer's Race, the furrow that led the water to the Blyde River power station, had been washed away. Neale reported that the bed of the river "had been quite altered and the valley, which was formerly one succession of Kaffir gardens, is now a stretch of gravel and boulders".

Every house in Pilgrim's Rest in those days, and all the mine buildings, were roofed with corrugated iron (they are to this day). It is a tribute to the enduring quality of this metal that it stood up to the storm, and that not one building collapsed beneath the weight of the water that poured down. For this was more than a rain storm. It was a cloudburst. Had the rain gauges in the valley been big enough there seems no reason to doubt that they would have registered at least 20 inches that night. At the height of the downpour the few who ventured out found it difficult to breathe in the heart of that solid sheet of water.

The flood cost the company R64,000 in loss of profit during the three months that followed, when the mill was closed down and the damaged adits repaired. It also incurred extraordinary expenditure of R24,902 in rebuilding bridges and getting the tramway in order again. The dividend was reduced that year to 7½ per cent.

It was now clearer than ever that the mines could no longer rely on the Blyde River power station at Pilgrim's Rest. The flood had put it completely out of action, and brought all the mines to a standstill between January 20 and March 15. And it was not until may 1, 1909 that the central mill was working to its full capacity.

A flood such as this could be regarded as abnormal, but there were also the difficulties of the winter season to be taken into consideration, times when the flow of water was so low as to make it difficult to keep the power station going. There had to be more power, and since the railway line was still no more than a light in the railway engineers' eye there would be no coal, so that another hydro-electric scheme was necessary.

Another factor in the calculations that the directors were making at this time was the promising results that had been obtained on the farm Vaalhoek, 13 miles to the north of Pilgrim's Rest. The company's claims there had been thoroughly proved, and there was no doubt that there were the makings of a very rich mine. Power would be needed to run the plant, and it was obvious that it could not come from the Blyde River station, which had its work cut out to keep the Pilgrim's Rest mines going.

The company's consulting electrical and mechanical engineer, Mr. A.M.

Robeson, went to the district and he, with his eye on the prospecting that was going on on the farms Willemsoord and Buffelsfontein, recommended a power station on the banks of the Blyde River on the farm Dientjie, adding a rider that a scheme which used the Lisbon-Berlin waterfall to the east would probably be cheaper.

In the end a fall on the farm known in the district as Bourke's Luck, adjoining the concession farm Belvedere, was chosen as the site of the power station. It was an ideal situation, not far below the point where the waters of the Blyde and the Treur meet and enter the Blyde River Canyon. It guaranteed the necessary flow throughout the year. The power line to be built to Vaalhoek, and eventually to Pilgrim's Rest, would run largely over the company's ground.

The scheme was estimated to cost R248,000, and the board decided to raise the money by issuing first mortgage debentures at 5 per cent, which would be redeemed over the next six years. These debentures were issued in 1910, and were all taken up by the shareholders. Mr. Robeson having, in the meantime, retired, Mr. Elsdon Dew was appointed consulting engineer, and work began on what was to become the largest hydro-electric generating station in the southern hemisphere.

Vaalhoek was not one of the original concession farms. It had, therefore, to be proclaimed as open for digging once the company had decided where its mynpacht would be, and which discoverers claims it wanted.

But Vaalhoek was Neale's special "pet", and he kept Joe Needham, the company's chief prospector, hard at work there for some considerable time. Altogether some R54,000 was spent in prospecting and developing with the result that the position of the reef was well proved. When crushing began on May 5, 1910, the ore reserves were estimated to be four years ahead of the mill.

The proclamation of Vaalhoek, when at last it came, was a disappointment to the diggers and the small syndicates in the district. They had held high hopes of the results that might be obtained from claims in the vicinity of the company's discovery, where Joe Needham had been getting consistent values of 18 dwts. and more. But in the end few crumbs fell from the table. Neale had neatly "cornered" most of the payable gold in the area.

It was a different story in the Sabie area, where the Elandsdrift Mine was producing remarkable results. Here there were patches of gold throughout the district, and syndicates that could afford a small battery and some form of reduction plant made money. There was a rush of diggers to the district, and claims were pegged over almost every square yard of the farm Waterval, north of Sabie. Quite a number of men who started with some capital made small fortunes. While it lasted it was called the "Sandstone Reef Boom", The Buchanans, Willie McLachlan, L.O. Bright and Exley Millar were among the small mine owners who achieved success.

Elandsdrift Mine produced some of the most spectacular values the district

118

has ever known, including a reef of pure white quartz studded with nuggets of gold which it was possible to extract from their beds by hammering the quartz.

The new tube mills at Pilgrim's Rest started work in 1910, and had the immediate effect of increasing the mines' production by 1,000 tons a month. It was also estimated that they improved gold recovery by about 4 per cent. Despite the setback caused by the flood the company's results improved, and in 1910 it was able to declare a dividend of 27½ per cent. This was followed by a record profit of £204,861 in 1911 and, to the satisfaction of the shareholders, a dividend of 30 per cent.

The guiding genius behind these developments and the architect of the vastly improved results had been A.L. Neale, who by sheer hard work and enterprise had developed no less than five new mines, and who had also succeeded in cutting costs by 7s. 4d. a ton, a saving of nearly R70,000 a year.

He ought, at this time, to have reaped the reward of his endeavour. Unfortunately his health began to fail. In 1910 he had a serious operation, from which he made a slow recovery. His doctors had then to tell him that he could no longer undertake the strenuous work demanded of the general manager of a mining company whose properties extended over thirty miles of rugged country. His days in the saddle were over. He could no longer climb mountain sides and crawl about in adits.

To Neale this news was heart-breaking, but he took it like the man he was. He wrote to the board tendering his resignation, and every line of his letter conveyed the very real regret he felt at giving up what he regarded as the most interesting job in South Africa, and leaving the valley he loved.

The board accepted his resignation with great regret and, as some small indication of how highly they valued the services he had rendered the company, voted him a bonus of £4,000.

He was succeeded, in 1911, by a man who could hardly have been more different in temperament — an Italian named Stefano Carlo Bianco Aimetti who, up to that time, had been manager of the New Heriot Mine on the Rand.

CHAPTER XIV

THE COACH ROBBERS

The years from 1910 to 1915 were the golden years of the company, and of the whole district from Vaalhoek to Sabie. Profits were of the order of R400,000 per annum and it had been announced that work was to begin on the railway line from Nelspruit. The mines were employing some 250 white men and 3,000 Africans, and the company was spending at least R200,000 a year in the district. In addition to this the discoveries at Elandsdrift and Vaalhoek, and the proclamation of a number of farms owned by the Government, had attracted both individuals and companies to the district.

All told the population must have been bigger than it was in the days when diggers "rushed" the alluvial gold field. It was a steadier population, too. There were now wives and families in the houses at Pilgrim's Rest, a more certain source of income for most of the inhabitants and more sobriety (though let it not be supposed that the village was by any means a Sunday school camp).

The concession on Morgenzon was soon to expire, and the Clewer Mine was being worked for all it was worth to remove the last ounce of gold. It had been a steady producer for close on sixteen years now, though the values were low, it was still giving good payable ore. The Peach Tree Mine at that date looked as though it might take Clewer's place. There were 164,000 tons of ore in sight, of an average assay value of 21.41 dwts. over 30 inches.

A.L. Neale made one of his few miscalculations in his last report in 1910. "The Beta Mine is now exhausted after a life of 19 years," he wrote.

It was never safe to say that of any mine in the Pilgrim's Rest area until you had honeycombed the hill under which it lay. In due course the Beta Mine was opened up again, and continued to produce gold until 1971.

The company imported a number of Welsh and Cornish miners in those days for the conditions at Pilgrim's Rest, particularly the timbering that was necessary in almost every drive, were not unlike those to which they were accostomed.

Here are some of the names from the pay sheets fifty years ago: E. Randolph, G. Edwards, R. Griffiths, P. Shepherd, A. Glinister, R. Longstaff, R.K. de Boer, J.J. Meyer, J. Jones, J.N. Southgate, W.T. Jones, T. Barton, J.N. Franck, M. Davies, Idris Giles, E. Edwards, G. Tudor, John Giles, J. Williams, J.C. Turner, J. Wagner, N.R. Cheeseman, J. Harris, W. Latimer, P. Vermeulen, F. Walker, Dai Rees, R.W. Jones, J. Craney, H.D. Dewey, W. J. Jones, D. Price, M. Thomas, G. Roberts, E. Jones, I. M. Giles and H.W. Watkins.

Observe that there are no less than five Joneses in this list – all of them from Wales. W.T. Jones became the mine captain of the Jubilee Mine, and

Randolph is still remembered as the driving force at Theta and Brown's Hill.

Most of the Welshmen grew to love the valley which was so like the valleys they had known at home. Once they had a football field and a male voice choir established they were as happy as Welshmen ever are. They brought their own brand of lilting English to Pilgrim's Rest, but wherever three of them gathered they spoke their mother tongue. There wasn't a child in Pilgrim's Rest in those days who did not know a word or two of Welsh, or could not sing some of the old ballads.

Ah, the singing! To this day you have to be pretty good before you dare to sing in public in Pilgrim's Rest, and of even the best of tenors the old inhabitants will say: "He's not as good as Dai Rees when he was at his best in the old days."

Every male inhabitant of the district owned a horse and the hitching rails lined the main street of the village where the cars are parked today.

On Saturdays the miners, dressed in riding breeches, jacket and cap, used to assemble on their mounts at a particular point — Fullard's Corner, Darke's Gulley, Geoff Edward's Corner or Brown's Hill. When they were all there someone would cry: "Last man in pays for the drinks."

That was the starting signal for a wild race to the Royal Hotel or the European (now the annexe of the Royal). They would gallop flat out up the main street, dismount, tether their horses and bolt into the pub — and the last man to reach the bar counter paid for the first round.

Long before closing time their voices would be raised in song. And late at night the horses would carry some of the revellers home, riding knee to knee, the reins hanging free, their arms round one another's necks and their heads thrown back as they gave a final rendering of "The Ash Grove". A miner's mount had not only to be able to gallop but also to know how to find his way home on Saturday night.

These cavalry charges through the village led to keen competition for fast horses. The miners scoured the countryside for good-looking colts, and even imported retired race horses from Johannesburg. So enthusiastic did they become that they established a symkhana course on the other side of Brown's Hill, and held Saturday race meetings.

There is one delightful story of Pilgrim's Rest's Welshmen which belongs to later years but is worth telling here. It happened at the beginning of the first world war.

Beyers, De la Rey, Maritz and others had gone into rebellion and General Louis Botha, the Prime Minister of the Union, had declared martial law. A young constable of the South African Police, newly posted to Pilgrim's Rest, had made a very careful study of what was permitted and not permitted under martial law. One Saturday night he was patrolling in the village main street when three miners emerged from the bar, talking to one another, rather loudly, in Welsh.

The constable stepped forward and barred their way.

"It is my duty to inform you that under the provisions of the Martial Law proclamation you are not permitted to speak a foreign language," he said.

There was a shocked silence.

"What was it I am thinking I heard you say, young man?" asked the senior member of the party.

"I said you're not allowed to speak a foreign language . . ."

A foreign language! This whippersnapper had the impertinence to call the tongue of Welshmen, the honoured language of Wales, known throughout the world and indeed to goodness the language all Englishmen would speak if only they could learn it . . . he called it foreign!

They fell upon that constable and, for the honour of Wales, they beat him up. Then they delivered him at the police station, his uniform in shreds, and told the sergeant-in-charge that they wanted to lay charges of high treason and of gravely insulting the Prince of Wales against him.

But instead they were charged with obstructing and assaulting a policeman in the course of his duty, and of damaging his uniform.

It would have been quite a case had it come to court. But the sergeant was a tactful man. There was a conference between the police and the accused, at which it was explained that the constable had never heard anyone speaking Welsh before, and how was he to know that it was the second language of Great Britain? To him it had sounded like a foreign language.

The Welshmen on their part described how deeply insulted they had felt and what the feelings of the people of Wales were about their language. They agreed to buy the constable two new uniforms — and there the matter ended.

I wish I could have visited Pilgrim's Rest in those days and seen the horses lined up outside the hotels, and the morning "tram" bringing the children to school from Clewer along the line that normally carried ore to the mill. It was a happy, friendly village (it still is), where everyone knew everyone else (they still do), where you had to walk no more than a hundred yards to do your shopping or visit both bank and post office or call on friends.

Imagine a row of corrugated iron houses, built on slabs of concrete on ledges cut from the side of the hill. The only street (it has never had a name) winds downwards between the houses and shops, and thirty yards below it lies the Creek where once the gold was found. At the far end of the village are the mine buildings and the homes of the mine employees. And beyond that lies the Blyde River and the Joubert Bridge (named after Commandant Piet Joubert), across which everyone who enters Pilgrim's Rest from Lydenburg must pass. The road turns left-handed not far beyond the bridge and winds in a series of hairpin bends to the summit of Pilgrim's Hill, 2,000 feet above. It climbs the hill above the Clewer Mine and on, above the hillsides which are scarred by prospectors' pits and mine workings.

To this day in Pilgrim's Rest you step up to reach the houses and the shops on one side of the main street, and down to reach the houses on the other side. The surface of the road presents the only really level surface in the village. Here and there on its verges may be seen the remains of a water race that led water to the sluice boxes eighty years ago. Below the road big boulders line the banks of the Creek. Every one of them was moved from its bed by the diggers searching for the nuggets that they hoped would lie in the gravel below.

The proprietor of the Royal Hotel in those days was "Honest John" McIntyre, a Scotsman who knew the value of money and made his hotel pay. He owned property in Lydenburg, and there his wife and daughters lived. Pilgrim's Rest has always had rather a grudge against them because they preferred the amenities of Lydenburg to the "rough" life of Pilgrim's Rest. Legend has it that they used to send "Honest John" food parcels as though he were living in an internment camp, and that never once in all the years he lived there did they visit the Royal Hotel. It is a legend I find hard to believe.

"Honest John" persuaded one of his brothers in Scotland, Neil McIntyre, to come out to South Africa and help him run the hotel. Cameron MacFarlane, their nephew, followed. He married Sheila Lilley, daughter of the Maud Mary Purcell who was the first white child born on the diggings. Mrs. MacFarlane, now a widow, remains one of the village's direct links with its adventurous past.

Managing the Royal Hotel in those days cannot have been an easy task. It required what "Honest John" had, a firm hand and an intimate knowledge of the financial standing of everyone in the district.

To the hotel at one time or another came every celebrity in the Transvaal — the judges and barristers on circuit, the consulting engineers, the company promoters, the redoubtable Colonel Steinacker and Colonel Stevenson-Hamilton, Warden of the Sabi Game Reserve as it was in those days. To it also came some of the "old timers", the prospectors and diggers who were still working claims in the district and who still spent their money freely when they had it. Add to these visitors the miners who were regulars, and you will see why "Honest John" and his brother had to be on the spot at closing time, and also why the hotel made money.

The bar of this hotel has an interesting history. It was once a small Roman Catholic mission church in Lourenco Marques. When it grew too small for its mission it was bought, lock, stock and barrel, by the then proprietor of the hotel, loaded on to a wagon and hauled up that impossible track which climbed the Berg. In Pilgrim's Rest it was assembled and erected as a sort of annexe to the hotel. It became, in the course of time, the bar. It is there to this day, and to look at it you would never guess that it once housed an entirely different type of congregation.

The Government of the day was pepresented by some strong personalities. Whoever chose them must have known the district. The magistrate of Lydenburg was Colonel H.A. Damant, who had commanded Damant's Horse in the South African War and won a great reputation for fearlessness. He won the respect of everyone in the district, even those against whom he had fought.

One of the spectacles of the day, provided you were not a passenger, was to see Colonel Damant driving a team of mules and a wagon down Pilgrim's Hill. He was eventually to become Chief Magistrate of Pretoria.

The district commandant of police was Captain Billy Scarth, a Canadian who had served in the South African Constabulary. Colonel Damant was his hero and his inseparable companion, and there is no doubt that they both spent some of the happiest years of their lives during their tour of duty in the district.

Napier Devitt, author of *Memories of a Magistrate,* was appointed magistrate at Pilgrim's Rest in 1912. On his first day in the village he met one of the old-timers and the conversation, as he recorded it, went like this:

"You're the new magistrate? "

"Yes."

"You have come to a queer place."

"How so?"

"This is the Pilgrim's Rest Republic. There is no law here except what we make ourselves."

However, alarming as that must have sounded, it turned out to be a comparatively law-abiding community and Napier Devitt, like everyone else who has lived there, succumbed to the charm of the district.

The coach to Lydenburg, and thence on to Machadodorp, ran twice a week. Of the relays of mules which the Zeederberg Coach Company provided none worked harder than those stationed at Kruger's Post, whose duty it was to haul the coach up and down Pilgrim's Hill.

On the days when there was no coach service, native runners carried the mail from Pilgrim's Rest to Lydenburg and back again. In all the years they dog-trotted on this arduous journey, using footpaths and byways that only they knew, no letter or parcel was ever lost.

They travelled in pairs, and were armed with a rifle and assegai apiece. They used to cover the distance from Lydenburg to Pilgrim's Rest in the incredible time of seven-and-a-half hours — incredible, that is, if you have seen the mountainous country they had to cross.

As they came over the crest of the hill and sighted the village they would pause and one would blow a bugle, a signal that meant: "The mail is on its way". Everyone who was expecting a letter would drop whatever he was doing and saunter to the post office. Twenty minutes later the "post boys" would canter up the main street, their 30-mile run completed.

Twice in the first thirty years of its history Pilgrim's Rest heard the alarming cry: "There's been a robbery . . . Highwaymen have held up the coach!"

It happened the first time in 1899, right at the top of Pilgrim's Hill. There was bullion valued at £10,000 in boxes in the coach, four passengers and their luggage.

As the straining mules rounded the last bend at the top of the hill two masked men stepped into the road with pistols in their hands.

The coach is robbed at the top of Pilgrim's Hill. It happened in 1899 and the thieves got away with bullion worth R20 000.

"Get off the coach and stand in the road or we'll blow your brains out," said one of them.

Piet du Plessis, the driver, and the passengers hastily disembarked. They were handcuffed and made to lie down under the coach. Meanwhile one of the highway men unharnessed the mules.

In a matter of minutes the bullion was taken out of the boxes, loaded on to a pack mule, and the robbers galloped away.

On that particular afternoon A.T. Darke, son of a man employed by T.G.M.E. after whom Darke's Gulley was named, was riding near Clewer when the Native who rode on the coach as brake man and baggage hand came running towards him.

"Baas, baas, the coach has been robbed and Baas du Plessis and the passengers have all been handcuffed," he cried.

He showed young Darke a bullet hole in his hat.

The youngster told the man to get up behind him, then galloped for Pilgrim's Rest and the police station. Having told the man to report the robbery, he galloped back to his house.

"I found my father busy in the garden," he says. "But as soon as I told him what had happened he yelled to the stable boy to saddle two fresh horses. We mounted and galloped up the road to the bottom of Pilgrim's Hill.

"We made our way up the hill as fast as we could by giving our mounts constant breathers. At the crest of the hill, where the "Jock of the Bushveld" bronze now stands, we found the coach with one of the six mules missing and the driver and four passengers lying underneath it, handcuffed. There were empty bullion boxes scattered around.

"My father and I questioned the passengers as to the route the robbers had taken.

"Within a few minutes two policemen arrived. We followed the spoor of three horses and a mule, and in the fading daylight we saw the gang in the distance, just moving round the head of a gorge about two miles away.

"But it was past 6.30 p.m. and getting dark rapidly. The pursuit was hopeless."

There you have a first-hand account of the robbery from a man who was then a schoolboy but who, nevertheless, was first on the scene.

It would seem impossible that two men and a mule loaded with bullion could have made a clean getaway through wild country. But that is what happened. The bullion was never seen again.

It must be remembered that there were no police patrols and no telegraph lines in those days. It is generally believed that the highwaymen had fresh horses hidden somewhere on the route, and that they went straight through to Lourenco Marques.

But Mrs. Joubert, the oldest inhabitant of Pilgrim's Rest, never believed this. She told me that the men of her family formed the theory that the highwaymen either buried their loot or dumped it in a dam and came back for it when the hue and cry had died down.

The first coach robbery undoubtedly inspired the second, which took place at almost precisely the same spot near the top of Pilgrim's Hill in 1912. The difference was that the first hold-up was carried out by professional gangsters who had planned every detail of their coup. The second one was the the perfect example of the muddle an "amateur" can make of his first attempt at larceny.

Normally the proper technique in telling the story of a crime is to leave the reader guessing as to the identity of the criminal until the very end. But the normal rules do not apply in this case, and there is no harm in telling you that the highwayman who held up the coach the second time was Tommy Dennison, once a private in the British Army, and bugler and despatch rider to the Earl of Athlone on active service in the South African War.

Dennison was wounded and took his discharge from the army in South Africa. In due course he drifted to Pilgrim's Rest, where he became the village barber.

When a more enterprising barber, who talked less and cut hair more smoothly, put him out of business, he became laundryman to the bachelors of the village and the mine. What this meant was that a bevy of African maidens did the washing and Tommy Dennison collected the cash.

Then it was that he thought up his scheme for holding up the coach . . .

The scene was almost precisely the same as that of 1899. The coach turned a corner and there, in the roadway, was the masked highwayman mounted on a dappled grey horse (which anyone from Pilgrim's Rest would have recognized as the horse that Tommy Dennison had bought from the Reverend Maurice Ponsonby).

"Keep yer 'ands up but kick off them money boxes," said the highwayman in an accent that was a queer mixture of Cockney and stage "American".

There was only one passenger in the coach, which was on its way from Lydenburg, carrying cash for the banks.

Piet du Plessis, the driver, kicked the boxes off the coach and as the first one hit the road it burst open, scattering half-crowns and florine in the dust.

"You ———— fool! I thought you said it was sovereigns?", the highwayman is reported to have shouted at the driver.

Nevertheless he began picking up the silver and loading it into a sugar bag.

The coach tore into Pilgrim's Rest with the driver shouting: "Send for the police! The coach has been robbed!"

Statements were taken from him and from the solitary passenger.

The next morning Dennison appeared in the village street with his retinue of washerwomen carrying the clean washing on their heads. But it was not only laundry he had come to deliver.

He stopped at each of the shops where he owed money, extracted a small bundle from the pile of clean linen and then paid his bill — in half-crowns.

And as he left each shop the proprietor sent a message to the police to say: "Tommy Dennison has been in here, paying his bill in half-crowns. It looks suspicious."

He was in the bar of the Royal Hotel, counting out 160 half-crowns to pay his bill of £20, when the police walked in and arrested him. He went quietly, as they say.

Du Plessis, the coach driver, turned King's evidence against him, though it was scarcely necessary. He admitted his guilt.

Tommy Dennison's reasoning seems to have been that, in view of the very poor financial return on his hold-up and the fact that he liked living in Pilgrim's Rest, his best tactics were to pretend that the whole affair had been a huge practical joke carried out by a man renowned for his sense of humour.

The betting in the village was that he would get six months hard labour when he came up for sentence.

But the judge at the Criminal Sessions at Lydenburg had no sense of humour. He took a grave view of the crime of highway robbery and sentenced Tommy Dennison to five years' imprisonment.

Dennison served his sentence in the Pretoria Central Prison. When he was released he returned to Pilgrim's Rest, but no one could say that he was either a sadder or a wiser man. On the other hand, no one in the village held his conviction against him. Most of them, except possibly the bank manager, thought that he had received a rather more severe sentence than he deserved.

127

He took up his life where it had ended four years before, and was only too happy to discuss the details of his famous "hold-up" with anyone who cared to listen.

He worked for T.G.M.E., became a cartage contractor, and then one day announced that he was going to open a garage. He did — and all Pilgrim's Rest went into fits of laughter when he erected the sign above the door. It read: "The Highwayman's Garage".

Tommy was eventually lured to Johannesburg by an offer of a part in a film that was to tell of his escapade. But the film was never made, and Tommy became a barman and eventually a parking attendant in Pretoria.

Ever afterwards he used to refer to the time he spent in prison as his "college days".

When I first set out to write the story of Pilgrim's Rest twelve years ago I was fascinated by the story of Tommy Dennison. Who wouldn't have been? I made every effort to get all the details and tell the story in full. I had dozens of advisers. Everybody in the village lent a hand in producing "our" book. But no one thought of mentioning to me that Tommy was still alive and flourishing. Everything that had been said to me was in the past tense. Naturally, though perhaps a little carelessly, I presumed that he was dead. Imagine my astonishment, and dismay when, a week after the book appeared, someone telephoned me from Pretoria and said: "That Tommy Dennison you write about. He's still alive, you know".

The old reprobate was not in the least upset by the fact that all the details of his crime had been recalled in my book though this, in the eyes of the law, was defamation of his character.

He was pleased to have his own copy of the book. His only request was a simple one: Would I please sign it?

Pilgrim's Rest has one other story that it loves to tell about this cheerful character. It dates back to the days when Lord Selborne, the Lieutenant-Governor of the Transvaal, visited the district.

There was an official banquet at the Royal Hotel and Tommy was roped in as a wine waiter for the evening.

At the appropriate moment he appeared at Lord Selborne's elbow and said, with all the suavity of Luigi of the Ritz: "What can I give you to drink, my lord?"

His lordship asked for wine, and it was poured into his glass.

Then Tommy, beaming happily, leant across the table and, addressing Mr. Bob Sutherland who, as acting general manager of the mines, was the official host that evening, said:

"And what's yours, Bob?"*

Tommy is part of the history of Pilgrim's Rest.

---

* I heard several versions of this story. Sometimes the chief character was Tommy Dennison. At other times it was either George Bates or the Bosun. Mrs. Joubert, the oldest inhabitant of the village, said it was Dennison.

CHAPTER XV

WHERE THE ORE WAS RICH

The Transvaal Government or, more accurately, its department of mines, was never very happy about the concession held by the Transvaal Gold Mining Estates Ltd. The Concession farms represented a "kink" in what the officials regarded as the neat pattern of their application of the gold law. Then, too, there were individuals and companies who spent their time telling the mines department, and the newly-elected members of the Transvaal Parliament, that the company was "sitting" on vast, undeveloped mineral resources that ought to be opened up for the benefit of the district and the treasury.

They depicted the T.G.M.E. as a heartless octopus which was keeping the "small man" out of ground that he could work profitably.

These misrepresentations were based on the fallacy that the company's general managers knew exactly where the gold was situated and could at any time, if they so wished, produce large quantities of rich ore. However, for mysterious reasons, which were alleged to be part of the policy of big mining companies, they were keeping these reserves dark. The irony of all this lay in the fact that the rumours were circulated and half believed at a time when the shareholders were clamouring for a dividend and the company was hard put to make ends meet.

T.G.M.E.'s right to its concessions was unassailable in law. It had been granted to Benjamin and his successors by special resolution of the Volksraad and the Milner administration had re-enacted all the resolutions of the old Raad that affected property rights.

It was tacitly hinted to the company more than once that it might be to its advantage voluntarily to surrender these properties and re-establish its rights to them under the normal provisions of the gold law. But the board, with ten years' experience of the difficulties of mining in the district, thought otherwise.

The proposal was formally made to the company when the negotiations for the building of a railway line were at their height. It was then pointed out that the government was reluctant to build a railway line that would exist primarily to serve a gold mining company and might, in fact, run over land owned by that company. If the company would surrender its concession there would be no difficulty about the construction.

Put in this light it may have seemed to some people that the T.G.M.E. was the dog-in-the-manger, holding up the development of the district. But the truth was that the company *was* the district, and that the prosperity of almost everyone who lived there depended on the mines and the revenue that they provided. This had been explained time and again, and for seven years the company had argued, begged and pleaded for the building of the line in the interests of all concerned.

A deputation representing the claim holders and property owners in the district eventually met the directors of the company at the Corner House in June, 1909. Sir Percy FitzPatrick, acting as spokesman for the board, explained why they could not give up the concession.

He pointed out that what the government had ignored was the fact that the company had paid with some 400,000 shares for the concession when it acquired it from the Transvaal Gold Exploration and Land Company in 1895. The shares now stood at R18. That meant that they had paid the equivalent of over R6,000,000 in cash for the concession. It belonged not to the board, but to the shareholders, of whom there were between 3,000 and 4,000. Could anyone expect them to surrender it just as the mines on these properties were beginning to give them a dividend?

The members of the deputation, all of them practical men, saw the point. One of them suggested that a way out of the difficulty might be to guarantee to make up any losses that the new line might incur. This suggestion was accepted by the board of T.G.M.E. They formulated a proposal by which the company would rent the line and undertake to guarantee interest at 3 per cent on the capital cost of building it, the cost being estimated at a sum not exceeding R800,000.

Armed with this most generous proposal, which might well have meant an expenditure of R20,000 a year, a joint deputation representing the company, claim holders and property owners, then interviewed Sir Thomas Price, general manager of the Central South African Railways. Mr. Robert Kotze, the Government Mining Engineer, was present at the interview.

Sir Percy FitzPatrick again explained why the company could not surrender its concession. He then outlined the proposal for guaranteeing the interest charges on the capital cost of the line. Sir Thomas Price, though impressed by the terms of the offer, said that he was against any proposal by which the administration shared with a company the costs of building and running a line.

A member of the deputation not connected with the company said that the people he represented were prepared to pay a freight rate equal to that which they were paying the transport riders (it was 40 cents a 100 lbs.) if that would help the railway administration to make up its mind to build the line. They made this offer simply because they knew that if the railway line was not built all the claim holders in the district would be ruined.

The discussions continued for some time. Sir Thomas Price made no promises but the deputation left his office feeling that they had made a favourable impression on him.

They were right. The money for the line from Nelspruit to Graskop was voted next year, and the work at last began.

To this day the company operates under the terms of its concession, and of all the various concessions handed out by the Kruger government eighty years ago this alone survives.

Though the concession came under heavy fire from the diggers and would-be mine owners in the early days, and was undoubtedly open to criticism at the time, as were the other "monopolies" which the old South African Republic created, one sees today that it was really a blessing in disguise.

Neither Paul Kruger, who granted the concession, nor the enterprising David Benjamin who applied for it, knew anything about the gold-bearing reefs of the district. The former was simply anxious to increase the State's revenue by R2,000 a year, while the latter was gambling on getting at the rich source of the alluvial gold. Yet, unwittingly, they hit on the only form of tenure that could have brought about the methodical mining of the gold there.

It is not hard to imagine what would have happened had the mines been proclaimed under the system that then prevailed. The owner of each farm would have selected his mynpacht and the rest of the area would then have been pegged by prospectors. Where there were indications of gold there would have been wild speculation, followed by the flotation of dozens of companies — and disaster for all when the rich "patches" were worked out.

This was precisely what happened at Barberton in 1882, where all the farms except Moodie's were proclaimed. Almost anybody who had succeeded in pegging a claim, and quite a number of people who had no ground at all, proceeded to declare that they needed capital and to sell out to hastily formed companies.

No one is quite certain how many of these companies there were, but the names of more than a hundred are recorded. Between them they must have sold some 5,000,000 shares to the public who, at that time, were prepared to buy anything provided that it gave them an interest in ground that was near Bray's Golden Quarry or the Sheba Mine.

The result was disaster. Three-quarters of the shares sold were worthless. Many of the shareholders lost every penny they possessed, and some of the men who had rushed to the field died of starvation. As for the mining, it was a muddle from start to finish. Thousands of tons of quite useless ground were excavated and where there was gold the ore was often incompletely treated.

The Barberton boom and the subsequent crash gave the South African gold mining industry a bad reputation with overseas investors which it took years to live down.

The concession farms at Pilgrim's Rest may have provided the company that had the exclusive right to work them with a "gold monopoly", but they also provided the only sound basis for this type of mining. They were the focal point at which a central mill and a power plant could be established and from which the whole district could be thoroughly prospected. Rich patches of ore, however short lived, helped to finance exploratory work in unpayable ground. Peter was robbed to pay Paul, and a percentage of all the gold won went to develop new mines which, in their turn, later helped to

Prospectors in the hills.

finance the re-opening of old mines and the prospecting of new areas.

That was the pattern of the company's mining operations in the district for nearly 80 years, forced upon it by the inconsistency of the reefs of the area. In that period it worked some 30 different mines. From some of them it extracted as little as 1,000 tons of payable ore. But others, notably Theta, Beta, Duke's Hill, Columbia Hill, Clewer, Jubilee and Elandsdrift, were worked for more than sixty years and each produced a million tons or more of payable ore. The Theta Mine held some of the richest lodes ever discovered in the Transvaal or, for that matter, in the world. For the best part of fifty years it helped to carry the marginal mines and finance prospecting and development.

It was this process of balancing the rich ore against the unpayable development work on new mines that made it so difficult to explain to the layman the art of mining in the Pilgrim's Rest district. He was baffled by the constant recurrence of the names of some twenty different mines in the reports, and of references to at least twelve different gold-bearing reefs which kept reappearing in the story. Now the Beta Mine was "worked out", then it was producing again; the Theta Reef would suddenly be "struck" in a spot six hundred feet from where it had last been worked; Brown's Hill went on producing new patches of gold-bearing ore; Vaalhoek shut down in 1928, reopened in 1938, shut down again in 1943, reopened once more in 1946. What did it all mean?

Probably the only way to appreciate the extent to which the skill of the prospector, combined with an element of luck, dominated all mining operations in the district was to climb the hills and inspect the thousands of pits and adits which told and still tell, the story of the search for payable ore. The Theta mine plan shows no less than 152 adits and drives of various lengths that mark the pursuit of the reefs through a positive maze of faults and folds. The hills in which the lodes were worked had been scooped out as though they were ripe melons. Millions of feet of timber lie buried in the old drives now fallen in. And though the Theta was the most sought after of all the reefs the same process was repeated in other reef zones throughout the district.

Mining men still speak with awe of the "jeweller's boxes" that were found in the Theta Mine, where the visible gold taken from a particular spot would probably have assayed 50 ounces to the ton.

The ore was so rich, and could so easily have been extracted by anyone who knew where it was situated, that iron gates were installed in the drives and locked at the end of the day's work.

The Elandsdrift mine, south of Sabie, was famous for its quartz "blow", known throughout the district, as "The Blow", in capital letters. A "blow", it should be explained, is a section of a quartz reef which suddenly widens out as though it had been inflated by pressure from an immense pump, rather in the way that a balloon of inner tube used to emerge from a badly torn tyre.

The Blow at Elandsdrift was 200 feet in width, 20 to 30 feet thick and some 5,000 feet in length. It was composed of a pure white quartz, almost like marble, in which were embedded nuggets of pure gold, clearly visible and extracted simply by crushing. The mine recovered 94 per cent gold from this quartz without the use of cyanide.

It was immensely rich in places and rather poor in others, depending on the concentration of gold. It attracted the attention of geologists throughout the world and provided some of the most beautiful quartz specimens ever seen. Indeed, there are so many specimens of Elandsdrift's gold-bearing quartz scattered about the world that one some times wonders how the mine was made to pay. Nor were the native mine workers above knocking out a specimen or two for their collections when they were unobserved. Many of them were seeing the gold for which they dug so diligently for the first time in their lives. The temptation must have been irresistible.

Here is a description of The Blow by a man who saw it for the first time more than 50 years ago.

"Would you like to have a look at my jeweller's shop in the morning?" asked Patrick (W. Patrick, the first manager of the Elandsdrift mine).

". . . Rain had fallen during the night so that when Patrick showed me his 'jeweller's shop' the morning sun had risen sufficiently to make the nuggets of pure gold scattered about in the pure white quartz look like plums in a Christmas pudding. And in the sunlight they began to shine like the candles on a Christmas tree.

"This otherwise 'hungry' reef of white quartz, eight feet thick, was exposed in an open quarry about fifteen feet deep and about 300 feet in width. I stood there amazed at this bonanza of wealth . . ."

This is also the area where the famous "hatful of gold" was found.

It happened years later in Horseshoe Creek, to the north east of the main Elandsdrift workings. The mine management had ordered prospecting there, and in one cross-cut on what was known locally as the T.B. Leader some exceptionally rich quartz was unearthed.

"I've got a rich patch here, Mr. Diering," said H.C.F. Bell, the sectional manager to the then general manager who was inspecting the work.

"Well, take a sample and let's have a look at it," said Diering.

There was no pan available so the miner used his helmet into which he scooped a few handfuls of the gravel.

When he washed it there were 29 ounces of gold in the bottom of the helmet.

But, such is the luck of the draw in the district, that this particular section of the farm produced only a small tonnage of payable ore.

If you have followed the story from the beginning you will be interested to know that the Elandsdrift mine was established not very far from the spot where Tom McLachlan, Valentine and Parsons made their original discovery in 1872, and thus established the Pilgrim's Rest field.

The alluvial diggers gave the whole area a very thorough "going over" and took out a great deal of gold. They were succeeded by the Rosshill Gold Mining Company, registered in 1883, which erected a mill and remained in operation for the next eight years. It is recorded that Aubrey Woolls-Sampson, then digging for a living but afterwards a director of T.G.M.E., actually camped on the sub-outcrop of The Blow at Elandsdrift, but missed finding it by a matter of feet.

When the company acquired the concession over the ground they did a good deal of prospecting in the area, but decided that it was not worth working. It was then let on tribute to one Gus Stiebel, who worked it for a number of years and was reputed to have made R3,000 a month when things were going well. But he, too, failed to find The Blow.

When his agreement with the company expired he gave up, and in later years lost most of his money in a tin mine in Cornwall, of all palces.

A.L. Neale sent Joe Needham, the company's prospector, to Elandsdrift, and he it was who unearthed the quartz reef. That was in 1906, and by that time the ground had been prospected and worked for 23 years. Yet the Elandsdrift mine produced 329,894 ounces of gold and showed a profit of over R1,000,000 in the course of its working life between 1906 and 1947.

To Stefano Aimetti, most temperamental and brilliant of mine managers, goes the credit for the rediscovery of the Duke's Hill Channel at Pilgrim's Rest.

This channel contained a rich lode of the Theta Reef in decomposed dolomite. It was found on Clewer in the early days and worked extensively until 1904, when it came to an end. A great deal of work was done at the time in an effort to find an extension of the ore body which everyone on the property felt must be there. But it could not be found.

Aimetti began a big prospecting programme towards the end of 1911, and almost his first discovery was the extension of the Duke's Hill Channel that had been lost for seven years. What is more, it was found only some 600 feet from the old channel and, as luck would have it, was on Ponieskrantz, whereas the old channel had been largely on Morgenzon, the farm to which the company's title was due to expire in 1913.

This channel produced some exceptionally rich ore. It was from ten to twelve feet wide and assayed over an ounce to the ton. It played its part in the excellent results achieved by the mines in 1912, 1913, 1914 and 1915, when the company's net profit soared over the £250,000 mark, and it paid dividends that ranged from 30 per cent to 37½ per cent.

Then, having done its duty for years, it vanished once again. One day there was an eight foot vein of rich ore and the next there was nothing — a blank face in which there was not a pennyweight of gold. A fault? A down throw? They searched high and low. A diamond drill was brought in and set to work to probe the neighbourhood.

Drilling was often ineffective in the Pilgrim's Rest district owing to the extensive faulting of the reefs and to the difficulty of recovering a core in the decomposed dolomite. In this case, however, it seemed possible, in view of the known width of the channel and of the knowledge that had been acquired of the reef horizon, that the drill might pick it up.

Not a trace of it was found. All that can be said is that the Duke's Hill Channel has vanished into thin air and no one can explain what happened to it. It may still be there, waiting to be re-discovered.

There are some eight miles of drives in this section of the hills. If they had not caved in, it would have been possible to walk underground from Peach Tree right through to the old Clewer Mine by making one's way through the old workings from which the Theta reef was worked. But it would have been a very complicated journey, through a maze of long forgotten passages that twisted and turned and rose and fell in the eccentric pattern of the reefs that once were there.

You ought now to have some idea of the financial switchback that the man who looked for gold in the Pilgrim's Rest district had to ride. I have described some of the ups and downs of a company. There are a hundred other stories of the adventures of individuals to match these.

There is, for example, the extraordinary stroke of luck that befell the O'Donovan brothers. They were butchers in Lydenburg. One day they were on their way to Glynn's Lydenburg mine at Sabie to put in a tender for the meat supply. They were on horseback, and took the old track that led over Mount Anderson. Near the top of the mountain they off-saddled to give their horses a rest and to smoke a pipe.

Joe O'Donovan noticed something gleaming in the grass near his brother's feet. It was a nugget!

The O'Donovans pegged twenty claims on this spot near the summit of Mount Anderson, 7,000 feet above sea level. They carried all the necessary apparatus, including pumps and sluice boxes, to their lofty eyrie and proceeded to dig. They found gold in the grass roots and then they hit a rich

The O'Donovan brothers find gold on Mount Anderson.

vertical leader. They made, so it is said, R2,000 a month, for two years on end, and their discovery started one of the strangest of all gold rushes — a rush to the top of the highest mountain in the Transvaal.

And then there were the partners McLanigan and Tucker. In an earlier chapter I have said that very few of the diggers and syndicates who pegged claims on Vaalhoek made money. But McLanigan and Tucker, who found gold on Ledouphine to the east, were the exceptions. They made a fortune.

Mr. Henry Niven Scott, who lived in Pilgrim's Rest for over fifty years, remembered Tucker coming to him with a chit in 1913 and asking to be supplied with a wheelbarrow, two picks and a bag of mealie meal. He could afford only half of the R12 that these supplies cost him. He promised to pay the other half at the end of the month.

Thus equipped, he and his partner, McLanigan, started digging. They were both thirsty characters, but there was no money over for gin when they began.

Then, by an incredible stroke of luck, they found a rich leader. Within a comparatively short time they made R126,000.

It was wealth beyond anything they had dreamed of, and they did not really know what to do with it. The tent in which they lived on their claims was piled high with cases of whisky. There were times when they had as many as half-a-dozen jam jars lying about, filled to the lid with nuggets they had taken out.

To their credit it must be said that they both joined Botha's Natal Horse during the first world war, and gave their comrades-in-arms a riotous time. After their period of active service they went back to their claims — and to the whisky bottles.

Then one day the leader they were working pinched out. What had seemed an unending flow of gold ceased overnight.

Neither of them could face the prospect of life without money and without whisky.

They both committed suicide by taking cyanide. And thus ended a partnership that was a throw-back to the old days of the diggings. The death of these two unhappy men may be said to mark the end of an era.

CHAPTER XVI

A CAR CLIMBS THE HILL

The record years of the mines of Pilgrim's Rest were 1913 and 1914, when the net profits were R554,828 and R570,936. The grade was then 12 to 13 pennyweights to the ton and, with the new Belvedere hydro power station at work, the crushing plants were handling 14,000 tons of ore a month. But December 1914 and January 1915 were two of the wettest months in the history of the district. The rainfall that January was 26 inches — and once again there was a disastrous flood. Bridges were washed away and the lower levels of the Vaalhoek mine were flooded. Nevertheless the new power station, built on a site chosen by Mr. Elsdon Dew above the raging torrent that was the Blyde River in full spate, was not affected by the flood and its turbines hummed cheerfully throughout the storms.

The staff of the power station had a nerve-racking time for a day or two, for they were like men in a lonely lighthouse at sea. The roar of the river as it raced through the gorge above which the station was built drowned all other sounds. But the dam, its sluice gates wide open, stood the test, and after that flood no one ever doubted that it would stand anything the weather could do, and last for a hundred years or more. The power station is still at work, still has a generating capacity of more than 2,000 kilowatts.

There was value for money in those days. The whole power scheme had cost R250,000. It supplied power to Vaalhoek and the central mines at a cost estimated at less than one cent a kilowatt and had sufficient reserve, at any rate in the early days, to make power available to other undertakings in the district. A similar installation today would cost at least R1,000,000.

Despite the fact that the old Brown's Hill power station was destroyed by fire in November, 1913, despite the setback caused by the flood the following year and the closing down of the Clewer mine, these were the years when the output of gold reached its peak. A production of 112,000 and 113,000 ounces of gold in two successive years drew the attention even of the experts who had firmly stated their opinion that "small mines never pay". T.G.M.E. shares were in great demand. These production figures may seem insignificant to the present generation but 60 years ago they represented a triumph of mining under difficult conditions.

In 1914 the railway line, which had crawled slowly to Sabie and then on, up the Berg to Graskop, was officially opened to traffic. There was still an eight-mile haul over the mountains to get the freight to the mines at Pilgrim's Rest, but that was child's play compared to the journey from Machadodorp via Lydenburg.

Almost the entire population of Pilgrim's Rest trekked over to Graskop to see the first train pull in and, once the service was established, it became a popular amusement to make a train journey to Nelspruit or to Lourenco Marques.

Though 42 years had passed since the pioneers first trekked to the diggings from Delagoa Bay there were men of the older generation who remembered that dreadful journey. The old wagon track, over which MacDonald, the first Gold Commissioner, had led an expedition in 1873 and on which Alois Nellmapius's and FitzPatrick's wagons ran, was still to be seen when the Kruger National Park was first opened to the public. A series of beacons now mark what has come to be known as "The Jock of the Bushveld Road".

It was a road that was rightly described as "The worst 150 miles in Africa". It is no exaggeration to say that it was paved with bones of the thousands of oxen that died on the route, to say nothing of the transport riders, the carriers and the footsloggers who died of fever. These men, whether they walked it or rode in wagons, took from eight to 10 days to reach Mac Mac from Lourenco Marques and as often as not arrived more dead than alive. The train to Graskop covered roughly the same distance in six hours. To the old-timers who assembled at Graskop on the day in 1914 when the train came in it must have seemed that civilization had at last reached their valley.

The Pilgrim's Rest mines had suffered rather more than their share of misfortunes to that date. But they were spared the disasters of the 1913 miners' strike. That upheaval began with a strike on the New Kleinfontein mine at Benoni and spread to the entire Witwatersrand. It was an anxious time for Aimetti, who knew that some of the men felt that they ought to strike in sympathy.

He decided to take the bull by the horns, and in doing so acted very wisely. Attempts were being made to pull out the men on the T.G.M.E. properties, most of whom scarcely knew what the strike was about.

Aimetti called a meeting at Pilgrim's Rest at which Napier Devitt, the magistrate, presided. The situation on the Rand was fully explained to the men and they were asked to state their grievances if they had any. Spokesmen for the miners said that they were quite satisfied with the conditions under which they worked at Pilgrim's Rest, and had no intention of joining the strike.

"It was apparent to me that the good feeling which had always existed on the property was not to be impaired either by missioners from the disturbed areas or as a result of repercussions from elsewhere," said Napier Devitt afterwards in describing this meeting. "The result was that the labour troubles on the Reef did not affect Pilgrim's Rest."

It was at about this time that the first motor car made its appearance in the district. This new form of conveyance was fairly common in other parts of the Transvaal, but there the roads were level. The two problems that faced the would-be motorist at Pilgrim's Rest were whether these new-fangled machines could climb the last stretches of the road from Lydenburg and, if they did and made the journey down Pilgrim's Hill into the valley, whether they would ever get out again. The general opinion was that no horseless carriage would ever climb that precipitous road, which in those days was a great deal steeper than it is now, since it followed a more direct route to the summit.

These doubts were justified. Aimetti, the general manager, bought a five-seater Hispano-Suiza, a car that was the Marilyn Monroe of its day, positively gleaming with highly polished brass. It fairly spanked along the road between Clewer House, where the Aimettis lived, and the Royal Hotel in Pilgrim's Rest. But on Pilgrim's Hill it roared, puffed, panted — and gave up.

It was thus that when the general manager of the mines wanted to go to Lydenburg by car a span of oxen had to be stationed half-way up the hill. The Hispano-Suiza then climbed the first two miles under its own steam (and "steam" was the right word), after which it was ignominiously towed by oxen over the most precipitous stretch.

The next car to reach the village was a much more humble model than Aimetti's lordly Hispano-Suiza. It was, in fact, a shiny black Model T Ford, owned by H.P. Valintine, the claims inspector. Until the day came when he took the coach into Lydenburg to collect his chariot Valintine had spent most of his life on horseback. He had, however, recently learned to ride a motor cycle and had made a careful study of a manual on how to drive and care for a Ford. Nevertheless he had much to learn from the moment that he poured the first gallon of petrol into the car's capacious tank.

How strenuous was the process of "learning while earning" way be judged from his description of his first encounter with the Ford.

"Although I wound and wound at the starting handle I could not get the car to start," said Valintine. "When almost exhausted I spotted a small key hanging from the steering wheel which I inserted into the hole marked 'Ignition' and returned to the starting handle. At the first swing the engine roared in delight and revved loudly.

"After rushing round and closing the throttle lever I climbed into the driver's seat where I released the hand brake-cum-topgear lever — and the engine stalled immediately.

"Having started the engine again I made sure to put my foot on the clutch pedal and started my career round the goods yard at the railway station. Having never driven anything but a motor cycle before, I continued to go round and round until I realised that I had to turn the steering wheel back again to regain a straight course."

However, he was a fearless man, and after a few hours' practice he set off for Pilgrim's Rest, descended the hill in bottom gear and drew up outside the Royal Hotel, where the car was much admired.

But the real test was yet to come. Would the car climb Pilgrim's Hill?

One Sunday morning, while the village was still asleep, Valintine and his stable boy set out to see whether it could be done. They crossed the Blyde River bridge and set the Ford's blunt nose at the hill. And, with only four stops to cool the engine and replenish the boiling water, she made it!

In a second test the car climbed the hill carrying the owner-driver and three passengers. She was the first car to get to the top of Pilgrim's Hill under her own power. After that the test of any car in Pilgrim's Rest became: Can it do what Valintine's Ford has done? Can it climb Pilgrim's Hill carrying passengers?

Many were tried but few were chosen. Enterprising motorcar salesmen who visited the district from time to time were allowed to talk and talk about the merits of their particular model without interruption. Then the prospective purchaser would say: "I'll buy it if it will climb Pilgrim's Hill with three passengers on board." As often as not that meant the salesman had to drive his demonstration model back to Lydenburg, vowing that never again would he visit this valley where the road "climbed the side of a house".

The early motorists in the district were among the first to discover that the reverse gear on most cars developed more power than the forward gears. It was not considered at all unusual to turn your car round and back up the hill, pausing from time to time to refill the radiator from the water bottle which was an essential part of the Pilgrim's Rest motorist's equipment.

General J.C. Smuts, then Minister of Mines in the first Union Cabinet, accepted an invitation to open the Belvedere power station in July, 1911. He had known the district in the South African War, but had never had time to visit it in all the years he served as Colonial Secretary in Botha's Transvaal government. He had no idea, therefore, what was in store for him, though it was the sort of excursion he loved.

The Belvedere power station stands in a remote spot some twenty miles from Pilgrim's Rest. It is reached by a rough track that leads from the Vaal-hoek mine to a point on the Blyde River where the force of the water has carved a gorge over two thousand feet deep. The Treur and the Blyde meet some distance above the power station and pour their combined weight into this wild and beautiful chasm. The stream, placid enough in winter, becomes a roaring torrent in summer when the rains come and the mountain streams are swollen.

General Smuts and his private secretary, Captain Lane, arrived at Pilgrim's Rest in a large and powerful motor car that looked as though it were designed for ceremonial occasions in Pretoria.

The inhabitants of Pilgrim's Rest studied it with awe and then, as one man, said: "It won't do." They knew the road to the Vaalhoek mine.

In those days on the 12-mile track to Vaalhoek there were five drifts to be crossed, and in most of them the water almost reached the hubs of the wagon wheels. The last drift near the mine was particularly deep. There the mine staff had erected a steel cable and a bucket on pulleys to get the distinguished visitor across. It was obvious that his heavy car with its low clearance would never get through the drifts without cracking its sump and flooding its engine.

141

The versatile Valintine and his Model T Ford were called in to help. Could they take the General to Vaalhoek? They could and would.

That night there was a banquet at the Royal Hotel at which General Smuts spoke of Pilgrim's Rest's picturesque past and of the great contribution the T.G.M.E. was making to the prosperity of the district, and of the bright future he saw for it.

The banquet is remembered as having marked one of the few public appearances of Schalk Burger, formerly Vice-President of the South African Republic, and one of the last links with the Voortrekker generation, who also delivered a speech, in which he recalled the early days of the Eastern Transvaal.

The next morning Valintine and his Model T presented themselves in "travelling kit". The radiator of the car carried an oil-cloth "hood" which could be lowered to keep the water out of the engine. To the exhaust pipe was attached a length of hose pipe which was tied to the tall light — a primitive form of "schnorkel" for the river crossings.

With General Smuts taking the keenest interest in the proceedings from his seat next to the driver, the car safely forded the first four drifts. At the fifth the General transferred to the bucket and was hauled across the river, while Valintine bravely headed into water three feet deep. The car stalled just as it had completed the crossing, was hauled out by oxen and once its plugs and carburettor had been dried out, proceeded on its way.

The last stage of the journey, down the rocky track that led to the gorge and the power station, was done on foot. The whole party, including Mr. Aimetti, Mr. Elsdon Dew, the consulting engineer, and Mr. R. Laroque, the manager of the Vaalhoek mine, camped at the power station for the night.

The next morning, after a short speech, General Smuts broke a bottle of champagne over one of the turbines and turned the valve that set the whole plant going.

Those turbines celebrated their sixtieth birthday — and sixty years of faithful service — in 1971.

There are many power stations in South Africa today, most of them bigger and producing far more kilowatts than Belvedere. But there are few that presented more problems in the building and designing than this one. And it is quite certain that there is no other installation of this type set in more beautiful surroundings. Indeed there are few scenes anywhere in the world to match the rugged grandeur of the Blyde River Gorge at this point.

Those who remember his visit say that General Smuts threw off the cares of office during his stay in the valley and thoroughly enjoyed himself. He was immensely impressed by the beauty of the countryside, particularly by the view across the lowveld from the top of Kowyn's Pass.

To Aimetti he said: "One day I shall have to come back here to stay. This is where I should like to live when I am old."

He spent the next forty years in harness, and he never returned. But he

The gold watch presented to M.W. Phelan, editor of the "Gold Fields Mercury", by "a few fellow British subjects" in 1877. Mr. Phelan supported the diggers' cause through thick and thin. He was the grandfather of Mrs. June Guest, the proprietress of today's Royal Hotel.

A photograph of Elizabeth Russell, the girl who went to the diggings and worked her own claim there, as she was in later life. She was then Mrs. W.A.B. Cameron, having married Cameron, an American whom she met on the diggings.

After morning service in the little Anglican church, built in 1886 - 87.

A car making its way through the water in the Vaalhoek drift on the way to Pilgrim's Rest in the early days.

They took General Smuts across
the river in a bucket.

never forgot the district and could always recall every detail of what he had
seen.

Valintine, who drove the brave little Ford, had one further interesting
memory of the occasion. He said that, even at that early date, Smuts was
thinking of founding a South African Flying Corps. He had been impressed
by Valintine's skill in handling his car. He told Captain Lane, his private
secretary, to ask Valintine whether he would care to join this corps and be
sent to France for training as a pilot. However, as the pay would have been
no more than his salary as a claims inspector, and as he was a married man,
Valintine reluctantly had to refuse.

Six years later he called on Smuts at the Savoy Hotel in London, and
asked for assistance in obtaining a commission in the Royal Flying Corps.
The General had not forgotten the man who took him over the rough road
from Pilgrim's Rest to Vaalhoek and, though skill in piloting a Model T Ford
was no longer quite the accomplishment it had been in 1911, he wrote the
necessary letter.

Stefano Aimetti, the general manager of the T.G.M.E. mines, was a loyal
Italian subject with great respect for the Italian Royal family. The outbreak
of the first world war in 1914 had a profoundly unsettling effect upon him.
Though he had an excellent job and had seen the production of the mines
rise to the highest level since the company was formed in 1895, he yet felt
that it was his duty to return to Italy, and serve his country and its allies,
Britain and France.

After much heart-searching and considerable personal unhappiness he came
to his decision. He wrote to the board tendering his resignation and announcing that he intended to return to his country and offer his services to the
Italian army.

The chairman replied that, while the directors deeply regretted that he had found this step necessary, they fully understood his motive and congratulated him on his patriotism. And so Aimetti left Pilgrim's Rest for Europe and was succeeded by R.A. Barry, who had been manager of Nourse Mines and was considered the outstanding candidate for the job.

Pilgrim's Rest proceeded to give him his baptism of fire at once. He ran straight into a loss of profit of £22,000 and all the other difficulties caused by the flood in January 1915. In addition to that he had to contend with rapidly mounting costs and a very considerable depletion of his white labour force. No less than 69 men from the T.G.M.E. mines joined the forces, and that represented almost twenty-five per cent of the white men employed. It was a record of which the company could well be proud. It promised the men that their jobs would be waiting for them when they came back.

The village followed the mines' example. All the able-bodied men joined up, leaving the older generation to work much harder than they ought to have done, not only in their various occupations but also in raising money for war funds.

The Pilgrim's Rest men were all horsemen and they flocked to the mounted regiments of the day. But before the end of the war they had forgotten they were ever cavalrymen and were serving in every type of unit, most of them overseas.

Nevertheless, and in spite of the absence of its young men, Pilgrim's Rest enjoyed quite a "boom" in those years. The shops were bigger and busier than they had ever been, and the output of the mines was soaring. There were even rumours that there might be motor buses running between Lydenburg and Pilgrim's Rest and Graskop and Pilgrim's Rest. Sure enough, the buses came, and Zeederberg's coaches and the post carts faded into the past.

My researches into the history of the village and the mines have led me into some strange byways. I could, for example, tell you why it was that an iron pelton wheel, weighing about 700 lbs. suddenly leapt from the stoep where it was standing at midnight one night and, gathering momentum as it went and sending out showers of sparks, rolled down the full length of the main street to crash through the wire netting of a tennis court and break into a hundred pieces. I might name some of the members of the Ku Klux Klan, which had a short but effective career in deep secrecy. And I could certainly tell you who it was who gave the editor of the *Pilgrim's and Sabi News* a black eye. He, it seems to me, had more justification for his assault than the Irishman who rode all the way to Lydenburg to beat up the editor of the *Lydenburg News* simply because that paper had published a paragraph about his wife which read: "Mrs. ——— ——— arrived from Australia last week. Children will follow later".

To add to this small talk of history there is, too, the story of the occasion when the mine secretary set out in a trap to deliver bullion to the bank. As he jogged along the road that leads from the mine offices to the village main

street the back of the trap came open and, one by one, the bullion boxes fell into the roadway. A mine official who passed that way a little later saw what he thought looked like a bullion box lying in the road. He stopped and examined it and found that it was indeed a box containing a bar of gold. And there, a little further on, was another . . .

He gathered up the boxes and set off in pursuit of the trap. He was just in time to save the mine secretary from heart failure.

One of the personalities of those days was Andrew Scrymgeour, a versatile Scotsman who was manager of the reduction plant at Pilgrim's Rest until 1913, when he fell out with the general manager.

When this happened he could without difficulty have found a job on other mines, but he chose to settle in Pilgrim's Rest and become a prospector and small mine owner. He was one of the founders of the Pilgrim's Rest Small Mines and Claimholders Association, and he also acted as editor and chief contributor to the *Mines and Claimholders Quarterly,* the journal from which some of the information about the early diggings in these pages has been drawn.

From all accounts Scrymgeour was an extremely skilled reduction expert and metallurgist. He was also a good amateur journalist with a pawky sense of humour, and he wrote some excellent verse.

The Association existed to look after the rights of the "small man", to get the Gold Law altered in his favour and to have more farms in the district proclaimed and thrown open to prospecting. This gave Scrymgeour every opportunity of pulling the company's leg, and the journal was full of references to "the locking-up of auriferous ground by concessionaries" and to the "dog-in-the-manger policy of not working workable ground while preventing others from doing so". As everybody knew that the company had not the slightest intention of surrendering its concessions these remarks did no harm and made good reading.

Today Scrymgeour certainly ranks as Pilgrim's Rest's "village Hampden", for he was always battling for the rights of the underdog. However he was at his best when he was being ironical.

In one issue of the quarterly he published an article on mealie meal in which he said. "Pending the promulgation of a new Gold Law, which may perhaps allow of the prospector retaining a small proportion of his cash to vary his diet, it will serve a useful purpose to give a few special mealie meal recipes for the prospector's benefit. If the Government really intend to keep the present Gold Law in operation for any length of time it would be advisable for them to incorporate with it a small manual on the art of cooking mealie meal".

He then gave some excellent recipes.

An article on the nomenclature of the reefs at Pilgrim's Rest said: "The fact that the reefs worked by the Transvaal Gold Mining Estates Ltd. have names bearing a striking resemblance to the letters of the Greek alphabet undoubtedly points to those reefs having been originally worked by the early Grecians, and finally disposes of the theory that the descendants of Solomon and the Queen of Sheba were the original discoverers of these fields . . .

"The old Lisbon-Berlyn company having utilized the name of one of its directors in the Bevitt's Reef, an indignant shareholder objected and suggested that the long-suffering shareholders should be given a chance. In accordance with this the next reef discovered was called the Pigeon Reef . . .

"Heddle's Gorge, it is well-known, derived its name from the size of the luncheon basket which accompanied the late Professor Heddle when he was engaged in geological investigations in the canyon".

I suspect from the style that it was Scrymgeour who wrote the entertaining reminiscences of Mathias Mockett, better known as The Bosun, some of whose adventures I have described.

The Bosun's story, a mixture of fact and fancy, is a South African classic and I wish I could have been on the scene to take it down in full. Here is an extract from the diggers' journal in 1915:

"Mathias Mockett, otherwise the incomparable Bos'n, is one of the best representatives of the Fields . . . Several of the plums of leader digging have fallen to his share and he has always been in the happy, healthy position of enjoying the plum, flicking away the stone and starting afresh. The Bos'n is as nearly an old tarpaulin as ever sailed the seas. He is now 82 years old, but his broad frame, clear complexion, blue eyes and dense white beard show him good for many years to come while the voice that cultivated its stentorian bellows in the Roaring Forties can still be heard over half of Graskop . . . .

". . . In September, 1873, Mr. William Trafford, a miner, reported the discovery of payable gold in what was afterwards termed Pilgrim's Creek and this he duly notified at the Commissioner's camp at Mac Mac. The Bos'n, however, claims the credit of the discovery some time previous for a digger, Alec Patterson, who worked on his own in the Creek and was eventually given a discover's claim opposite the Pilgrim's Hotel. Patterson afterwards worked at Spitzkop and was noted for his theory that the Old Digger method of "humping the swag" was out of date and that a barrow gave the higher mechanical efficiency. He never at any time obtained any converts to his theory, but once a month this staunch pioneer of vehicular traffic was seen trundling his lonely barrow between Spitzkop and Pilgrim's Rest.

". . . The Creek contained three camps; the Lower Camp, the Middle Camp and the Upper Camp. The diggers themselves had each his tent. Canteens and stores were either wattle-and-daub or galvanised shanties.

"In an interesting chapter of Dr. Theal's History of South Africa the doctor traces with some unction the gradual development of a Dutch dorp, from two or three farmers meeting at some central place for Divine Worship, eventually some edifice being erected and a few of the older farmers settling near the church. It must be a matter of pained regret to the Anglo-Saxon that the Bos'n believes the choice of different camps was due to the proximity of the various canteens. (It is pleasing, however, to record that in the one camp that survives the English Church may have been the extra source of permanent attraction).

"There were at least seven canteens in the valley while at most of the stores strong drink could be obtained. The most important canteen was Stent's Cathedral, opposite the present National Bank. "Stent's Cathedral" was christened by the Bos'n owing to the extreme devotion of the worshippers as evidenced by their prostrate forms . . ."

In this journal Editor Scrymgeour also quoted from W.C. Scully's account of how Major MacDonald and 25 men from the diggings made their way to Delagoa Bay in 1874 to collect arms and collected ammunition landed there for the Government.

"The country was teeming with game", says Scully. "Lions were much in evidence and their rumbling groans were at night often audible on three sides of the camp at once.

". . . The first notable incident occurred after we had crossed the Komati and were approaching the Lebombo range. Early one morning we were astonished to find a tent wagon standing in a somewhat thickly wooded hollow. Around it lay putrefying carcases of several oxen. A few low mounds were also visible. Under the wagon lay four white men in the last stage of exhaustion from fever. All were raving in delirium. There were no signs of water in the vicinity.

"We camped close to the spot, wondering what could be the explanation

147

of the strange phenomenon. Hours passed but we could discover no clue. The unhappy creatures under the wagon mowed at us and raved in French. We gave them water which they greedily drank. The stench was frightful; the mounds we had noticed were human graves. But no excavations had been made, the sand being simply heaped over the bodies.

"Then a gigantic, bearded man emerged from the bush, and approached carrying a small demijohn in each hand. I recognised him as one Alexandre, a Frenchman I had known on the Diamond Fields. He explained matters. The expedition, originally eight strong, had started from Lydenburg some six weeks previously. The whole team of oxen succumbed more quickly than usually to tsetse bite. All his companions went down with fever. Three died, and had been laid to rest under the mounds. But even there rest had been denied them, for the lions used to come at night and tear open the graves; they had actually rooted out one of the bodies. Every night jackals and hyenas snarled and fought over the carcases of the oxen, but it was the lions that were the chief source of terror. A lioness had carried off a dog from the fireside immediately behind the wagon. As though aware of the helplessness of the party, the great brutes became bolder, walking round and round in a ever-narrowing circle.

"The nearest water lay 10 miles away, and to the spring Alexandre wended with his two demijohns every day. We loaded the sick men up — leaving the wagon in the waste, like a stranded ship — and took them on to Delagoa Bay."

This terrible story is a reminder of the toll of the Lowveld took of those who travelled there in the early days. In leaving us some record of the early history of the field Scrymgeour performed a service for which historians and collectors of Africana are grateful. Later he left Pilgrim's Rest and became reduction officer at the Nestor mine near Sabie. When finally he retired he lived at Sabie, and died at a ripe age in 1955.

CHAPTER XVII

"BOSS BOB'S" TREES

Stefano Aimetti was not only a skilled mining engineer but he also had more than his fair share of luck. And let no one deny that luck counts when you prospect at Pilgrim's. He enjoyed four years of steadily increasing profits and an uninterrupted flow of good, payable ore to the mills. His successor, R.A. Barry, inherited the difficulties.

In the year he took over, Pilgrim's Rest had 67.6 inches of rain. This led to the 1915 flood, of which we have already heard. The war put up the costs by as much as 18s. a ton, and profits began to fall.

From the record figure of R570,936 in 1914 they fell to R334,674 in 1916, R277,354 in 1917, R187,518 in 1918 and finally R31,102 in 1919, at which point the dividend was only 2½ per cent and the shareholders became a little restive.

The flight from gold in 1919 and the premium that it earned all producing mines then came to the rescue of the company. Its profits rose again to R199,000, hovered at that mark for two years and then sagged to R56,832. The following year, 1923, the mining operations showed a loss despite a production of more than 60,000 ounces of gold. Revenue from a variety of sources enabled a profit of R3,000 to be shown but, as far as the shareholders were concerned, that might as well have been a loss. They grumbled about an expenditure of some R40,000 on prospecting and were told by the chairman that the company had no intention of changing its policy on this point. It had either to prospect or die.

And, as though to prove what a sound policy this was, the mines produced 71,000 ounces of gold the following year, and showed a profit of R106,000. Barry had pushed the total quantity of ore mined and milled up to over 190,000 tons, but he was getting only six pennyweights to the ton, which was half the return of the palmy days. And, as the inevitable sequel to the rise in the price of gold, costs had risen and were now considerably higher than they had been before the war.

It was J.H. Curle, the mining engineer turned author, who, looking at the company's returns at this time described the Pilgrim's Rest mines as "Nature's three-card trick . . Now you see it, now you don't". It has to be confessed that there was some justification for the comment in these years, as the annual profit sank, rose, sank again and then soared.

The power station at Belvedere and the tube mills had brought about a vast improvement in the crushing capacity of the plant, but the rich ground had been worked out. There were no longer "jewellers' boxes" from which ore assaying well over 18 dwts. to the ton could be fed into the mill to improve the grade. Such rich patches as were found were small. For the rest it was good, payable ore, but unspectacular. In addition to this a great deal of water was being encountered in the dolomite at Elandsdrift, and also at Vaalhoek.

Mr. Max Honnet, who had succeeded Mr. H.C. Boyd as chairman of T.G.M.E. and Glynn's Lydenburg Estates in 1920, bore more than his share of worry at this time. The London shareholders, many of them of the second generation, asked exactly the same questions that their fathers had asked. Why were working costs so high as compared with costs on the Rand? Why was it not possible to find a "steady" source of gold? Why was so much being spent on prospecting?

At one annual meeting Mr. Honnet, normally one of the most courteous and patient men the mining industry has ever known, let his indignation get the better of him. It was "ridiculous" to suggest, he said, as one shareholder had suggested at a meeting in London, that the costs in the T.G.M.E. mines should be the equivalent of the R1.60 a ton which was the figure on the Rand in those days. Anybody who made such a suggestion simply did not know what he was talking about. As to prospecting, the whole art of mining in the district lay in a constant search for new areas of payable gold, and it needed only a discovery such as the Duke's Hill Channel or an extension of the Theta Reef to repay all the costs of such development. The company had 150,000 acres of undeveloped land, and it proposed to explore every acre.

At this time ore was being drawn from no less than thirteen different mines and the annual expenditure on prospecting was some R35,000. Everyone from Mr. Honnet downwards believed that it was only a matter of time before new sections of reef would be found and new mines opened. This was always the impressive feature of the company's operations in the district. Everybody remotely connected with the mines — the directors, the general manager, the mine captains, the boss boys and the people of Pilgrim's Rest — believed that there was far more gold in the hills than has ever come out of them. "Don't worry. We'll find it again," they used to say. And for more than seventy years they found it. But such was the pattern of mining in the area that even a company with all the resources of The Corner House behind it had to accept the ups and downs of fortune as the early diggers did. Yet there was something in the air at Pilgrim's Rest that bred an unquenchable spirit of optimism. The diggers had it. The company had it.

In the difficult years after the first world war the company discovered that it had another asset. This was timber. The first trees in the district had been planted almost casually, as an experiment. It was found that they flourished, as well they might for they were planted in the mist belt and had anything from forty to sixty inches of rain showered down upon them every year. The tree planting programme grew. The time came when the plantations were producing almost as much profit as the mines — more in some years.

But the story of the beginnings of a great Transvaal industry is not to be dismissed in a few words. It is one that deserves a book of its own, for what

Hauling out the timber from T.G.M.E. plantations on mountain slopes.

began almost as a by-product of the gold-mining at Pilgrim's Rest has grown into a national enterprise — and it was fathered by T.G.M.E.

Very early photographs of the Pilgrim's Rest district and the Blyde River valley show that the hillsides were covered with low shrub, comparatively dense on the river banks and growing more and more sparse as it climbed the mountains. There were areas that were thickly wooded with indigenous trees. On the farm Belvedere there were even some ancient yellowwood trees against which elephants had once rubbed their trunks. It is not difficult to imagine what happened when some 1,500 diggers settled in the district. They needed timber for their fires, their shacks and their sluice boxes, and they were not prepared to walk very far to get it. It is astonishing how much wood a thousand camp fires can consume.

Within a few years the area surrounding Pilgrim's Rest had been swept bare of wood, and the hauling of timber to the camp had become a profitable business. When mining started in earnest it was found that the adits needed a great deal of timbering. Belvedere Bush, as it was called, became the principal source of timber, and thousands of feet were cut at contract prices that were very high.

How long this process could have continued without disastrous results is anybody's guess. The indigenous trees were small and slow-growing. Vast bare patches began to appear on the hillsides and erosion grew. In the rush to get at the gold no one worried very much about the future. It was a here-today-and-gone-tomorrow policy.

However, after the South African War, when the mill was going again, it

151

occurred to Hugh Hughes, the general manager, that it might be sound policy to plant some wattles within reasonable distance of the mines to supply props. He went ahead with the project, and in 1904 reported that 370 acres of land on the farm Driekop had been ploughed and planted with eucalyptus and black and white wattles. He was a little diffident about the scheme, which he seems to have thought the board might regard as a waste of money. Rather optimistically he reported that he estimated the value of this "new asset" at R100,000.

No one seems to have been particularly hopeful about this tree planting. The district had never been regarded as suitable for farming, for it is an area of sour veld. The indigenous trees grew slowly and, except at Belvedere and in some of the kloofs where there were streams, seemed satisfied to achieve a height of six feet.

But the results of that first experiment in afforestation were astonishing. The seedlings imitated those mysterious peach trees that lined Pilgrim's Creek and grew and grew. Everybody who saw that first rough and ready plantation was deeply impressed. The directors authorised more plantings, though on a strictly limited expenditure, and a modest paragraph about the number of acres ploughed and trees planted began to appear in the general manager's report.

Mr. Robert Gardner, universally known as "Boss Bob", who was the compound manager at the central mines, was placed in charge of the plantations. It was a part-time occupation, but he was an enthusiast and enthusiasm is an essential ingredient in any tree planting programme. Soon "Boss Bob's trees", which was what the Bantu called them, were the talk of the district. They seemed literally to leap out of the ground in their eagerness to grow.

"Boss Bob" may have been an amateur, but he certainly proved that this was a district that was perfectly suited to the trees that he planted. How far he stuck to his budget no one knew. He had ways and means, known only to compound managers, of marshalling a labour force far in excess of that officially authorised. He lived for his plantations, found joy in the astonishing rapidity with which the trees grew and dreamed of the day when every mountain side would be clothed with forests.

Thus was born what became known officially as the company's "afforestation policy", but which Pilgrim's Rest was always to call "Boss Bob's trees". It began with the planting of quick-growing gums to supply mine props, and some wattles. In 1911 an extensive wattle growing programme got under way, and finally in 1919 a large commercial timber scheme was launched with the planting of thousands of acres to Pinus patula and Pinus caribaea (the swamp pine).

In 1927 Mr. John Martin, then chairman of the board, was able to announce that the company had 3,664 acres under wattles, planted at a cost of £12,000. The first profits appeared in the balance sheet in 1919, and by 1927 the entire capital cost had been recovered and profits totalling £29,224 had been made. In that year alone the plantations had earned £15,649.

What, in fact, had happened was that from these small beginnings the T.G.M.E. had established a new industry in the Transvaal – an industry that was to reach its peak of production at precisely the moment when it was most needed.

As the plantations grew it became obvious that the general manager at Pilgrim's Rest, whose preoccupation was mining, could no longer control the activities of the "forestry division" of the company. The leading authority on afforestation at that time was a Norwegian with American training, Mr. Nils B. Eckbo, who had come to the Union to advise the Department of Agriculture. He was offered the position of consultant to the T.G.M.E., and accepted. Like "Boss Bob" he was an enthusiast who lived for the day when every mountain side would be covered with trees. But he was also a highly trained forestry officer, and he proceeded to put the whole tree planting programme on a scientific basis which, though it increased the costs, doubled the areas planted and vastly reduced the fire risks.

Within a few years the company had 40,000 acres planted and was easily the largest timber company in South Africa.

The modest profit that Mr. John Martin had thought worth mentioning in 1927 was soon eclipsed. By 1945 its plantations were earning over R120,000 a year. This rose to R196,000 in 1946 and R202,000 in 1947.

It was as Nils Eckbo had said years before: "With timber you plant and then you wait. But in the end the profits astonish you".

To deal with the ever-increasing quantity of timber that was now being produced a saw mill and a box making factory were established on the farm Hendriksdal.

In 1939 the company entered into an arrangement with the Acme Box Company of Durban by which this firm agreed to take the saw mill, erect another of its own and handle the entire output of timber from the T.G.M.E.'s plantations at contract prices. The war had begun and the directors of T.G.M.E. were at a loss to know how they would deal with their rapidly growing output. They saw the agreement with the Acme Box Company as a very profitable solution of their problems. Two companies which were specialists in timber, Moshal Gevisser Holdings and Hillman Brothers, owned the shares in the box company. To ensure a permanent outlet for their timber products and to increase the efficiency of their plantations the T.G.M.E. directors also began to consider the possibility of an alliance with the Acme Box Company.

No one criticised the contract with the box makers at the time it was made, but five years later it led to the most stormy meeting, indeed the only really stormy meeting, in the company's history. A gentleman named G.J.V. Clarence had acquired a large number of T.G.M.E. shares and in 1945, after circularising the other shareholders, he led what is best described as a "filibuster" against the Board. It was his contention that for 30 years the company's afforestation policy had been wrong and that it had made a grave error in entering into the agreement with the Acme Box Company. Verbally he clothed every mountain in the district with millions of trees producing millions of cubic feet of timber. Why, he asked, had these trees not been planted? He seemed not to realise that for years the mine staff had managed the plantations, that the whole operation in its early days had been run "on a shoestring" by people who loved the district.

After some discussion, one of the biggest timber merchants in Johannesburg rose to his feet and said that he thought the directors ought to be congratulated, not criticised. He pointed out that the company's forestry operations had shown a profit of £66,000 that year. He wished that he could run a timber proposition half as economically as this one had been run. Had he been able to do so he would be on his way back to Scotland with a fortune.

Mr. Clarence stuck to his guns. He nominated four new directors and accepted nomination himself.

The new nominees were narrowly defeated in the poll that followed. The old directors were re-elected. Mr. Clarence continued to protest for the next three years. The company continued to make large profits on its timber.

But it was clear that a company that had been formed to mine gold was rapidly becoming a timber company, the biggest in South Africa. The once stumpy tail was now wagging the dog, for the profits from timber were bigger than the profits from gold. It was decided that T.G.M.E. had better stick to its last and divorce its timber production from its gold mining activities. Accordingly, in 1948, a new company called S.A. Forest Investments Ltd. was formed in which the shareholders were Moshal Gevisser Holdings, Hillman Brothers, The Central Mining and Investment Corporation, Rand Mines and the Transvaal Gold Mining Estates Ltd. It had a capital of £125,000 in £1 shares.

The T.G.M.E. Assistant Manager (Forestry), Mr. G.J. Hofmeyr, was appointed manager of the new company, a post which he held with distinction until he retired early in 1961.

The next step was to increase this capital to R1,550,000, divided into 2,500,000 shares of 50 cents each and 150,000 5½ per cent preference shares, and buy out the assets of all the participating companies.

In the case of the T.G.M.E. this meant buying some 99,000 acres of freehold property, of which 40,000 had been planted with pine, gum and wattle trees, together with equipment, buildings and vehicles.

The price set on these assets was some R680,000, and the T.G.M.E. was allotted 1,360,000 shares. This made the company the majority shareholder in S.A. Forest Investments. However, at a later date, in accordance with the policy of the directors by which T.G.M.E.'s activities were to be restricted to mining, these shares were distributed to the shareholders. Thus T.G.M.E. retired from the timber business, with the extraordinary effect that shareholders who had invested in a gold mining company found themselves holding shares in a timber company, as well as retaining their interest in the gold mines of the district. Few of them have regretted the change.

It was agreed that the mineral rights over 99,000 acres sold to S.A. Forest Investments should remain the property of T.G.M.E. Though the company lost the freehold of 99,000 acres in this transaction it still held approximately 53,000 acres and owned the mineral rights over another 72,000. In this period the total number of claims registered in its name was never less than 7,500 which, with its three huge republican government mining concessions, meant that it was easily the largest gold mining property in South Africa and probably in the world.

In these days there are afforestation schemes throughout South Africa. But the company can claim to have led the way in the Transvaal. That first experiment in producing mine props was the foundation of a great and useful industry.

In 1930 Barry, who had served as general manager for fifteen years, retired, and was succeeded by Mr. J.H.A. Diering, best-known of all the T.G.M.E. managers. Diering's name is honoured from Lydenburg to the Lowveld, and he is remembered with affection by all who knew him during the thirty-three years he served the company.

He was a South African of German descent who qualified as a mining engineer at Freiburg in Germany. On his return to the Union he worked on the West Rand Consolidated, the May Consolidated, the Van Ryn Deep and on the Messina Copper mines. Then he added alluvial gold digging in the Western Transvaal to his experience and later prospected for Dr. Hans Merensky and Von Dessauer on Pienaar's River and also on the Komati.

His first job after joining T.G.M.E. was in the survey office. Later he was successively a prospector, mine captain at Ponieskrantz North and the Chi mine and resident manager at Vaalhoek. He was then lent to the Glynn's Lydenburg company to complete the sinking of the South shaft. From 1923 to 1927 he was resident manager at Elandsdrift and was then appointed manager of Glynn's Lydenburg.

He had been in Sabie less than three years when Barry retired. No one was in any doubt as to who would succeed as general manager.

Diering was at Pilgrim's Rest as general manager for twenty-one years, and there is no one in the village or, for that matter, in the district, and in all reminiscences of the "old days" in Pilgrim's Rest the phrase "Mr. Diering said . . ." tends to recur. He decided everything from how the school should be enlarged to who should be permitted to shoot on the company's property.

He was a methodical, meticulous man, who demanded accuracy and method from his staff and got it. He set very high standards both in work and personal behaviour, was grave and courteous in his manner, knew the name of every employee of the mines and made them all feel that he took a keen personal interest in their welfare. In one way and another he stamped

155

his personality on the district.

It was his custom to change three times a day. He would appear in the morning, often devoted to visits of inspection, in khaki. After lunch he re-appeared immaculate in white duck, with which he wore a white solar topee, a blue tie and a blue handkerchief in his breast pocket. At sundown he changed again for dinner.

Pilgrim's Rest, never noted for high sartorial standards, was impressed by the immaculate attire of the new general manager. It found itself tidying up in the afternoon. Mr. Diering was never known to speak to any of the staff in the mine office on this subject. But he had a way of looking at a man which said: "Slovenly" more clearly than words. It was all that was necessary.

Although Diering did not know it, many a member of the mine staff watched with close attention the little ceremony that took place on the afternoons when Mrs. Diering drove to the mine office with him, as she sometimes did.

Mr. Diering, immaculate in his white suit, would step out of the car, walk round to the other side, open the door for Mrs. Diering and hand her out. He would then conduct her to the other side of the car and hand her in. There followed a formal little bow, after which he would stand with his topee raised as she drove away. It was a ceremony that taught many a young man a lesson in good manners.

Good manners and punctiliousness are all very well in their way, you may say, but they do not help in the production of gold. In Diering's case they were backed up by immense efficiency, attention to detail and a great capacity for hard work. The phrase that the men who worked under him use is: "He kept us all up to the mark".

The years preceding his appointment were not among the Company's luckiest. In 1924 both Mr. Max Honnet, the chairman, and Sir Aubrey Woolls-Sampson, a director, died.

In 1927 there was a flood in the Elandsdrift mine when blasting opened a fissure in the dolomite and "a great, uncontrollable body of water" rushed into the workings. This was followed in November, 1928, by the closing down of the Vaalhoek mine which had been then in production for eighteen years. The whole district regarded this as a blow to the company. So did the shareholders.

Diering made two resolutions as to what he would achieve when he took over. One was that he would reduce working costs, and the other that the Vaalhoek mine would again produce gold for the company. He was by way of being a Glynn's Reef "specialist", and it was from the upper and lower Glynn's Reef that Vaalhoek and drawn most of its ore. He believed that there was still much gold to be won from the reef at Vaalhoek and that it was worth fighting the persistent flooding in the mine.

The trouble at Vaalhoek lay in an underground stream which the workings below the sixth level in the mine had punctured. In normal weather this did

"The devaluation of the £ was the shot-in-the-arm that the mines needed . . . ."

not matter as the underground channel was big enough to carry the water on its course. But when there were heavy rains the channel could not hold the full volume of the swollen stream. Then the water poured into the workings and flooded the mine to third level. It was this problem that Diering set himself to solve.

He succeeded in reducing working costs within eighteen months of his appointment. But it took him much longer to get Vaalhoek going again. The problem was finally solved by fitting watertight doors which were shut as soon as the underground stream began to flood. In this way the flood water was confined to a comparatively small section of the mine and the great expense of pumping was reduced.

To everybody's delight Vaalhoek was re-opened in 1938, and began steady production again. Its life was lengthened by accelerated development to the south which opened up large tonnages of payable, though refractory ore in the Lower Glynn's Reef Horizon. It was as Diering had said it would be.

Fortune favoured the company earlier than this. South Africa abandoned the gold standard in the last days of 1932 and the ratio of working costs to production was vastly improved. It meant a new lease of life for the T.G.M.E. mines.

And, to the delight of generations to come, Vaalhoek is likely one day to be reopened yet again. Next time, however, it will not be for the gold that may lie hidden inaccessibly but to open up to public view the beautiful caves which are said to rival the best in South Africa in beauty of the crystalline structures clustering the walls.

CHAPTER XVIII

UPS AND DOWNS

The devaluation of the pound, delayed until the entire economic structure of the country was at breaking point, was the shot-in-the-arm that the mines at Pilgrim's Rest and Sabie needed. For nine years they had been struggling to make ends meet. The net profit, even with the timber sales thrown in, ran at about £3,500 a month. The company was just able to pay a dividend but there seemed no prospect of improvement. Never before had a full nine years passed without some discovery, same new stroke of luck.

Then at last, in December 1932, Mr. Havenga made his announcement. The pound was to be allowed to find its own level. The price of gold rose from 84s. 10d. an ounce to 124s. Pilgrim's Rest breathed again. Its luck had held!

Immediately large quantities of ground that had been abandoned became payable. The task was how to get the ore to the mill. The tonnage crushed rose to 227,400, to 243,000, 288,000, and finally topped the 300,000 mark in 1938.

"We wouldn't have used this stuff even for tennis courts in the old days," the miners said contemptuously as yet another load of ore rolled off to the mill.

The profits rose to R151,956 in 1933, though the new gold price had prevailed for barely ninety days of the financial year. The following year they doubled. However, this was the peak. Costs began to catch up with profits and, though the mills worked as they had never worked before in all the long history of the valley, profits sank to more humdrum levels. Nevertheless they showed a vast improvement on the figures from 1929 to 1939, and there was excitement in the air. Vaalhoek might open up again, a rich find was reported from Willemsoord, the Bourke's Luck Mine, purchased by the company in 1932, was promising, and Elandsdrift had a new lease of life.

It is difficult for anyone who has not lived at Pilgrim's Rest to realise how completely the success or failure of the mines dominated the lives of all its inhabitants in those days, and how much a rise in the price of gold meant to them. The names I have mentioned so frequently — the Beta, the Theta, the Peach Tree, Vaalhoek, Elandsdrift, Ponieskrantz, Bourke's Luck, Columbia Hill — were household words in the village. They talked of output as we talk of the weather. If a prospecting party "struck it rich" the grapevine fairly twanged with excitement as the news went from house to house. The values shown by the samples would be discussed that evening in the Royal Hotel bar. And when you said: "They've hit the Trixie on Willemsoord and it's showing 11 dwts. over 73 inches", even the schoolchildren knew what you meant. An old resident, returning to the village to visit relatives, after asking

Mr. A.R.C. Fowler, a former general manager of the Pilgrim's Rest mines, and now consulting engineer to The Rand Mines group.

This is the Burgers Cross presented by President Thomas Francois Burgers to Mrs. Tom McLachlan, who had nursed men suffering from malaria and black-water fever on the Pilgrim's Rest diggings 100 years ago, and to Mrs. D. Austin who looked after men of the commandos wounded in the Sekukuni war. Only two of these crosses are known to exist. They are made of gold and, by reason of their rarity and the quantity of gold they contain, are very valuable. In his letter to the recipients and President said: "May God reward you for your noble self-denial."

about Aunt Maud's health would say: "And what are they getting out of Theta these days?" Since everybody knew that Theta was the barometer of the company's prosperity it was the most natural question in the world.

Every house, every shop, every building (except the post office and the police station) in Pilgrim's Rest was built on the company's land, and everyone in the village was a tenant. They told you that this was why all walls and roofs are of corrugated iron. "Who's going to spend money on a proper house when he doesn't own the land?" they say. But the truth is that the fate of Barberton has always hung like a cloud over the valley. No mining engineer in the Transvaal would have dared to prophesy that the mines would last for ninety years, and that Beta would still be producing in 1971. For as long as anyone can remember men have thumped the counter and said: "Well, I give them another ten years." They were giving them another ten years as far back as 1875.

When the company was first formed in 1895 plans were drawn up for the township of Pilgrim's Rest. At the annual meeting in 1896 the chairman mentioned that the company expected to derive quite a considerable revenue from the sale of trading sites in Pilgrim's Rest. But the government of the day rejected the township plan. Paul Kruger is said to have ordered the refusal of the application because he would not have a "nest of uitlanders" established in the district — but more probably because Phillips, Bailey and Fitz-Patrick had been involved in the Raid. Another attempt to establish a township after the South African War failed because the residents declared that they did not want to pay rates. Then the irregularity of the reefs was revealed and no one was certain that it might not be necessary to mine under the village.

So the township was never established and the company remained the landlord of the district to the end, owning even the ground on which the the churches stand. And how the tenants have grumbled down the years!

As time went by the company found itself not merely the landlord but, whether it liked it or not, the father and mother of the village. Its expenditure in the district rose to R1,000,000 a year, of which some R600,000 was paid out in wages. The sons of men who had worked for it in the early days turned to the mines for employment and were taken on. If someone was down on his luck he went to the mine office and asked for a job, and usually he got it. Tommy Dennison worked for the company, so did the Bosun, Herbert Lilley and George Bates, all of whom had been diggers in their day.

Thus mining in the district was very much a "family affair" in an old-fashioned way that has almost vanished from the modern world. It was a pleasant, friendly atmosphere in which everyone was happy, and naturally everyone took the keenest interest in the grade of ore that went to the mill.

I think it is no exaggeration to say that, dating right back to the days of Lionel Phillips, the directors of The Corner House had what is known as "a soft spot" for Pilgrim's Rest. Certainly they devoted a great deal of time and energy to the difficult task of "keeping things going".

Once you have visited the village you understand this. Pilgrim's Rest is a very personal place where, whatever your occupation, you are a neighbour and a friend. When the bus that brought the older children back from school was due at the end of the term everyone turned out to meet it. When an old friend died all those who were not going to the graveyard stood at their front doors with bowed heads as the funeral procession passed along the main street.

This was the responsibility that the company bore for close on 90 years. The health, wealth and happiness, the very life of the village, were largely in its hands. It never failed them.

Let us look at the names of some of the men who worked at Pilgrim's Rest in the twenties. We find among the "top brass" Milverton Ford, manager of Vaalhoek, R.D. Spillane, chief surveyor, W. Patrick, (resident manager of the Elandsdrift mine), W.G.A. Stein, metallurgist, C.G. Brink, J.R. Normand, (resident manager of the central mines) and E.M. Skea, assayer who worked for the company for 47 years. Mr. Skea lived at Graskop and made mineralogy his life work. His specimens of South African minerals, mounted for the microscope, won him an international reputation.

Milverton Ford was once blown clean out of his office by a cyclone that hit the mine buildings at Vaalhoek. It was a discriminating cyclone. It picked up the mine manager and the safe and deposited them both in the veld without damaging either. But the mine plans are still missing!

Then there were the Leadley brothers, H.R. and J.V., M.J. Owens, Hans de Jager (a giant of a man), W. Maritz and G.M. Maritz, Johan de Beer, J.S. Fullard, L.V. Knight, Tommy Dennison (you know about him), J. Ramsbottom, H.C.S. Botha and Frank Creese.

Creese became well-known in Western Province cricket. He left Pilgrim's Rest to join his brother Bill Creese, who was professional to the Western Province Cricket Club at Newlands. For years he did the catering at the Newlands cricket ground. He had learnt the art at mine functions on the T.G.M.E. property.

I see also the name of D.C. Diespecker and suspect that he is a link with the Lowveld, surely a son of Jules Diespecker who was stationed at Komatipoort as manager of the old Selati Railway company.

The most interesting name on the list is that of Johan de Beer, son of "Maboompie" de Beer, once leading citizen of Pilgrim's Rest and owner of the Desire Mine. He was the grandson of the original Johan Muller who owned the farm Geelhoutboom on which McLachlan opened up the Mac Mac diggings. His mother's family owned Kruger's Post and the concession farms that David Benjamin acquired and sold to T.G.M.E.

"Maboompie" de Beer had a financial setback before he died and Johan had to earn his living the hard way. He became a miner, learnt the trade on the Rand and then joined T.G.M.E. in 1918. He had worked in the mines at Pilgrim's Rest for 42 years. Later he developed phthisis, but he was still able

"The mules trot in and out of Beta Mine . . . ."

to work as a prospector in the open air. To my mind up to the time of his death in 1965 he had the most interesting job in Pilgrim's Rest. Officially it was described as "cleaning-up". What it actually meant was that he roved the hills round that area taking samples from old workings, putting in prospects here and there or digging out the ground round an old mill site.

It is astonishing how much gold there was to be found in these odd corners. When he "cleaned-up" on the site of the old Kameel's Creek mill, burned down in 1907, some of the samples he took from the channels that once led the water off from the old plant assayed 160 dwts. This residue of gold and gold-bearing ore which escaped the stamps long ago tends to sink into the soil and may be six feet down. De Beer estimated that from the soil he excavated round the foundations of the ancient mill at Kameel's Creek gold to the value of at least R30,000 was extracted.

When I first met him eleven years ago he had a gang at work on the remains of a leader that the miners of long ago had missed. It looked as though he would have to follow it right under the ruins of what used to be Clewer House, which in its day housed Legett Neale, Aimetti and Barry. He had another gang at work on the spot where a small battery once served a mine called "Uncle Bill" on Jubilee Hill. There he panned some samples that showed a very nice tail of gold.

I was interested in the site of the old mill at Brown's Hill from which a couple of hundred tons of top soil had produced a great deal of gold. In the process an old gas engine had been unearthed, unlike anything I had ever seen before. It must have weighed ten tons, and I pictured its component parts sliding down Pilgrim's Hill in 1884 or thereabouts. I scratched the soil from one of the rusted girders and found the inscription "Shanks & Co., Arbroath and London". Further scratching revealed a name — "The Caledonian". Even this ancient engine, it seemed, preserved the Scottish tradition.

Another old employee of the company is Michael Owens, son of M.J. Owens, who worked at Pilgrim's Rest for 47 years and still lives there. He

161

looks very little older than he did when he joined his father on Jubilee in 1923, and his Welsh accent is just as marked today as it was then.

M.J. Owens came out from Wales in 1913. Having looked the district over he decided that he liked it, and sent for his family. They liked the valley, too, once they got used to the thunderstorms, and settled down happily. Michael Owens now has a family of his own, and it is unlikely that he will ever return to Wales. But his father did. After 23 years at Pilgrim's Rest he won a half share of the first prize in the Lourenco Marques lottery and decided to retire. He still owned the family farm on the slopes of Mount Snowdon, where the Owens had lived for four hundred years. It is called Llwyncoed (which means the Wood Grove), and while he was in South Africa it was managed by his sister.

When Mr. Owens announced that he was going back to Wales and to the farm his family said "no". They had grown to love South Africa and Pilgrim's Rest, and Michael Owens saw that he had a future in T.G.M.E.

So the father and his family parted, and the old man went back to the foot of Snowdon to die where he was born.

Michael Owens is today almost the last survivor of the Welsh colony that once lived at Pilgrim's Rest. He still speaks Welsh, writes it and reads Welsh newspapers but, though he also speaks Afrikaans, Fanagalo and English with an accent that says "Carnarvon", he has become a South African and Llwyncoed will have to get along without him.

No one at Pilgrim's Rest had a better memory than Mr. V.A. Frankish, the T.G.M.E.'s engineer who was born there and whose reminiscences I have used throughout this book. He had known the valley and its people since he was a child. He was born there and he died there in 1971. Like everyone else who grew up in the valley, he had a deep and abiding effection for the place. And had I to choose a representative citizen of Pilgrim's Rest, one who embodied all the sturdy qualities of its citizens, their kindliness and generosity, he would have been my man.

Now, to round off this gallery of portraits, let me present one more personality of the village who died comparatively recently. His name was George Bates. He was a coloured man, who was the court interpreter and the last of those who had been actively connected with the old diggings.

George Bates was born in Pilgrim's Rest in 1883. His father was an alluvial digger who pegged his claims at Mac Mac before George was born, and later moved to Pilgrim's Creek. As a boy he played about among the claims and knew such characters as Bismarck, Harry Cossor, the Bosun, Lilley and Purcell. He saw nuggets weighed on the scales and was always proud of the fact that his father contributed a 2½ ounce nugget towards the cost of building the Anglican church. He knew George Roy, who built the Royal Hotel and eventually sold the lease to "Honest John" Macintyre. He remembered the wonderful month in which his father, working a claim at the foot of Jubilee Hill, made R800.

He was educated at Marianhill and intended to become a carpenter. But in 1903 a court interpreter was needed and because he spoke English, Afrikaans and twleve Bantu languages he got the job. He reached the retiring age in 1944, bade farewell to the magistrate and the police, and went off to supplement his pension by working for an estate agent. His retirement lasted exactly eight weeks. Then one morning a policeman appeared at his house to say that he was urgently needed to do some interpreting as the new official was not available.

George Bates went back to his old job and was there in a "temporary" capacity for many more years. If we accept the two months of his "retirement" as a temporary absence, he had 60 years of continuous service in the magistrate's court at Pilgrim's Rest and at circuit courts. If there was any civil servant in the Transvaal with a better record than this I have yet to hear of him.

All the judges of the Transvaal division of the Supreme Court had known him since the days when they were young barristers on circuit. Mr. Justice Maritz, the former Judge-President of the Transvaal, never visited the district without asking: "Where is my friend George Bates?"

He interpreted in thousands of cases dealing with every sort of crime, not least among which was that of illicit gold buying which sent many a man to gaol. He can even remember the days when the rangers in the Sabie Game Reserve marched the poachers they had caught all the way to Pilgrim's Rest for trial.

For all its "toughness" in the early days the village holds a record which I think cannot be equalled by any other community of its size in the Union. No white man has ever been charged with murder in the Pilgrim's Rest court. The only crime of this description that anyone can remember was caused by jealousy. A young man went berserk and shot his rival in a love affiar. Having done so, he committed suicide before the news reached the police.

Even in the early days when men settled their quarrels with fist fights there were no murders. It is true that the thief who returned to the diggings after he had been expelled was shot in his tracks and buried in a nameless grave. But that was simply the rough justice of the day, which no one ever regarded as murder.

On the other hand Pilgrim's Rest is the only magisterial district in South Africa, as far as I know, where there have been two cases of highway robbery carried out in the Dick Turpin manner.

George Bates used to shake his head sadly over the wickedness of human beings he had seen revealed in the 58 years he had spent in the courts, but that was because he was a kindly man who had lived all his life in a country district. He had been spared the horrors of a city court.

In my mind's eye there is a picture of him as a barefoot boy running about among the claims, helping his father clean up his sluice box and listening to gossip about nuggets, leaders and the cost of a five-stamp battery. He was twelve years old when the T.G.M.E. took over Benjamin's concession in 1895. He died in 1965. When I met him he was the only man living who could truthfully say that he remembered the "good old days".

CHAPTER XIX

ABE BAILEY – THE LAST TO GO

The mines went on yielding what a sarcastic engineer had called "their widow's mite of gold" to the central plant in the village. But the old order was changing very rapidly. One by one the men who had known Pilgrim's Rest in its early days were dying – all, let it be noted, having lived to a fairly ripe old age despite the hardships they had endured when gold mining was in its infancy. Friedrich Eckstein died in 1930, Percy FitzPatrick in 1931, B.T. Bourke in 1932, Lionel Phillips (aged 82) in 1938 and Abe Bailey, the last of the pioneers, in 1941.

In the end he and Phillips were the only survivors of the group of young mining men who had taken part in the original discussions between the partners in the Corner House and the claim-holders at Pilgrim's Rest. Bailey, now probably more wealthy than he had ever been before by virtue of his holdings in the Orange Free State, had outlived all the men he had known at Barberton in 1884 and 1885 and his interests had spread to many other companies. But his holdings in the Clewer and Jubilee mines were the foundation of his fortune. The chairman of T.G.M.E., Dr. Hans Pirow, in recording his death at the annual meeting in 1941, said that he had been a director of the company since 1917. In fact he had been interested in the mines of Pilgrim's Rest for very nearly 50 years, though I have never succeeded in finding out how he acquired his holdings.

One of the earliest descriptions of Sir Abe as a dashing young man at Pilgrim's Rest is supplied by a man who was a schoolboy at the time.

"On one occasion I was riding my favourite horse, a young bay stallion," he says. "I was having great difficulty in preventing him from bolting with me when round the corner swept Abe Bailey in a Ralli cart drawn by a pair of zebra.

"The sight of their striped coats was too much for my frisky mount who bolted with me from the Blyde River valley, past the Clewer mine and up Pilgrim's Hill where, about half way up, he stopped of his own accord, frothing at the mouth and dripping with sweat.

"I suppose Abe was going to his mine at Clewer to show off his zebras and possibly collect a few pounds in the bets he had made as to the possibility of training them to harness."

In all the 45 years he was associated with the company Sir Abe seems never to have made a speech at an annual meeting or attempted to have any hand in the running of the company. This was unlike him, and must be taken to indicate that he was a satisfied shareholder.

The complicated pattern by which ore was drawn from thirteen different sources became a little less complicated as the older mines were worked out. Ponieskrantz North closed in 1942, Peach Tree in 1945, Desire in 1946 and Jubilee, one of the steadiest of producers, in 1947. Vaalhoek, which had been reopened in 1938 closed down in 1943 — but came back into action in 1946.

The last had not been heard of any of these mines, for in most of them there were patches of ore that later became payable with the devaluation of the pound and the higher price of gold in 1949. But until that day the company's revenue was mainly drawn from Beta, Bourke's Luck, extensions of the Theta reef and various open-cast workings in the Pretoria shales at Columbia Hill that produced quite a reasonable quantity of gold.

The old Elandsdrift mine at Sabie, which had been a steady producer since 1905, was nearing the end of its life, though from time to time new strikes such as the short-lived leader in Horseshoe Creek, which I have described, kept it going for a year or two. When at last, in 1944, it seemed certain that it must close, the company bought its next-door neighbour, the Malieveld mines, in the hope that a vigorous development programme would produce a new source of gold to replace Elandsdrift. But Malieveld did little more than repay the R104 006 it had cost.

When Elandsdrift finally closed in 1947 it had produced 329 894 ounces of gold from 1 306 449 tons of ore milled and had shown a working profit of R1 054,276.

It was a mine in which all the geological problems of the district were represented, not least of them being fissures and caves, some of which contained vast quantities of stored up water and mud.

The flood in Elandsdrift mine in 1927 was caused by blasting that opened up a great underground lake fed by streams that ran through ancient channels in the dolomite.

A heading of the eighth level at a distance of 3 300 feet from the outcrop, measured on the dip of the reef, was suddenly inundated. The pilot holes had shown no sign of water but, some time after blasting had taken place and when the water-tight door had been opened to allow the working party to get at the face, there was a sudden, mighty inrush. In the dash for safety that followed, the water-tight door was left open and as millions of gallons of water poured in from the vast, underground reservoir the mine was flooded up the second level.

After this disaster the collapse of some of the caverns, which had probably been filled to roof level with water, caused sudden waves that overwhelmed the pumps. At midnight one night a few days later, when dewatering of the mine had begun, there was another sudden surge of water in the workings and the level rose eight feet in a few minutes, as though it had been pushed by the piston of a gigantic pump.

This meant that the roof of a particularly big cave had collapsed, forcing the water up the fissures. The next day a native called at the mine office to say that "the mountain had collapsed". He guided Mr. Diering, the resident manager, to a spot on the ridge above the mine and showed him a chasm more than 100 feet wide and 80 feet deep, the biggest sink hole in the district.

These underground floods and mud rushes caused great damage and sometimes endangered life.

Mr. Diering recorded an occasion on which he had an exceptionally narrow escape in getting out from a flooded section of one of the mines.

"I reached a place of safety with such a narrow margin that, in swimming I had to turn on my back to breathe and scraped the skin off the ridge of my nose against the rock roof of the drive," he says.

It happened in the flood at Elandsdrift in 1927. At that time work was being carried on in a heavily waterlogged area of the mine.

"I expected to be called out — and frequently was — at any hour of the night and to avoid having the rest of the household disturbed every time this happened had my bed made up on the verandah," he told me in an account of the incident.

"On this particular occasion I was roused at about 2 a.m. by a runner from underground (in those days we had no telephone between surface and underground) who handed me a note from R.J. (Tommy) White who was in charge that night.

"The note read: 'Come quickly. Have struck the Indian Ocean!'

"I scribbled below: 'Impossible. You're driving west. It must be the Atlantic. Coming', and sent the note back, following as rapidly as I could.

"When I joined White at the bottom of No. 7 incline the main pump chamber was already flooding. We managed to struggle through the surging and rapidly rising water in the main cross-cut to the water-tight door. But we could not shut it because floating timber had got wedged against it.

"We left our return till rather late but got out by the skin of our teeth — or, in my case, by the skin off my nose!"

At one stage at Elandsdrift 85 tons of water had to be pumped out for every ton of ore recovered. After the flood in 1927 the miners set out to drive a drainage tunnel into the mine from Palmer's Creek on the boundary of Waterval, the neighbouring farm. This was a long job, though it was considerably assisted by a series of caves that ran in the right direction. On one occasion a developer at work on the tunnel drove into one of these caves and claimed an advance of 85 feet in one "round"!

This tunnel, completed in 1931, drew off the water in the fissures and underground caves and brought about a considerable reduction in costs at Elandsdrift.

They had the same trouble in the Glynn's Lydenburg mine. There the drainage tunnel had to be cut through three miles of rock.

It was begun in January, 1935 and completed in May, 1940 at a total cost of R282 000. Its length was 12 900 feet and the internal dimensions were 15 feet x 8 feet in hard formation, and 20 feet x 8 feet where concrete lining was necessary. Over 2 300 feet of the tunnel were concrete lined and arched.

Much water was met at various stages of the work and mud rushes made it necessary to deviate from the originally planned route. The total footage involved, including development, crosscuts and raises was approximately R16 600 feet.

Before this tunnel was built some four million gallons of water a day were being pumped out of the Glynn's Lydenburg mine workings. When completed, the tunnel delivered over 11 million gallons of water a day to the Sabie river, and eliminated the need for major pumping installations. With the consequent lowering of the water table in the area the flow from the portal dropped considerably.

The whole Pilgrim's Rest-Sabie district is honeycombed with these underground caves, which extend for miles and have never been properly explored.

As far back as 1875 a great chasm opened in Pilgrim's Creek after floods and literally "swallowed up" the stream.

An account of this happening, written by the renowned Dr. Atcherley, whose book *A Trip to Boer Land* published in 1879, says: "A very heavy rainfall had taken place, accompanied by one of those fearful thunderstorms so frequent in these latitudes. The quiet creek was converted into a roaring torrent which was rolling boulders along like wisps of straw. The terrified inhabitants of the camp stood by horror-stricken, watching the destruction, when by some marvel, and without sign of warning, the boiling flood suddenly ceased and where, a moment before, an enormous volume of water had been rushing by, an insignificant rivulet now trickled lazily along."

What had happened was that a fissure had opened up in the very bed of the creek and the water was pouring into it. When the flood subsided the stream was diverted round the mouth of this opening, beams were put into position and a man carrying a torch was lowered into the depths.

He went down ninety feet and returned to the surface, pale and shaken, to report that he had heard rushing water and the "crashing of rocks", but had not been able to see the bottom of the cavern.

Then a weight was sent down at the end of a rope, and finally touched bottom at two hundred feet. It seemed probable that there was a whole series of caves and an underground river below the creek.

The diggers, who needed a steady flow of water for their sluice boxes, closed up the mouth of the cavern with stone work and did their best to forget about it.

An even more ancient legend says that, in the days before the Voortrekkers reached the district, the Portuguese sent trading missions there. One of these early explorers, having persuaded some Bantu to act as porters and carry the gold, ivory and other goods back to Lourenco Marques, made slaves of them.

The next expedition paid the penalty for this breach of trust. After they had exchanged their trade goods for gold and ivory they called for porters but there were no volunteers. Instead the natives attacked them and they were forced to withdraw into a cave. The natives then built fires at the mouth of the cave and suffocated them.

One man from this expedition is supposed to have survived by retreating far into the caves. He managed to get back to Lourenco Marques, where he told the story and drew a map of the situation of the cave. He was convinced that the natives, having revenged the kidnapping of their fellow tribesmen, would not go near the cave which, to them, had become "a place of death". He believed that the gold and ivory would still be there if anyone had the pluck to search for it. But he died of the privations he had endured before he could lead an expedition to the cave.

The legend persists to this day, and there have been many attempts to find the cave which is supposed to lie on the farm Olifantsgeraamte, not far from Glynn's Lydenburg mine.

No one has ever found a trace of it, and for all I know a fortune in gold and ivory lies waiting for some latter-day explorer. All he has to do is to find the entrance to the cave in a district where there are thousands of such caves, the entrances to which are buried by rubble and vegetation.

The caves seem not to have been used by the Bushmen for, though there are some fairly well preserved Bushmen paintings on sheltered ledges along the banks of the Treur, no traces of occupation have been found in the large dry caves of the district. It is believed that the native tribes used them as places of refuge when, as frequently happened, they were raided by marauding bands of Matabele or Swazi. In their wars with the tribes of the eastern Transvaal the Boers often found that, when the battle went against them, the natives would hide in caves.

Mr. Diering records that he once received a report that a cave "full of skeletons" had been found on the farm London, north of Graskop. He took the sergeant of police, Mr. W.G.A. Stein, the T.G.M.E. geologist, and the inspector of mines to the spot, and they made a thorough investigation.

The floor of the cave was littered with human remains. They counted over fifty skulls. There were no signs of injuries such as might have been inflicted by knobkieries or assegais and they came to the conclusion that these unfortunate people had either died of some infectious disease or, more probably, had been trapped in the cave by Swazi raiders and been suffocated by the smoke of fires built at the mouth. They found beads of ostrich shell, copper and glass which were not of particularly ancient origin. The skulls proved to be those of Bantu men and women. However, this is one of the very few cases in which human remains have been found in a cave, though there are probably hundreds that have yet to be discovered and explored.

There is a large cave system on Jubilee Hill a few miles from Pilgrim's Rest. It consists of a great central cavern, with lofty passages running off to the east and west.

A man named van Niekerk, who set out to find where the eastern passage led some seventy years ago, was lost in the caves for a week. He entered them equipped for a thorough tour of inspection. He had a candle lamp, a good supply of matches and provisions in the form of bread and biltong, but he seems not to have blazed his trail or used a guide string.

He lost himself in the eastern section of the caves, but kept his head and husbanded his food supply.

"He reasoned that, as long as he moved against the prevailing air current, he must reach daylight somewhere," says Mr. Diering, who has recorded the history of this adventure. "This line of thought might well have been his undoing for, had the weather conditions on the surface changed, the underground air flow would probably have reversed its course and he would have been hopelessly misled.

"Fortunately this did not happen and, after a week of underground wandering, he emerged, almost completely exhausted, at the foot of the mountain range overlooking the Graskop plateau."

The spot where he at last staggered into the open air was only three to four miles, in direct line, from the point where he had entered the caves. The fact that he spent seven days getting there gives you some idea of the labyrinthine wanderings of these underground passages.

Though these caves and the water-bearing fissures in the district have often added to costs, and complicated the miners' task, there have been times when they have simplified it. Quite often a drive has entered a system of dry caves that has taken it forward some distance without the need for blasting. They have also provided natural ventilation shafts. In some cases they proved useful for dumping hundreds of tons of waste rock which otherwise would have been trammed to the surface.

Mr. Diering records that, in the Desire mine at Pilgrim's Rest, they once advanced a stope into an area where dissolution of the footwall strata had left a cavity into which the ore body, separating cleanly from the hanging wall, had fallen and broken up. All they had to do was to collect this large quantity of payable ore and send it to the surface.

As the years went by not only did the mining at Pilgrim's Rest become more difficult, but the recovery of gold from the ore became more and more complicated.

In the very early days the alluvial diggers found nuggets that were almost pure gold and washed the free gold from the sand in their sluice boxes. "Pilgrim's Rest gold" in those days was distinguishable by its peculiar radiance, that "ashblonde" colour I have described, which was due to the high percentage of silver it contained. The gold from the quartz leaders was almost as easily extracted as the alluvial. Then, when mining proper started, the ore near the surface was largely oxidised and was easily dealt with by the cyanide process.

But the day came as the mines went deeper when it became more sulphitic. At Vaalhoek and in the Beta mine at Pilgrim's Rest there were large quantities of this refractory ore. As the more easily worked lodes were used up it was clear that the future of the mines would depend more and more on these refractory ore bodies.

A flotation plant was set up at the central mill in 1940 and the concentrates obtained were shipped to America or wherever there was a market. Before that the product of the refractory ore had been sent to Japan. But the war brought increased freight rates and very high insurance charges. The only possible solution of the problem was for the company to instal its own roasting plant and treat its own concentrates. This was done in 1942. The necessary equipment for roasting, leaching and cyaniding the concentrates was installed, and T.G.M.E. became a producer of some tons of copper as well as gold. As a war measure the plant was satisfactory, but it gave the general manager another headache.

The difficulty lay in disposing of the sulphur dioxide fumes which were released during the roasting process. To take them clear of the mine and the village a flue was built to the top of Kaalkop, a hill behind the plant. This carried the gas some seven hundred feet above the houses. But even so there were times when there was sulphur dioxide in the air. You shall hear how the problem was solved.

The feature of the later years of the "Diering era" was the remarkable quantity of ore this most energetic of managers managed to pour into the mill from failing mines. Even the closing down of Elandsdrift in 1947 was not allowed to affect this figure . . . 292 000 tons in 1946, 285 000 tons in 1947 and 255 000 tons in 1948. Where it all came from only Diering knew. When the gold price rose from 172s. 6d. to 248s. with the devaluation of the pound in 1949 he pushed production over the 300 000 ton mark and, in 1951, achieved the remarkable figure of 336 000 tons.*

Thus when the time came for him to hand over the reins to Mr. A.R.C. Fowler, after twenty-one years as general manager, he went out with flying colours. More than that, he took with him the affection and respect of everyone in the district. He was to live and take a fatherly interest in Pilgrim's Rest and all who lived and worked there for twenty years after his retirement.

In 1950 T.G.M.E. increased its capital and took over the assets of Glynn's Lydenburg mine, now at the end of its long and honourable career. In the course of fifty-five years of production it had paid its shareholders more than R2-million in dividends, and had been a model of what a small mine ought to be. It could no longer be run profitably as a separate undertaking, but there was still much gold to be won by the reclamation of the old workings, and this T.G.M.E. could undertake in conjunction with its development of the Malieveld mine across the boundary.

*This was almost, but not quite, a record. In the financial year 1941-2 375 000 tons had been milled, to which total Elandsdrift contributed 69 000 tons and Bourke's Luck 36 000 tons. If to this total is added 28 000 tons from the Rietfontein (T.C.L.) mine, at that time under the administrative control of T.G.M.E., the final figure of 403 000 tons is easily the highest ever reached by an "outside" mine. Even greater production would have followed but for the war.

For a time T.G.M.E. profits, including a good return from its plantations, remained over the R200 000 mark, but in 1951 there was a marked decline. The chairman, Mr. G.V.R. Richdale, issued what sounded like a final warning.

"Operations during the last three months resulted in a small loss," he said in his address at the annual meeting. These figures clearly indicate the precarious position in which the company's mines are placed. Mining operations will be continued therefore so long — but only so long — as they can be maintained on a profitable basis, however marginal it may be."

It was the first time that anyone had put into words the thought that had been in most people's minds. To mining men it looked like the writing on the wall. In Pilgrim's Rest they weighed the chairman's words and gloom settled on the village. But it lasted only a week or two and then the optimism of the district asserted itself.

To everyone's astonishment, except possibly Mr. Fowler's, the gold won the following year showed an increase of no less than 3 321 ounces, and the complexion of the accounts was much more healthy.

When 1955 came round and it was time to celebrate the company's diamond jubilee there was life in the old dog yet. The valley from which so much gold had been won had not stopped yielding, and the rockets that soared into the air from Brown's Hill on that night in May were cheerful symbols of the hope that was in the air. It was not quite the party it would have been if all the Welshmen had been there and the Bosun had been present to serve the drinks. Nevertheless it was an occasion that no one who attended will ever forget. This was the birthday of a company, born in 1895, whose mines, despite their erratic production record, had outlived most of their contemporaries on the Rand.

In 1956 the mining operations of the T.G.M.E. and the forestry development of South African Forest Investments were finally divorced. The company's holding of 1 392 000 fifty-cent shares in the latter company were distributed to shareholders in the proportion of three S.A.F.I. shares to two of T.G.M.E. Any twinge of regret that the shareholders may have felt at this parting of the ways was probably mollified by the announcement that there had been a loss of R2 366 on the gold mining in the district while S.A.F.I. were in a position to pay a dividend of 5 per cent.

There was no improvement in T.G.M.E.'s affairs in the year ended 1957. Mr. P.H. Anderson, now chairman of the company, had to announce a working loss of R4 800 and also to make the ominous statement that the directors were considering the advisability of liquidating the company.

Probably, had The Corner House not had an attachment to the district that went far beyond the bounds of normal financial ties, that would have been the end of the company. The mines would have closed down, the plant been sold and the sturdy individualists of Pilgrim's Rest might have had to earn their living by selling tea and scones to tourists bound for the Kruger National Park, a procedure that would have made the Bosun turn sharply in his grave.

Instead the consulting engineers of the Corner House came up with a "keep-it-going" plan. In addition to the gold that was still being won from odd corners of the property the Beta mine, over which two generations of managers and geologists had said the prayers for the departed, proved still to be alive. Mr. Fowler, whose uncanny knack of finding gold that his predecessors had missed equalled that of Leggett Neale, had reported that the mine was far from exhausted and everyone in the district breathed again.

After another five years there was left only the Beta mine and a considerable reserve of pyritic ore which showed an average value of 11 dwt. to the ton. At that point the mine's consulting metallurgist, Mr. Frank Bath, recalled the old roasting process and the great volume of sulphur dioxide it gave off. In these days you no longer got rid of your sulphides. Instead you converted them into sulphuric acid. At Phalaborwa, in the Lowveld, the Phosphate Development Corporation (Foskor) had begun the production of phosphate concentrate from the immense natural deposit there. If sulphuric acid produced at Pilgrim's Rest could be used to treat this concentrate the company could establish an inland superphosphate plant within easy reach of a very large and prosperous agricultural area, said Bath.

With remarkable rapidity a fluo-solids roasting plant, combined with a small sulphuric acid plant, was designed and erected near the central mill at Pilgrim's Rest. Simultaneously a superphosphate plant was built at Graskop. In 1959 the T.G.M.E. became a producer not only of gold and copper but of some 16 tons of sulphuric acid a day and 12 000 tons of fertilizer per annum.

This was to win another reprieve for the mine and the village.

CHAPTER XX

THE END OF MINING BUT . . . .

The story of the ingenuity, the elaborate planning, the economies and the unceasing search for new sources of payable ore that kept the company afloat in its old age is, in its way, a mining epic. There was really no financial gain involved as anyone can see by comparing the R8-million-a-year net profit of Blyvooruitzicht, the Group's top mine, and the almost negligible R6 000 or so annual return for all the work put into keeping this old stager on its feet. But the board of Rand Mines felt that there was more at stake than profits. Apart from the mine there was virtually no avenue of employment, and no other source of income, in the district. Men who had grown old in the service of the company could not be uprooted and sent away from the village where they had spent most of their lives. It was quite true that the little community of citizens of Pilgrim's Rest had shrunk considerably but there was still a population of about 200 white people who were there because the mine was there. In the compound there were more than 100 Bantu mineworkers, including some who had been there a very long time. One of these men, John Meshego, was believed to be nearly 80. He had come to the mine as a boy in 1905 and had been continuously employed ever since.

Despite the warnings of successive chairmen of the company most of the inhabitants of Pilgrim's Rest flatly refused to believe that "their" mine would die before they did. Over and over again in the past something – a rise in the gold price or the discovery of a continuation of payable reef – had come along at the eleventh hour to save them. They were confident that this would happen again.

Perhaps it should be added that the former shareholders were not involved in the various expedients adopted to keep the mining operation going. In 1959 they had been offered an exchange of shares on a generous basis by a newly formed subsidiary of Rand Mines, The Corner House Investment Company, Limited. The shareholders accepted this offer almost to a man. In 1968 Rand Mines established Rand Mines Properties Limited, a property development company. The T.G.M.E. land in and close to the village was sold to that company in 1971.

However, whatever dispositions were made as to shareholdings and freehold property the main problem remained the same. What was to become of Pilgrim's Rest – its quaint houses, its winding main street, its four churches, its schools and its historic graveyard? The directors of the company and all who knew and loved the village felt that, even when the mine closed down, as close it must, the houses would have to be preserved if only because there was nothing quite like them anywhere else in South Africa.

Fortunately, thanks to the efforts of the directors of Rand Mines, and also in part to the publication of the early editions of this book in 1961, the village and the valley in which it stood had, from being comparatively unknown to tourists and holiday-makers, begun to acquire some small measure of fame. The roads of the Transvaal were rapidly improving and the detours to Pilgrim's Rest, either from Lydenburg or from White River, could no longer be described as off the beaten track. Also the historical background of the district was becoming better known.

Up to that time South African historians had been rather vague about the origins of the great South African gold mining industry. To this day you will find that most history books declare that the first discoveries were made at Barberton. The historians are also fond of the splashes of gold found at Marabastad, Leydsdorp and even at Knysna in the Cape Province. Pilgrim's Rest? Well, there was a diggers' camp there, they say . . . .

But the truth is that there had been no *payable* gold field in South Africa before Alec Patterson panned the gravel in the creek at Pilgrim's Rest in 1873. Edward Button undoubtedly found gold on the farm Eersteling at Marabastad in 1871 and also undoubtedly did float the Transvaal Gold Mining Company with a capital of R100 000. This was the first gold mining company in the Transvaal to work a mine but, in the absence of any record of its achievements, it seems improbable that it produced enough gold even to pay for the expensive battery Button had ordered for it.

Gold was found in many strange places in those days but most of these discoveries merely produced enough of it to finance the flotation of a company and a little further development of the mine. Then the gold would peter out and the company would collapse, having made no profits for anyone but the promoter. Such was the difference between discovering gold and discovering "payable gold".

Pilgrim's Rest, if one regards the entire area from Sabie to Bourke's Luck as a gold field, produced payable gold from 1873 to 1971, ninety-eight years in all. The only gold mine in the world that has ever equalled this record of consistent production is, as far as I know, the Homestake Mine in South Dakota, U.S.A. The Homestake Company was incorporated in 1877 but gold was mined in the area much earlier than that so that Homestake can probably claim more than 100 years of production.

This leaves the Pilgrim's Rest district as the second "long service" gold field in the world. The only gap in its production record occurred during the South African War. Thus it has earned itself an honoured place in mining history.

However, even more important than this, is the fact that it served as the launching pad of the South African gold mining industry. It brought to the Transvaal an army of gold-seekers, among whom were skilled prospectors from the Californian and Australian fields. These men then found more gold at Barberton, after which the search began in earnest. Finally in 1886 came what was then regarded as the discovery to end all discoveries — the Main

175

Reef, outcropping over a distance of more than 30 miles on the Highveld, less than 40 miles from the capital of Kruger's Republic.

These facts had not been widely known but once Rand Mines drew attention to them, and the whole story had been published, mining men began raising their hats to the miners of Pilgrim's Rest. In any other country, particularly if it had been the United States, the village would at once have become a place of great historical importance and attracted thousands of visitors to see the birthplace of the industry that had kept the world supplied with gold. But South Africans are not as yet very historically minded. To many of them history means battlefields and ancient guns mounted on concrete pedestals. The fact that our mines produce three-quarters of the Western World's gold stocks, and that South Africans have built the largest mining city in the world and sunk the deepest shafts, gets less mention in our history books than Simon van der Stel's journey to inspect a copper prospect in Namaqualand.

Nevertheless Pilgrim's Rest is where it all began and the district is now officially recognised as the birthplace of South African gold mining. By the time these words are in print the central section of the village will have been declared a national monument. I hope that it will assume this mantle just in time to celebrate its 100th birthday — and the 100th anniversary of the beginning of payable gold mining in South Africa. At about the time that happens the total gross value of the output of our gold mines since mining began should soar very close to the fabulous figure of R16 357 000 000. The first R2-million came from the alluvial diggings at Pilgrim's Rest.

The village's status as a national monument means that the little whitewashed houses and the winding road will be preserved in perpetuity and the charm of the village will remain. The old Royal Hotel has also been declared a national monument so that too, will survive exactly as it is today.

This historical accolade will probably mean more and more to the village as the years go by. But of more practical importance at the moment to the people who live there is the interest which the Transvaal Provincial Administration now takes in the tourist potential of the countryside. The "Pilgrimites", as they call themselves, have enjoyed for many years the privilege of living in one of the most beautiful tracts of unspoilt country in the whole of South Africa. Their little kingdom extends from the top of Pilgrim's Hill to the escarpment of the Drakensberg, the last massive rampart above the Lowveld. Across it flows the Blyde River sometimes a calm, clear, swift-running trout stream, at others a raging torrent carrying all before it. It rises on the farm Hartebeesvlakte, behind the village, and makes its way towards the escarpment flowing fairly gently. Suddenly it begins its descent into a mountain gorge and is joined by the Treur River just above the T.G.M.E. power station which served the mines and the village for more than 60 years.

The mountain gorge through which the river runs widens until it becomes a mighty canyon 2 500 feet deep and a mile wide. It has taken an angry river fighting its way to the sea, hundreds of millions of years to carve itself this passage. Looking down into the canyon one can almost visualise a colossal saw biting out a solid segment of the rock to make a causeway through which the water can flow.

Having thus set its course the Blyde pours down out of the portal at the base of the escarpment and makes for the mighty plain below, where eventually it joins the Olifants, which in turn joins the Limpopo and thus finds its way into the sea off the coast of Mozambique. If there is a more impressive rock canyon anywhere in South Africa I have yet to hear of it. In carving itself a way of escape from the mountains the Blyde has produced a masterpiece of natural sculpture.

The canyon is something that every visitor to South Africa should see for it presents a wonderful example of the might of the elemental forces that shaped our land. Here even the ancient rocks of Africa had to give way to the raging torrent that poured down from the mountains.

A portion of the Blyde River Canyon was once the property of the Transvaal Gold Mining Estates which owned the farm Belvedere on which this scenic wonder is situated. However, in 1964 Rand Mines, the parent company decided that it would not be right to retain these natural beauty spots as private property in perpetuity. The company therefore presented the farm to the provincial administration of the Transvaal, and through them to the people of South Africa, to be preserved as a holiday site and a nature reserve for all time.

The canyon was off the beaten track and up to the time when Belvedere was given to the province it formed part of the wonderful domain of the people who lived in the district of which I have already written. They used to cross the canyon, if they were brave enough, by means of a swaying suspension bridge of steel cables and narrow planks. (This bridge is situated at Bourke's Luck and miraculously, though the Bantu mineworkers used it every day, no one ever fell from it into the chasm below.) Now the province has made a scenic road along the top of the escarpment and built a wide concrete bridge across the canyon so that motor cars and pedestrians now stream across it every day. All the area along the escarpment has been proclaimed a nature reserve. At almost any point on the magnificent new motor road you can get out of your car and walk to the top of the precipice which is the last great shelf of the table land above the Lowveld. But the favourite spot here is the rocky platform, above a sheer drop of some 2,000 feet, which a romantic surveyor in the early days named God's Window. From this vantage point you look down on what appears to be a vast, wooded plain above which, in the early morning, wisps of mist hang giving it an ethereal look that makes you realise how it got that name. Somewhere down there, you know, is the Kruger National Park, teeming with wild life. On a very clear day you may even see in the distance the peaks of the Lebombo Mountains that mark the border of Mozambique.

177

There is no view such as this in any of the other provinces of the Republic, magnificent as some of their view sites are. Here you are looking down from a great height on that new, so different, land, the Lowveld, which has harboured some strange characters in its day. Across this area ran the wagon tracks that served this part of the Republic before the railway line from Lourenco Marques was built. This was the view that the Voortrekker, Hendrik Potgieter, gazed upon before he led his men on their perilous ride down the escarpment and on to Delagoa Bay more than 100 years ago.

The new road, this road of wonderful views, serves as a connecting link between two of the main highways that take the motorist from Highveld to Lowveld. One is the road down Kowyn's Pass to Sabie and to the Numbi gate of the park. The other is the Strijdom Tunnel route that takes you to Tzaneen, Gravelotte, Phalaborwa and the Phalaborwa gate in the northern regions of the park.

It also takes knowledgeable tourists to the Blyde River Canyon holiday resort where there are comfortable cabins and a first-class restaurant in one of the most beautiful spots on Earth.

"Such comfort where we once walked and slept on the hard ground," say the old-timers. "It can't be right. Everything is made too easy for them."

But it *is* right. This wonderful nature reserve now belongs to the people of South Africa and here are sights that all should see. The Blyde River Canyon and the other attractions of the Pilgrim's Rest district ought not be the preserve of the young and active. If the teenagers want to camp and climb they can. But if father wants to fish he must be allowed to do that here, too, provided he has a licence. And if granny wants to gaze endlessly at the breathtaking, ever-changing view she should be allowed that pleasure as well — and also the comforts that befit her age.

This is what the provincial authorities have recognized and they have established the Blyde Poort holiday resort that in time may well become world famous because it is so ideally placed — and open to all.

In 1967 what sounded like the death knell of the Beta mine at Pilgrim's Rest was sounded. The company gave notice of its intention to curtail operations, a formality that usually means that the end is in sight. Those of the inhabitants of the village who were young enough to look for jobs elsewhere began packing up. There weren't many of them.

But there was one more miracle to come. In the following year a reprieve for the old mine suddenly materialised frim an unexpected source. The Government in its Budget announced special provisions to subsidise "marginal" mines, which meant dying mines. T.G.M.E., the Pilgrim's Rest company, was to have special treatment. The State assistance it was to receive would be made retrospective and would be back dated to January, 1968.

Once again the mine was saved. It rose from the bier that had been prepared for it and went back to work. In the bar of the Royal Hotel they called this generous measure of State assistance "the corpse-reviver". But the roar of the stamps (not that there were many of them at work) was music in their ears.

Well, it worked for a time and the mine looked busy. But it was not a case of mining a lower grade or going back and finding ore that had been left behind. The truth was that there was virtually no gold to find. The Beta mine had been scooped as clean as an empty melon. The output fell, and fell again. There was not one corner of the property that had not been scraped bare and had its residues put through the mill. There simply was no more gold and it was no use pretending that there was.

So the end came in June, 1971, when there were only two years to go to Pilgrim's Rest's centenary. Everybody on the mine knew that the worst had happened long before they were told the news officially. Nevertheless the man who was then chairman of Rand Mines, Mr. P.H. Anderson, and a number of the directors, made the journey to Pilgrim's Rest to offer such consolation as they could and to make presentations to some of the veterans. Virtually every adult member of the community was in the mine recreation hall that evening. It ought to have been a wake and it began that way, but before the night was out it turned into a surprisingly cheerful gathering at which old friend shook hands and men who had worked together for years, slapped one another on the back and said: "I wonder when we'll meet again?" Essentially it was a party for the elderly and the middle-aged, most of whom had spent part of their lives there.

Mr. Anderson said that the function marked the end of mining operations.

"But it is not the end of Pilgrim's Rest — just another milestone in its history," he added. "In saying farewell to the past we can welcome the future. There may be a bit of a hiatus before the village achieves the bustling activity and prosperity associated with an important tourist centre but that is what is planned."

Mr. "Buster" Fowler, the consulting engineer of the Rand Mines Group, who had once been general manager of T.G.M.E. and lived in Pilgrim's Rest for twelve years, struck a chord in many hearts when he said that "something happened" to everyone who came over Pilgrim's Hill and lived in the district for any length of time. The place had a fascination that could not be denied. Everybody loved the district and went on loving it all their lives and that was the only way in which he could account for the fantastic efforts that had been made to keep the mine going.

It was a speech that was cheered until the rafters rang. Virtually everyone present was a Pilgrimite.

But in the weeks that followed the last rites began — the dismantling of the plant, the closing down of the mill and the selling off of such battle-scarred material as could be sold as scrap.

Waiting in the wings while this was going on was Rand Mines Properties Limited, the company that now owned the village and some of the T.G.M.E. company's neighbouring land.

Rand Mines Properties was formed for the specific purpose of taking over the freehold ground of some of the older mines in the central Witwatersrand area that were nearing the end of their lives, and of developing the surplus land for industrial and residential use. Crown Mines, City Deep, C.M.R. and Geldenhuis Deep are all now owned by Rand Mines Properties. The new company's task was to produce plans for the orderly development of valuable land that might otherwise be thrown on to the property market to be exploited by anyone who could afford to buy it in at an auction. To the R.M.P. planners this worked-out mine in the Eastern Transvaal and the village that the mining company owned presented the most complicated, but at the same time the most interesting, of all the problems with which they had to deal.

They soon found that everyone who had ever been there — mining engineers, accountants, irrigation experts and nature conservationists — had ideas about what should be done with Pilgrim's Rest. At first their task was to listen patiently. Then they went there themselves, lived in the old hotel and looked about them. Soon the magic of the valley gripped them and, tentatively, they began to plan the future of the village, of the old buildings, of the winding roads and of the Pilgrim's Creek from which the diggers' gold had come.

At that point in the story — the date was June 25th, 1971 — there was a dramatic change in the affairs of Rand Mines and all the companies it controlled. A take-over bid by Thomas Barlow and Sons, one of the industrial giants of South Africa, was successful and, once the necessary formalities had been completed, the two groups were merged to become Barlow Rand Limited. Rand Mines, the oldest mining house in the country, became a subsidiary of the new group for whom it has continued to administer the various mining interests.

There were many changes in the structure of the large conglomerate of companies that Barlow Rand now controlled. Among those that underwent reorganisation was Rand Mines Properties which at that time had many half-completed plans on its drawing board. Among these, of course, was the plan for Pilgrim's Rest. The new management took a hard look at the overall scheme for the future development of this area and the preservation of the village. There followed a long silence while the planners waited to hear the fate of this particular plan. Finally it was announced to all concerned that, with some modifications, the plan would stand — another reprieve, this time for the village.

The top brass of Barlows had visited Pilgrim's Rest and studied this acquisition of theirs. It is not every day that a large business organisation finds itself in *loco parentis* to a country village. But apparently the magic was still in the air that day. They came, they saw and they were conquered. So once again the village has wagged its tail like a friendly dog and won new friends and influenced people. As a result the best brains in regional planning have been at work to assure the future of this lovely countryside. Let us, therefore, try to picture Pilgrim's Rest as it will be in 1980 when all today's plans may have come to fruition.

The village will still be there, the upper portion of it exactly as it is today except that there will have been some refurbishing of the exteriors of the houses with white paint and flower boxes. Further down the main street there will be new houses but they will conform externally to the old-world pattern. The result will be a much bigger, brighter village with perhaps twice as many houses as there are today, but it will still be a village that looks as though it had come into being when Paul Kruger ruled the old Republic and every foot of timber and iron was hauled to the site in wagons.

On the hillside there will be holiday houses, some big, some small. Near the present golf course, which will be extended, there will be a hostelry outwardly conforming to the tradition of the coaching days, inwardly a modern hotel with every known device for providing good food and other creature comforts. There will also be a motel to cater for the caravan trade.

High up on Mount Sheba the Mount Sheba Hotel and Nature Reserve will be flourishing. This is the courageous venture of A.L. Evans, a young man who came to Pilgrim's Rest seven years ago and, because of his faith in the beauty and peace of the place, has succeeded in establishing a wonderful mountain resort. Mr. Evans is still young enough to enjoy the rewards his pluck and enterprise will earn him.

Some sections of the old Beta mine will be preserved so that visitors can form an idea of how the gold was won from the surrounding hills. There will also be an exhibition of the equipment of the early diggers and you will be able to try your hand at panning river gravel — with a sporting chance of finding a trace of gold. A section of the electric tramway that once carried ore to the central mill will come to life again and there will be tram rides into the hills where guides will point out some of the old workings — a great attraction this tram-ride.

Just off the main street of the village there will be a magnificent swimming bath — the old concrete pool in which three generations of Pilgrimites have swum in somewhat more modern dress. Round this will flourish a botanical garden in which there will be many picnic spots.

And then all the other attractions of an unspoiled country place — bridle paths for horsemen, the best trout fishing in the Transvaal, mountain climbing, forest walks . . . . There is no need to catalogue these things for those who have already visited Pilgrim's Rest.

Naturally all these developments will come slowly. Indeed it is the deliberate policy of Rand Mines Properties that progress in the district must be at the pace of the horse or, when acceleration is necessary, of the bicycle. Pilgrim's Rest is to be preserved as what it has always been — a place where time has stood still. The proprietors propose to keep a firm hold on the sites they sell for holiday houses in this respect. Houses will have to match the general pattern of the village so that as years go by the hillsides will be dotted with what look like old-world cottages, many of which will probably be the height of luxury once you have passed through the front door.

There will also be as little noise as possible. No sirens, no loud-mouthed bells or hooters or clattering internal combustion engines. And as little smoke as possible, please, and no litter at all.

What this really means is that the planners have gone back to the wisdom of Paul Kruger and acted on his advice. "Take what is best from the past — and base your plans on this."

They hope that what was once the Valley of Gold will now become the Valley of Peace and Beauty.

EPILOGUE

If you had not read this book and if you drove to the top of Pilgrim's Hill to-morrow, pausing at the spot where the coach was robbed, you would never know that this was once a mining valley. The scars on the hillsides are vanishing under a coverlet of green. Even the boulders in the creek, where once more than a thousand men scrambled for gold, look as though they have been in place since the beginning of the world. The beauty of the valley was there before the first wagon crawled down the hill. It will still be there a thousand years hence. Nothing can ever alter the enchantment of its mountains and its streams.

However, lest you think I have romanticised its history and imagined some of the stories I have told, pay a visit to the old graveyard on the hillside above the village and see the unmarked graves of the diggers. They paid for these plots of ground, their last claims, with the two-and-a-half ounce nuggets which were their "gold reserve". Often this was all they had left when they died. Above one of the graves is a tombstone inscribed: "Edwin Blacklaw,* of Launceston, Tasmania. Died 1890". No need to say where he died, for this was the Teddy Blacklaw who found young Percy FitzPatrick sitting forlornly outside a store without money, without food and very close to tears. "Come along 'o me, young 'un'," he said and, though his claim was producing barely enough gold to pay for his own food, he kept him there and fed him. Fitz-Patrick never forgot this kind-hearted Australian and you will find the story in the first chapter of *Jock of the Bushveld.*

Let Andrew Scrymgeour, the poet of Pilgrim's Rest, say the last word. One of his poems, written in 1915, described how a Voortrekker, who had buried his wife and children at Ohrigstad, "spanned his oxen at the drift and took the river course". He came at length to the hills above the Valley of Gold and:

> He saw the mountains in their strength
>   Bow down before the Lord.
> He saw the river joyous run,
>   The little hills that laughed and sang
> With gladness unto God.
>
> There came a strangeness on his soul;
>   A cry within his breast:
> "Behold the Gates of Paradise!
> For there the Happy River lies,
>   And there is Pilgrim's Rest!"

---

*On the tombstone the name is spelled "Blacklow", an obvious error by the mason.

INDEX